general editor John M. MacKenzie

Established in the belief that imperialism as a cultural
phenomenon had as significant an effect on the dominant
as on the subordinate societies, Studies in Imperialism
seeks to develop the new socio-cultural approach which
has emerged through cross-disciplinary work on popular
culture, media studies, art history, the study of education
and religion, sports history and children's literature.
The cultural emphasis embraces studies of migration and
race, while the older political and constitutional,
economic and military concerns are never far away.
It incorporates comparative work on European and
American empire-building, with the chronological focus
primarily, though not exclusively, on the nineteenth and
twentieth centuries, when these cultural exchanges were
most powerfully at work.

The other empire

AVAILABLE IN THE SERIES

The other empire

METROPOLIS, INDIA AND PROGRESS IN THE COLONIAL IMAGINATION

John Marriott

MANCHESTER
UNIVERSITY PRESS
Manchester and New York

distributed exclusively in the USA by
PALGRAVE

Published by Manchester University Press
Oxford Road, Manchester M13 9NR, UK
and Room 400, 175 Fifth Avenue, New York, NY 10010, USA
www.manchesteruniversitypress.co.uk

Distributed exclusively in the USA by
Palgrave, 175 Fifth Avenue, New York NY 10010, USA

Distributed exclusively in Canada by
UBC Press, University of British Columbia, 2029 West Mall,
Vancouver, BC, Canada V6T 1Z2

British Library Cataloguing-in-Publication Data
A catalogue record for this book is available from the British Library

Library of Congress Cataloging-in-Publication Data
A catalog record for this book is available from the Library of Congress

ISBN 13: 978 0 7190 8047 0

First published in hardback 2003 by Manchester University Press
This paperback edition first published 2009

Printed by Lightning Source

To the memory of the last member of a generation

Lena Margaret Marriott (1913–2002)

and to those of a new one

Molly Marriott Haresign
Ira Marriott Haresign
Jude Marriott Haresign
Niah-Jane Marriott
Arjun Singh
Simran Kaur

CONTENTS

CONTENTS

GENERAL EDITOR'S INTRODUCTION

When the Rev. Dr Robert Laws was preparing himself for missionary work in Central Africa in the 1870s, he went to work in a Glasgow medical mission. He was taken by the Superintendent to visit houses in the slums, 'frightful dens of viciousness and dirt', in one of which a 'Roman Catholic virago attacked them as heretics, flourishing a long knife in their faces, and threatened to murder them' (W.P. Livingstone, *Laws of Livingstonia*, London, Hodder and Stoughton, n.d. [*c.* 1924], p. 29). Later he was involved in 'drives' in which students of divinity and medicine would act as decoys to lure prostitutes to a hall for a late-night revivalist meeting. On one occasion they collected together a hundred and 'about forty declared for a new life' (*ibid.*, pp. 32–3). In the same period and in another Scottish city, Dundee, Mary Slessor, preparing for missionary work in West Africa and herself a slum dweller, was caught up in the establishment of a mission in slums even poorer than her own. There, she and her fellow workers were subjected to violence and frequently found the mission room wrecked (W.P. Livingstone, *Mary Slessor of Calabar*, London, Hodder and Stoughton, 1916, p. 9).

In the 1950s, the same sense of social proselytization survived into my own lifetime and experience. In the West End of Glasgow, Finnieston (later Kelvingrove) Church of Scotland, a middle-class and upper-working-class congregation in a grand Victorian classical building adjacent to the great gates of Kelvingrove Park, continued to maintain a mission in the nearby slums of the Glasgow docklands. It was in a street appropriately named for a mission, but not for the poverty and misery to be found there, Grace Street. In my youthful mind, brought up to loathe the pubs, the drunkenness and alleged criminal fecklessness of such 'darker' regions of the city, there was unquestionably a parallel between the Grace Street mission and the stations of the missionaries who came, on furlough, to speak about India and Africa. Indeed, I soon made the connection myself by going to live in Northern Rhodesia (Zambia).

This analogy between missions to the 'heathen' poor of Britain and the 'heathen' peoples of Africa and Asia is now well known, though it has never been fully researched. In this book, John Marriott takes up this theme, and much more, in relation to the mutually constitutive aspects of encounters with the London poor and with the peoples of India. Travel accounts, topographical mapping, descriptions of the 'Other', the adoption of the language of 'tribe' and race, anxieties about 'nomadic' people who cannot be pinned down and rendered subject to the requirements of the bourgeois state, fears of revolt and revolution, anxieties about degeneration, all reveal striking parallels in the language, form and style used in relation to the London poor and to the inhabitants of India. In its breadth of source material and its range of illustrations, this book constitutes a notable study of these parallel phenomena.

There can be little doubt that similar studies, as indicated above, could be attempted for other parts of Britain and other continents, notably Africa. The

conclusions that we can draw include the extraordinary complexity of the processes of 'othering', which have too often been rendered in over-simplified form; the
fluid interpenetration of concepts of class and race; and the manner in which these
are written upon both urban and rural landscapes. This book is therefore about
spatial as well as demographic conceptualizations. It analyses the rhetoric of discovery as well as the rhetoric of forms of social and religious 'redemption', partially
bound up in the central notion of 'progress'. It also surveys a dynamic which spans
the eighteenth to the late nineteenth centuries, demonstrating the intellectual and
conceptual transformations that occur during this period. But it also reveals striking continuities, just as my Scottish examples do. The vision of a relationship
between 'darkest England' or 'darkest Scotland' and 'darkest' India or Africa was a
remarkably durable one.

John M. MacKenzie

ACKNOWLEDGEMENTS

For much of the time the writing of this book seemed a solitary affair as I became conscious of how little historical attention has been devoted to the question of the precise location of London within the British imperial formation. It is only now that the book is complete that I can reflect on the support and guidance of others. The early encouragement of John MacKenzie and Bill Schwarz was crucial. And at different stages sections of the book were read by Christopher Bayly, Tim Hitchcock, Frank Mort, Manas Ray and Barbara Taylor. I am in their debt. Discussions with numerous generous people at seminars and conferences were of real help, but particular mention has to be made of Gautam Bhadra, Anjan Ghosh, Tapati Guha-Thakurta and Manas Ray at the Centre for Studies in Social Sciences, Calcutta. More generally, David Green, Susan Pennybacker and Heather Shore have been supportive in different ways, as have colleagues associated with the Raphael Samuel History Centre at the University of East London.

I have relied principally on the Oriental and India Office Collection at the British Library, Cambridge University Library, the Bishopsgate Institute Library, the Indian Institute Library at the Bodleian, Oxford, and the library of the Centre for Studies in Social Sciences, Calcutta, and have to thank their staff for invaluable assistance in providing access to these outstanding collections.

My greatest debt is to Kanta Kaur Rhodes. Without her this book would not have happened, for it was through her that India entered into my imagination. And she was a constant source of intellectual and emotional support. Perminder Kaur, Harsharen Rhodes and Santosh Kaur also helped, probably more than they realize.

Some of the material in this book has appeared previously. The first three sections of Chapter 2 are based on my chapter 'The spatiality of the poor in eighteenth-century London', in Tim Hitchcock and Heather Shore (eds), *The Streets of London*, London, Rivers Oram, 2003. The first two sections of Chapter 3 are edited from my 'Introduction', in John Marriott and Masaie Matsumura (eds), *The Metropolitan Poor. Semi-Factual Accounts, 1795–1910*, 6 vols, London, Pickering and Chatto, 1999. Chapter 4 contains revised material from my 'Introduction', in John Marriott (ed.), *Unknown London. Early Modernist Visions of the Metropolis*, 6 vols, London, Pickering and Chatto, and from 'Racialization of the metropolitan poor', *From the Margins*, 1:1, 2001, pp. 103–28. Chapter 6 is a revised and extended version of 'In darkest England', in Phil Cohen (ed.), *New Ethnicities, Old Racisms*, London, Zed, 1999. I am grateful to the publishers for permission to reproduce this material.

John Marriott
East London

Introduction: metropolis and India

Whatever the precise nature of the shift in Britain's role from a trading to a colonial power in India, not in doubt was the dramatic increase in demand for knowledge of the nascent colony. After the decisive battle of Plassey, the various forms of knowledge production grew exponentially. In 1784 the Asiatic Society of Bengal was formed. In 1788 James Rennell published *Memoir of a Map of Hindustan or the Moguls Empire*. It was the first British work to chart details of India's inland topography instead of maritime routes. Control over land-revenue management gave access to important technical details and Mughal sources of information.[1] Travelogues and associated historical-philosophical surveys appeared, and proved popular.[2]

It was at this moment, states Bernard Cohn, that metropolis and colony were brought into a unitary epistemological field. In introducing this idea, he has argued elegantly that the eighteenth-century European state established its authority by codifying and controlling representation of the relationship between the past and the present.[3] The accumulation of vast amounts of information on finance, trade, health, crime and industry served this end. In Britain this cultural project was integral to the country's emergence as a colonial power, and since India was potentially the most important colony, the consolidation of the state brought the two countries into a relationship of mutual reciprocity:

> It is not just that the personnel who governed Indian [*sic*] were British, but the projects of state building in both countries – documentation, legitimation, classification, and bounding, and the institutions therewith – often reflected theories, experiences, and practices worked out originally in India and then applied to Great Britain, as well as vice versa. Many aspects of metropolitan documentation were first developed in India.[4]

This process reached its zenith with the establishment of the nineteenth-century Raj. India was the laboratory for the Enlightenment project that provided the pillars of reason. Many branches of the natural sciences were catalysed by the demands attendant on colonial expansion.[5] India was also the test bed for methods of domestic government, while British public schools manufactured the governing elite for service in India.[6] All this was set in motion, however, toward the close of the previous century, and lubricated by theories on the nature of Indian culture and society. Government was predicated on knowledge of the cultural forms of India – forms that came to be transformed by the very process that sought to understand them. Again reciprocity obtained. 'Culture was imbricated both in the means and the ends of colonial conquest', argues Nicholas Dirks, 'and culture was invented in relationship to a variety of internal colonialisms.' Colonial culture reached back to the metropolis, to emerge in and inform domestic concerns.[7]

Metropolitan histories were profoundly influenced by events in India. It is difficult to explain, for example, the emergence of racialized conceptions of the poor in the second half of the nineteenth century without acknowledging the impact of notions of Indian castes and tribes, and of the seismic rupture created by the 1857 uprising. Such questions command much of what appears in the following chapters, but as a prelude it is necessary to examine briefly the emergence of the 'unitary field' in the latter stages of the eighteenth century.

Prior to the establishment of the Raj, connections between India and England were evident in travel writings and imaginative literature. A cursory glance at these does suggest that travelogues entered into the expansive domain of poetry and drama.[8] Initially, perceptions of foreign lands and peoples derived from the mythical tales of Alexander, Marco Polo and Mandeville,[9] but with the flowering of literary culture and the accumulation of contemporary travel accounts the place occupied by the exotic changed. At the most basic level, contemporary authors drew upon such mythical tales as a means of embellishing references to the foreign and the exotic. Milton's *Paradise Lost*, Shakespeare's *Macbeth* and *The Tempest*, Spenser's *The Faerie Queene*, Locke's *Essay Concerning Human Understanding*, Marlowe's *Tamburlaine the Great*, Thomas Moore's *Lalla Rookh* and Donne's *The Embassy* all reveal knowledge of travel accounts and geographies. But these accounts were not used merely as a ready taxonomy of exotic characters and phenomena; they shaped geographical and ethnological imaginations. The trangressiveness of the exotic in Shakespeare, for example, reveals a struggle to contain the ambiguous or liminal in a commonwealth being forged by the age of discovery. Indeed, it is impossible fully to appreciate these imaginations in Shakespeare, unless they are located contradictorily between the new consciousness struggling for superiority over the ancient, and the abiding lure of the fabled past.[10]

Andrew Hadfield's more introspective study of the impact of travel writing in the early modern period reveals how such works reflected on problems within the English body politic at a time of change.[11] Because of the uncertain status shared by writers of prose fiction, dramatists and travellers, they chose consciously to disguise what were often radical critiques of the existing order using conveniently remote locations. Thus representations of foreign lands and peoples were used allegorically to address a host of pressing domestic issues around national identity, the constitution, the distribution of power and individual liberty. More generally, the seventeenth century witnessed a critical stage in the transition from narratives of pilgrimage and exploration to those of the secular traveller equipped with the new epistemology of scientific and rational inquiry.[12] Integral to this project was a heightened obligation to establish the historicity and authenticity of travel accounts, primarily through original documentation and reputable eyewitness testimony. Those relying on medieval notions of the fabulous and monstrous were increasingly discredited by sceptical narrative voices committed to rendering a truth securely based on empirical sources and methodologies.

Mutualities between early travelogues and popular writings on London are less evident. Even though the first body of popular, secular literature emerged toward the end of the sixteenth century, that is, at the moment when the first travellers to India were recording their observations, the writings of Robert Green, Thomas Dekker and Thomas Nashe articulated a distinct and jealously guarded urban mentality. In contrast to interpretations provided by the moral authority of church, court and City, the transitional metropolitan scene found expression in an eclectic range of destabilizing moral and verbal conventions.[13] In a host of hugely popular plays, pamphlets and ballads, London became a dangerous, labyrinthine landscape, the interpretation of which was possible only for figures occupying that liminal space between moral and criminal authority, who descended into the world of deception, fraud and temptation, subsequently to emerge and recount their experiences. There is a sense here that the metropolis provided all that an ambitious and inquisitive traveller could need. It is instructive that Nashe's *The Unfortunate Traveller* (1594) – one of the very few examples of crossing generic boundaries – was a hostile attack on the putative merits of (European) travel.[14] In certain respects, travellers to India shared the same sense of journey into a strange and unknown world, but their interpretative authority owed nothing to the transgressive rationale of the pamphleteers, and proved singularly incapable of expressing Indian culture except through the perspective of a mercantile elite in pursuit of commercial gain. Even the rabelaisian buffoonery of Thomas Coriat, struggling to define the generic boundaries of English travel writing, revealed little beyond this.

The narrative forms and the epistemological transformation evident in

travel accounts were a formative influence on eighteenth-century literature. It was not just that personalized accounts of (self) discovery provided
the narrative structure of the first novels, but also that the combination of
extreme scepticism and naïve empiricism constituted the self-conscious
critical theory necessary for their emergence as a genre.[15] With Defoe's
Robinson Crusoe and Swift's *Gulliver's Travels* the boundaries between
travelogue and fiction – always fluid – seemed to vanish. And in form and
content there are repeated references to travellers' accounts in Defoe's
Moll Flanders, Richardson's *The Negotiations of Sir Thomas Roe in his
Embassy to the Ottoman Porte*, Fielding's *Tom Jones*, Sterne's *Tobias
Smollet* and Goldsmith's *Citizen of the World*.

The relationship at this time between forms within the burgeoning literary culture of the metropolis is complex. For there were powerful
countervailing tendencies. In representing London's increasing dominance of national and imperial ambitions, the eighteenth-century metropolitan bourgeoisie 'contributed to a new form of imperial, august
urbanism that in turn redefined the bourgeois ideals and practices of the
merchant class'.[16] Through this process the values and styles of a metropolitan elite were consolidated and came to exert greater hegemonic control over the English ruling class as a whole. Tensions evident in the
previous century between elite and popular literature gradually dissipated.
The radical subversiveness of satire declined, to be replaced by hack writings seemingly incapable of transcending the tired, formulaic narratives of
tricks-of-the-town travelogues.[17] Lawrence Manley captures well the consequences of this shift:

> The national literature did not become homogeneous, not were its elements
> identical – a world of difference still separated Dryden's *Miscellanies* from
> Tom D'Urfey's *Wit and Mirth*, or Ned Ward's *London Spy* from Pope's
> *Dunciad*. But the general interorientation of various urbane *decora*, at least
> from within the institution, made this difference negotiable in ways that the
> differences between, say, *Astrophil and Stella* and Greene's cony-catching
> pamphlets were not.[18]

This negotiability was effectively realized with the creation of a unitary
field in the second half of the century, for the bringing together of
metropolis and colony was predicated on a convergence of different forms
of knowledge. Recent scholarship has suggested that the European imaginary of the late eighteenth and early nineteenth centuries was profoundly
influenced by a resurgent interest in the East, not all of which was dictated
by colonial imperatives.[19] To deal adequately with this complex issue we
would thus need to investigate the extent to which India entered into
Enlightenment and Romantic thought. Cohn's emphasis, however, is on
the 'investigative modalities' of the project of the British to classify,

categorize and hence control the new empire in India, that is, the 'procedures by which appropriate knowledge is gathered, its ordering and classification, and then how it is transformed into usable forms such as published reports, statistical returns, histories, gazetteers, legal codes and encyclopaedias'.[20] There were six interrelated and overlapping modalities:

1 The historiographic had ontological efficacy in rationalizing and thereby facilitating British rule. It comprised a number of strands. Historical inquiries were undertaken into customs and local histories which came to form the basis of land tenure, assessment and revenue collection. Indian civilization itself was explored in historical perspective, usually within a teleological framework that validated British rule. And British rule was the subject of popular histories of specific events such as the Black Hole of Calcutta. Although the most complex, this modality was pervasive, and generally seen as the most valuable.

2 The observational/travel involved particular itineraries that incorporated familiar locations and encounters. Accounts of these travels drew upon tropes made familiar by earlier travelogues, although their precise representation reflected changing socio-economic contexts.

3 The survey embraced a wide range of practices including, most significantly, the mapping of India, but also the collection and systematic classification of flora, fauna, ethnology and architecture.

4 The enumerative was driven by the perceived need to collect and classify data. Over time, those on prices, customs, duties and coinage were supplemented by more ethnographic concerns, realized in the massive compilation of information on caste, religion and occupation. After 1857 this totalizing project came to fruition in the series of censuses.

5 The museological was a by-product of land surveys and settlement proceedings. It identified and recorded archaeological sites, and collected artefacts, manuscripts and oral histories which were later housed in museums and national collections. This project helped to define India's past.

6 The surveillance refers to the means by which the British gathered information on those groups and practices that were perceived to threaten the social order. Thugs, dacoits, religious mendicants, and the various tribes thought beyond civilizing influence were singled out for attention. In the process, many tribes and castes were criminalized.[21]

If India did indeed become known to the British, these modalities provided the means. The whole immense project to gather, classify, categorize and order information brought India within a European imagination. Partial, incomplete and replete with contradiction this project may have been, but it possessed sufficient power to help secure and maintain British dominance. This power derived from its sheer ambition; few features of

Indian society were left untouched by the hands of surveyors, census enumerators, photographers and cartographers. What underpinned the project was an empiricism that, by reducing colonial knowledge to factual statements about observable reality, made possible the bringing together onto a common epistemological terrain not only of different forms of evidence (gazetteers, statistical returns, topographical surveys, oral testimony), [22] but also of different disciplines (anthropology, history, sociology, science), and of different spaces (Indian regions, London). More important, however, I believe that the knowledge field was constituted by and cohered around an articulating principle. This principle was *progress*. At that moment in the late eighteenth century when India became subject to the knowledgeable gaze of the British state, belief in the idea of progress took shape. This belief structured the ways in which both metropolis and colony came to be understood.

Through this process – complex, multivalent and pervasive – diverse peoples within the ascendant commercial empire were constructed as primitive and hence incorporated hierarchically into the European human order. This had profound consequences for the ways in which these subject peoples were represented throughout the nineteenth century. Differences would remain on whether savagery represented a prelapsarian state of innocence, or a state of degeneration into which peoples had fallen from a previously higher one, but the important point was that savages were so because they had not been subject to the law of progress. It was in this way that colonial subjects, black slaves and the urban poor were culturally constituted by the doctrine of progressivism, and their continued exploitation justified. The seeming paradox was that this unified project was launched at that moment when elements within Enlightenment humanism encouraged recognition of the longevity of non-European civilizations, and of the barbarity of slavery. As Christopher Bayly explains:

> Ironically, the growing and orchestrated contempt for Asian, African and even European subordinates was derived in part from the very same humanitarian drives which saw the abolition of the slave trade and the beginning of the moves for the emancipation of slaves. It was morally necessary to bring slaves back from social death into civil society. But if so, the hierarchy of civil society must be closely defined both through institutions and by an ideology which derived from the idea that cultures attained 'civilisation' by stages of moral awakening and material endeavour. The 'discovery' of the urban poor and the criminal classes in Britain were part of a very similar project and undertaken by the same civil and religious agencies.[23]

Identification of the uncivilized was thus made possible in part by the use of an older rhetoric of heathenism, savagery and paganism, and these were to continue as powerful motives late into the nineteenth century. As we shall see, in the age of imperial modernity race came to define the boundaries of progress, as subject peoples were perceived increasingly in terms of rigidified racial hierarchies.

In the chapters that follow I explore aspects of this process. To address the field in its entirety is well beyond the limits of a single volume. It would have been legitimate, for example, to examine mutualities between metropolis and colony in the development of education, public health, governance, municipal reform, policing and town planning. Instead I intend to focus on what was perceived to be the most threatening antitheses to progress, namely, the metropolitan poor and colonial peoples. In terms of their chronologies, rhetoric, narratives and agencies there were distinct homologies between the discursive appropriation of the poor and of colonial subjects during the long nineteenth century, suggesting that the London poor were an object of imperial and not merely domestic concern. These homologies were to be found in the diverse array of reports, inquiries, minutes and surveys that resulted from the quotidian processes of imperial rule. More significantly, however, they were evident in the published accounts that reached a wider audience, and so entered into popular consciousness. Among these, the writings of travellers and evangelicals were by far the most influential. Before considering this literature I wish to explore the rise of the idea of progress and how it structured British thought on the place of non-European peoples in the new world order.

Notes

1 C.A. Bayly, *Empire and Information. Intelligence Gathering and Social Communication in India, 1780–1870*, Cambridge, Cambridge University Press, 1996, p. 49.

2 Among these might be mentioned William Robertson's *An Historical disquisition concerning the Knowledge which the Ancients had of India* (1791) and Abbe Raynal's *Philosophical History of the East and West Indies* (1776). The latter was among the most borrowed travel books from Bristol Library over the period 1773–84 (Peter J. Marshall and Gwynn Williams, *The Great Map of Mankind. British Perceptions of the World in the Age of Enlightenment*, London, Dent, 1982, p. 57).

3 Bernard S. Cohn, *Colonialism and its Forms of Knowledge. The British in India*, Princeton, Princeton University Press, 1996, pp. 3–5. I have taken a small liberty with Cohn's arguments here; he talks of the desire of the state to represent the past, while I believe it was more concerned to locate the present in relation to the past.

4 *Ibid.*, pp. 4–5.

5 Nicholas B. Dirks, 'Introduction: colonialism and culture', in Nicholas B. Dirks (ed.), *Colonialism and Culture*, Ann Arbor, University of Michigan Press, 1992, p. 6.

6 See also Eric Stokes, *The English Utilitarians and India*, Oxford, Oxford University Press, 1959.

7 Dirks, 'Introduction: colonialism and culture', p. 4.

8 Balachandra Rajan, *Under Western Eyes. India from Milton to Macaulay*, Durham, Duke University Press, 1999, is an interesting reconnaissance into this neglected field.

9 Donald F. Lach, *Asia in the Making of Europe. Vol. II. A Century of Wonder*, Chicago, University of Chicago Press, 1993, p. 381. Lach does tend to understate the impact of travel literature on satire and poetry in Tudor England.

10 For a sophisticated study of the influence of cartographical poetics on seventeenth-

century theatre see John Gillies, *Shakespeare and the Geography of Difference*, Cambridge, Cambridge University Press, 1994, while Margaret Hodgen's *Early Anthropology in the Sixteenth and Seventeenth Centuries*, Philadelphia, University of Pennsylvania Press, 1964, remains the best account of the impact of the new ethnology.

11 Andrew Hadfield, *Literature, Travel, and Colonial Writing in the English Renaissance*, Oxford, Clarendon Press, 1998.

12 This whole question is explored with exemplary rigour by Michael McKeon, *The Origins of the English Novel, 1600–1740*, London, Radius, 1988, pp. 100–17.

13 Lawrence Manley, *Literature and Culture in Early Modern London*, Cambridge, Cambridge University Press, 1995, p. 301. Manley's fine survey of this literary culture makes no reference to travel writings.

14 Hadfield, *Literature, Travel, and Colonial Writing*, pp. 192–6.

15 McKeon, *The Origins of the English Novel*, p. 118.

16 Manley, *Literature and Culture in Early Modern London*, p. 516.

17 See below, pp. 47–9.

18 Manley, *Literature and Culture in Early Modern London*, p. 520.

19 Raymond Schwab, *The Oriental Renaissance. Europe's Rediscovery of India and the East, 1680–1880*, Guildford, Columbia University Press, 1984; Nigel Leask, *British Romantic Writers and the East. Anxieties of Empire*, Cambridge, Cambridge University Press, 1992; Alan Richardson and Sonia Hofkosh, *Romanticism, Race and Imperial Culture, 1780–1834*, Bloomington, Indiana University Press, 1996; Tim Fulford and Peter Kitson (eds), *Romanticism and Colonialism. Writing and Empire, 1780–1830*, Cambridge, Cambridge University Press, 1998.

20 Cohn, *Colonialism and its Forms of Knowledge*, p. 5.

21 *Ibid.*, pp. 5–11. To this list I am tempted to add the 'intelligence modality' through which extensive networks of Indian informers were created to provide military, social and political information. This added to the storehouse of information on Indian peoples and cultures, and was critical to the success of the Raj (Bayly, *Empire and Information*).

22 David Ludden, 'Orientalist empiricism: transformations of colonial knowledge', in Carol A. Breckenridge and Peter van der Veer (eds), *Orientalism and the Postcolonial Predicament. Perspectives on South Asia*, Philadelphia, University of Pennsylvania Press, 1993.

23 C.A. Bayly, *Imperial Meridian. The British Empire and the World, 1780–1830*, London, Longman, 1989, p. 7.

CHAPTER ONE

The antinomies of progress

The idea of progress came to captivate influential sections of British society in the second half of the eighteenth century. Times were propitious, for after the successful conclusion to the Seven Years War the nation embarked on a course of industrialization and unfettered imperial expansion that was to secure Britain a seemingly unassailable authority in the world order. Domestically, the state enjoyed an unprecedented degree of stability. Revolutionary turmoil of the previous century had been settled, and a unity was being forged by the incorporation of rival national elites into the state apparatus. Challenges to state power from below, while not entirely eliminated, were mitigated by a groundswell of popular patriotism. Control of international markets supplied the wealthy with novel opportunities for conspicuous consumption; a rebuilt metropolis provided public spaces for conviviality and intercourse. This was the impulse of modernization, and it augured well.[1]

The increasingly powerful hold exerted by the idea of progress, however, was predicated on neither consensus nor conceptual rigour. To the contrary, as secular doctrines gained favour, diversity and confusion flourished; the idea could be, and was, articulated in many forms. Taken in general (and retrospective) terms to mean 'the belief in the movement over time of some aspect or aspects of human existence, within a social setting, toward a better condition', its precise expression was determined by the particular assumptions made about historical change, human existence and improvement, and the nature of their interrelationships.[2]

David Spadafora has argued that two doctrines provided the intellectual framework within which the idea of progress developed in eighteenth-century Britain. The Judeo-Christian vision of history had an ancient lineage in Western thought and continued to exercise a profound influence in discussions on the future of humankind. The second, with a much more recent ancestry in the Renaissance, derived from secular beliefs in the advancement of knowledge. The immanent tensions between these doctrines, and the attempts to resolve them, effectively defined the boundaries of the debate on progress, in the process of which both were modified if not transformed.[3]

Christian theology displaced earlier conceptions of cyclical historical time with one that was essentially linear. Progress over time, however, was delimited to the spiritual sphere of human development. Thus while no argument was made for material progress, it was generally recognized among religious thinkers that spiritual improvement through the revelation of divine truth had occurred in the past and would continue in the future. Eventually and inevitably all human kind would benefit by being brought into the faith and wisdom of Christ. Seemingly in tension with this vision was an epistemology that from the time of the Renaissance launched a concerted assault on the authority of the ancients and the scriptures. Advances made in the sciences and in knowledge of successful civilizations beyond the reach of Christianity encouraged secular visions in which progress was attendant on the accumulation of empirically based knowledge of natural and later human phenomena.

The dramatic developments in industrial production, agriculture and transport strengthened the secular vision of progress but never to the extent that it overwhelmed religious orthodoxy. As was so often the case, the frontiers of Christian thought were extended to incorporate – perhaps annul – the challenge. In a deft move, mutually causal links were drawn between advances in the arts and sciences and in religious knowledge. Thus the gradual improvement in knowledge of the world was merely a precursor to the future progress of Christianity. Conversely, such advances in knowledge flowed from and were concrete evidence of the practical application of divine grace. These contrasting visions were therefore integral to the grand design for an earthly utopia, and for many clerics and scientists it was not only possible but desirable to hold on to them both in spite of their seeming incommensurabilities.

Applied to areas of the arts and sciences identified by Spadafora, these arguments are persuasive. Eighteenth-century advances in fine art, medicine, philology, philosophy, medicine and literature were perceived as the irresistible and divinely ordained triumph of the moderns over the ancients. This spirit had pushed back the boundaries of knowledge, and paved the way for future progress. Providentialism, however, was neither as pervasive nor as powerful as he suggests; in one neglected area crucial to Britain's ascent, namely, political economy, divine will featured much less prominently.[4] The rise of commercial society and the attendant problems of liberal governmentality demanded more systematic forms of knowledge.[5] Empirical observation combined with Baconian induction had fostered a political arithmetic that was peculiarly suited to the operation and accountability of commerce. Attempts to justify this new moral economy

by recourse to the anthem of progress, however, were replete with difficulty, most notably that associated with the unavailability of reliable data
on past societies. To overcome this, conjectural histories that explored the
origins of commercial society were forced to rely on distinctly unscientific
notions of human nature and providence. What resulted was an awkward
synthesis of mathematics, experimental sciences and faith that, in isolat-
ing concepts of human nature and mankind, dominated British
historiography and philosophy of the eighteenth century.[6]

The failure to provide definitive solutions to these fundamental questions encouraged other forms of knowledge production. Poetry thrived in
this period, and of course the novel was born. These imaginative modes of
inquiry and representation addressed themselves to precisely the same
intellectual concerns as moral philosophy. Thus the writings of Defoe,
Richardson and Fielding express in their various ways the valorization and
naturalization of commercial society by displacing absolutism with an
ethos of liberal governmentality, and promoting the market by stripping
individual capitalist activity of the sinful guises imparted by Christian
orthodoxy. Now material self-improvement was viewed as an objective,
universal and ineluctable principle of human nature and progress.[7] As we
shall see, the influence of these genres in disclosing the nature of poverty
and crime gained strength toward the end of the century, and although
challenged in the nineteenth by the emergence of systematic techniques of
observation and recording they remained a powerful influence on bourgeois and popular perceptions.

In the meantime, the foundations of political economy were being laid,
for it was Adam Smith who provisionally resolved many of the tensions in
moral philosophy, simultaneously establishing a modern science of commercial society. Smith was able to provide both empirical and theoretical
justification by subordinating observable and quantifiable phenomena to
abstractions such as society, the market and later the economy in which
the divine had no evident or necessary role. Over time, these abstractions
became *the* objects of inquiry, pursued by a professional cohort of social
scientists armed with an impressive array of mathematical and statistical
techniques.

It was on this intellectual landscape in the latter half of the eighteenth
century that certain disturbing features came to be recognized. Poverty,
slavery and colonial expansion emerged almost simultaneously as matters
of urgent concern, forcing massive shifts in historical consciousness. The
presence of the poor, after all, had been acknowledged for centuries; why
should anyone seek to challenge the eternal wisdom of Christ's epigram
that they would always be with us? Why was it that at this moment the
poor were removed from nature and brought into the forefront of history?[8]
Likewise, the existence of slavery had not seriously been questioned since

ancient times. And yet in this period forces were unleashed that in the space of decades were to bring universal opprobrium to bear on the institution. And why did colonial expansion, which for a time had promised unparalleled prospects of material gain, now seem increasingly a threat to the future of the British nation? This synchronicity has to be explained.

To claim that these issues had resonance because at times of uncertainty they became politically charged is without doubt legitimate. There is sufficient evidence to suggest, for example, that concern about the threatening presence of the poor on the streets of London mounted at those times when their numbers were swollen by large-scale demobilizations. Politics, however, cannot provide a complete answer. The sheer diversity of constituencies that were drawn into debates, and the complex ways in which their concerns were expressed, cannot be explained adequately using the crude analytical tool of political interest. I would like to propose that the idea of progress unified and shaped these anxieties. Within the orbit of modernity, poverty, slavery and colonial expansion came to be perceived as aberrant; the poor, slaves and colonial subjects as defiant. Progress thus acted as an antithetical articulating principle, as a result of which distinctly dystopian visions of degeneration, decline, failure and evil gained currency.

Poverty and progress

Ancient though the condition of poverty was, the eighteenth century inherited few of the ideological presuppositions that had framed societal perceptions of the poor. Poverty had been thought a state of grace, a misfortune to be borne by the 'holy' poor with pious fortitude and resignation, or a condition to be sought by the devout as an escape from earthly temptation.[9] Since it was a condition of divine rather than human providence, those who were able were charged out of a sense of Christian duty to provide charitable relief in the form of funds for gainful employment, alms houses and hospitals. Some viewed this as a natural opportunity to display benevolence. Such charity, however, at a time of widespread immiseration attendant on forced displacement from the countryside, proved inadequate, and for the next four hundred years poverty was perceived as a moral, social and political problem to be ameliorated through appropriate measures of relief or control.

Most influential in this were the Elizabethan poor and vagrancy laws, implemented to provide relief to the necessitous poor and suppress potential disruption from those falling outside its ambit. Although private charity remained the preferred option, the principle of a compulsory system of relief implicitly recognized the social nature of poverty. In so doing it also consolidated age-old distinctions between the deserving and undeserving poor. Those who, through no fault of their own, were reduced to destitution could legitimately claim relief. Others, 'able but unwilling' to work, were refused, and hence forced into beggary where they were subject to the harsh, even brutal regime of the vagrancy laws. In a thesis that has defined much of the subsequent debate, Richard Tawney locates these new legal forms within the shift that took place in the consciousness of poverty. Protestantism – or more precisely its urban manifestation, Calvinism – broke with a Christian tradition that had regarded commercial activity as sinful. In contrast to the damning indictment of profit as the illegitimate gain of parasitical entrepreneurs and usurers, Calvin and his followers preached that profit, if not excessive, was income accruing from respectable industry and diligence. Indeed, by seeking not personal salvation but the glorification of God, commercial activity was practical devotion. It was a theology that both expressed and drew support from an ascendant merchant class, for

> it no longer suspects the whole world of economic motives as alien to the life of the spirit, or distrusts the capitalist as one who has necessarily grown rich on the misfortunes of his neighbour, or regards poverty as in itself meritorious, and it is perhaps the first systematic body of religious teaching which can be said to recognize and applaud the economic virtues.[10]

These economic virtues had their basis in labour, not only of capitalists but also of the poor. In a move that enshrined economic progress in religion, idleness was now acclaimed as a sin against God and society. The putative state of grace of the pauper was no longer defensible, nor was indiscriminate alms-giving; instead, a system of secular relief dictated that those who could work but were prevented from so doing by economic depression should be set to productive work, and those who could not work should be aided with relief.

Much as the Elizabethan poor law was celebrated as emblematic of a modern civilized nation, its legacy was uncertain. It was never designed to be the principal means of relieving economic distress, merely one to be used as a last desperate resort. Its founders anticipated that private philanthropy would continue to meet most of the need; in the event it did not. Furthermore, successive cohorts of legislators, acting out of a belief that prevention of destitution was better than a cure, sought to guarantee regular income by stabilizing employment, and to control the prices of staple foods, in particular bread, by eliminating restrictive practices.[11] None of this was successful in mitigating distress, and as pressure mounted on the system in the seventeenth and eighteenth centuries, so its actuarial and administrative foundations began to crumble.

Attitudes toward the system of relief hardened. Puritan zeal of the seventeenth century turned the critical gaze of individualism on the causes of distress and found there moral deficiency. The result was a renewed assault on idleness. Relief, in whatever form, was thought enervating since it discouraged the poor from seeking work; the only long-term solution was to reform their character, if necessary by compulsion. Thus the idea of forced labour for all able-bodied poor made sound moral and economic sense, and found increasing acceptance among religious and business communities. Morally, such labour instilled the values of thrift, sobriety and acceptance of subordination within a rigid social order; economically, it reduced the pool of unproductive labour and the diversion of precious financial resources in relief of destitution to the benefit of nation and empire. It was an ethos that combined personal and national salvation. Thus were established in broad outline the principles that were to culminate in the 1834 Poor Law Amendment Act, not in the event for the salvation of the nineteenth-century poor, but their damnation.

Even if the agenda of the voluminous debate on poverty during the eighteenth century had been decided from the outset, sharp divisions of opinion emerged. The dialectic of the moral and economic was sufficiently expansive to allow, even encourage, diversity; indeed, it is only with difficulty that we can provide a degree of coherence to the mass of comment.[12] If there was a common theme it was that of labour, for in an age of mercantilism productive labour provided the key to national prosperity and stability. Most writers in the early decades who addressed themselves to the question of poverty used this as the touchstone. Thus when Daniel Defoe in his 1704 pamphlet *Giving Alms No Charity, and Employing the Poor a Grievance to the Nation* railed against proposals for a variety of schemes to put the poor to work, he did so on the grounds that the work created no new industry.[13] When Bernard Mandeville satirized the moral and social evil of the time in *The Fable of the Bees*, he castigated the idleness of labourers and the hypocrisy of charity.[14] And the Rev. Thomas Alcock, writing on the poor law in 1752, identified the baneful influence of luxury. Touching on one of the most significance debates of the time, he blamed the poor law for promoting the evil it was intended to remedy. Relief served only to promote indigence by encouraging a taste among the poor for luxuries such as tobacco, tea and dress of little service.[15]

This paradigm was challenged if not overthrown by the emergence in the second half of the century of writers associated with the Scottish Enlightenment, most notably Adam Smith. As we have suggested, although Smith's political economy tilted the balance of thinking on progress toward more secular perspectives, moral philosophy evidenced in concerns over the human condition was never excised completely. In no area was this more apparent than that of poverty. Because human progress and prosperity were believed to attend the pursuit of self-interest in a market economy untrammelled by state interference, this did not mean that responsibility for the poor could be abrogated. The 'wealth of nations', after all, referred not to their monetary power but to their peoples.[16] No nation could be 'wealthy' that condemned the majority of its people to a life of abject poverty, and so it was a matter of urgent concern that the conditions of the poor be improved. Any system guided by the principles of high prices and low wages could not guarantee the nation's wealth. Instead, fair and liberal rewards for labour should be promoted by a 'progressive' economy since they encouraged the poor to pursue self-interest actively and conscientiously. Interference in this 'natural' mechanism was to be resisted. Thus settlement laws limited the mobility of labour, and were an affront to liberty and justice.[17]

Trade cycles, war and settlement laws also exacerbated the seemingly intractable problem of vagrancy. Vagrants had first been defined as a source of social and political concern with the introduction of Elizabethan vagrancy laws; indeed, we tend still to think of vagrancy as a problem of early modern England. Agricultural dislocation swelled the ranks of so-called masterless men who were forced to take to the roads of the country in search of gainful employment.[18] More than the poor who fell within the cold embrace of the poor law, 'vagabonds and incorrigible rogues' were potent symbols of transgression in a society that increasingly valorized Protestant virtues of hard work, thrift, order and personal responsibility, and as such they were subject to a brutal regime of sanctions from whipping and branding to transportation and execution.[19]

Toward the end of the seventeenth century the problem of vagrancy seemed to ease. Enhanced economic prospects and increased poor law expenditure forced fewer into transient poverty. The disciplinary regime became less bloody. Vagrants were less likely to be identified and punished as vagabonds; rather, when apprehended, they were removed to their place of settlement where they were entitled to poor relief. By the beginning of the eighteenth century, the vagrant population in the countryside comprised largely itinerant Scots, Irish, gypsies, entertainers and the ex-military.[20] The large cities, however, presented a different problem. London in particular drew the desperate masses of the poor displaced from the countryside. Here was concentrated untold wealth to be tapped by the various skills of beggars, tricksters and thieves. In the climate of eighteenth-century improvement, it was this constituency that came to be seen as the principal barrier to progress.[21]

Slavery and progress

Although the existence of slavery had since ancient times attracted the critical attention of social and moral commentators, it was not until the eighteenth century that discussion featured prominently in the influential works of moral philosophy and political economy.[22] At the heart of this concern was a desire to explain why slavery continued to flourish in an age of progress, *and* in the New World which so embodied the ideal. For potential answers Enlightenment thinkers, political theorists and theologians looked to the historical record and the troublesome concept of the natural order. Many resolved that there was a fundamental contradiction between the perpetuation of slavery and human progress, and that any progress to a new era was predicated on abolition of the slave trade and emancipation of slaves.

David Brion Davis has convincingly demonstrated that the history of modern Western slavery and emancipation can be recast around the notion of progress. The relationships between changing conceptions of slavery and progress, however, are highly mobile and ambiguous. There was little evidence of anti-slavery sentiment before the eighteenth century. It is a profound paradox that while prominent thinkers, heirs to the seventeenth-century revolution, were laying the theoretical foundations for political liberty, they accepted slavery as a natural state. Thus when John Locke in the *First Treatise of Government* declared that 'Slavery is so vile and miserable an Estate of Man, and so directly opposite to the generous Temper and Courage of our Nation; that 'tis hardly to be conceived that an *Englishman*, much less a *Gentleman*, should plead for 't', the estate of man he had in mind was that found in a free and rational society governed by social contract. The enslavement of Africans, on the other hand, conformed with natural law since it derived from the legitimate purchase and domination of captives of war. Such slaves were private property and were subject to the same valid morality.[23]

The sources of anti-slavery thought in the eighteenth century were diverse and complex. British Protestantism was in the early vanguard, and because of this it is tempting to view the stirrings of abolitionism as part of a Christian philanthropic tradition galvanized by mounting concern over the poor. The chronologies, however, were discrepant. Furthermore, Protestant attitudes to private charity and institutional relief were weakened by the belief that undue zeal in the pursuit of benevolence and promotion of self-reliance among the poor would undermine the social order, and as such could not provide the basis of a concerted assault on slavery. Slavery, however, provided a sufficiently remote test bed for Protestant morality since, unlike the poor law, it was an institution that could be challenged without the same threat to domestic social and political relations.[24]

Quakers in Britain were the shock troops of the abolition movement. As one of the most powerful groups to emerge from the sectarianism of the seventeenth century, Quakers retained internal unity and identity against an intolerant religious order, and directed spiritual energies to the practical alleviation of social problems. Commerce was one of the few spheres from

which they were not excluded, and through extensive, mutually supportive networks and a reputation for honest trading, Quaker families were
able to build substantial banking and manufacturing empires. Initially,
their economic interests were so tied up with the slave trade that active
involvement was inevitable, but in the course of the eighteenth century
this became increasingly untenable. Unable to make the moral compromises of more orthodox churches, the Society of Friends came to view
slavery as a moral evil, and in the 1760s took the first steps on the path to
its eradication.

Within two decades the cause had attracted a rather larger body of converts. In the 1770s John Wesley was alerted to the nature of slavery by a
pamphlet written by the Quaker Anthony Benezet, and mobilized Methodists behind the abolition movement. To Wesley slavery represented the
ultimate violation of justice, mercy and truth, and everyone involved in
the villainous trade was stained with blood. Redemption was to be sought
in emancipation.[25] These ideas appealed widely to revivalist sentiment in
that they provided a way out of the spiritual difficulties faced by many who
thought that religious orthodoxy had reached a self-created impasse of
meaningless and abstract speculation. Anti-slavery was a cause that could
be used to express Christian devotion in direct and practical forms. Few
Methodists, however, could sustain Wesley's uncompromising stand.
Even his most notable follower, the slave ship captain John Newton, who
experienced conversion during one of many voyages, was initially reluc-
tant to condemn the trade. It was only later he decided to speak out pub-
licly in order to bring to public attention the evils of the trade. Such
faltering progress was emblematic of evangelicalism as a whole, and suggested its future course, for the 'main thrust of eighteenth-century revival-
ism ended with the missionary, not the abolitionist'.[26]

Slavery, like poverty, attracted the attention of more secular and
rational modes of inquiry in this period. Here again the influence of thinkers of the Scottish Enlightenment was of particular significance, in part
because it was rather less ambivalent than its French counterpart. Drawing upon the work of contemporaries such as Francis Hutcheson, John
Millar and Jacques Turgot, Adam Smith condemned slavery by locating it
within schemes of economic and moral progress. Slavery, he argued, confronted directly the laws of morality and utility. The development of
mutual identification and self-interest, upon which harmonious social
relations and economic progress depended, was threatened by the perpetuation of the slave trade. Its eradication would unshackle progress from
those artificial restraints that had been sustained by monopoly and special
privilege, allowing self-interest to be harnessed to the general good.[27]

As a result of these various impulses, mediated in highly complex ways
from the late 1760s, modern slavery was viewed with increasing concern

as an evil, regressive and inefficient institution. This constituted a profound shift in historical consciousness, leading eventually to the abolition of the slave trade and the emancipation of black slaves. Much historical attention has been devoted to the role of organizations such as the London-based Society for Effecting the Abolition of the Slave Trade, established by the Quakers in 1787, and the Clapham Sect loosely based around William Wilberforce after his famous speech in parliament on the slave trade in 1789. These bodies, however, were able to draw upon a groundswell of popular opposition to slavery throughout the country, much of it galvanized by the activities of countless women.[28] Campaign activists or those who provided its moral and economic rationale anticipated abolition would promote material and moral progress. In the event, the legacy of slavery and abolition was rather more ambiguous and uncertain.[29]

Colonialism and progress

In the first half of the eighteenth century Britain emerged as a mercantile, imperial and naval power to rival France, Spain and Holland. Structurally underpinned by mutually supportive relationships among the state, the navy, and financial and mercantile sectors, British influence increased not only in global markets, but also in those ancillary services such as insurance, shipping, banking and distribution that were vital to continued growth.[30] The series of naval and land victories during the Seven Years War established Britain's supremacy by effectively stifling the ability of rival powers to develop overseas trade while that of Britain actually expanded.[31] The triumph over the French in North America was so complete that France's presence in other parts of the European empire was greatly weakened; most importantly, Britain was able to make significant gains in India, most of them at the expense of French interests. The profound sense of confidence that prevailed at the close of hostilities in 1763, however, was relatively short-lived. Within twenty years the British empire seemed on the brink of collapse.

A number of circumstances combined to sap belief in the progress of the 'first' British empire. Loss of the American colonies had revealed the limitations of Britain's fiscal strength, for when the state attempted to recoup the enormous cost of the Seven Years War by taxing the colonies it had claimed to defend, resistance mounted, precipitating the American War of Independence. Furthermore, the nascent empire in India was threatened by the endemic mismanagement and profligacy of the East India Company, and a rising tide of anti-colonial struggles. And the French, strengthened after fiscal reform and through retention of the most lucrative of the slave colonies, St Domingue, began to challenge Britain's control of the Caribbean slave trade. Finally, nationalist unrest in Ireland served to remind the British state that its oldest and nearest colony continued to be a source of real concern.[32]

For many, these events flowed inevitably from the logic of a flawed imperial ethos. From the early stages of expansion in the seventeenth century Britain's role had been defined by a distinct sense of imperial authority, much of it derived from ancient and medieval legacies. The Roman notion of *Imperium* described the limited but absolute authority of a single individual over a territory embracing more than one political community. In medieval Europe, this was appropriated by an ascendant Christian church to forge an empire – Christendom – in which the cultural and religious diversity of the Roman empire was superseded by a single sacred authority.[33] Armed with this authority, and claiming a mission to civilize the rest of the world by converting its inhabitants to Christianity, European powers embarked on various imperial projects, notable for their brutal exploitation of indigenous peoples.

While elements of this universalism survived well into the nineteenth century, it came under increasing attack from elites in the imperial metropolises. Early writings like Bartolome de Las Casas's *A Short Account of the Destruction of the Indies* (1552) had expressed moral outrage at the genocidal Spanish conquest of America, and a fear that Spain would be visited by divine retribution if not stopped.[34] More influential, however, were the later critiques that such imperial ambition was politically and economically destructive. The experience of Spanish, French and British overseas expansion, it was argued, demonstrated that every settler community eventually came to demand political autonomy and economic self-sufficiency, and that exploitation of forced labour – either indigenous or imported slave – was economically inefficient, not least because it was massively destructive of human life.[35]

Perceived here was a tangible threat to progress of the imperial state. In a pleasing irony, the ancient *Imperium* was now used to confirm a teleology of self-destruction. Just as the Roman empire had collapsed under the inexorable logic of extravagant territorial expansion, so European empires would fall into ruin unless the relationship between colony and metropolis was reordered to prevent the needless drain of vital resources. As David Hume, one of the most consistent critics of expansion, stated:

> There seems to be a natural Course of Things, which brings on the destruction of great Empires. They push their Conquest till they come to barbarous nations, which stop their Progress, by the Difficulty of subsisting great Armies. After that, the Nobility & considerable Men of the conquering Nation & best Provinces withdraw gradually from the frontier Army, by reason of its Distance from the Capital & barbarity of the Country, in which they quarter.... Hence Disorder, Violence, Anarchy, & Tyranny, & Dissolution of Empire.[36]

Evidence for the corrosive influence of territorial expansion could readily be found at the limits of empire in America and India. Colonists in America, armed with the rhetoric of liberty, were pressing for a degree of political representation with such urgency that total separation and the attendant collapse of empire seemed only a matter of time. Meanwhile, the corruption, greed and inefficiency attached to the activities of the East India Company were seen to threaten not only British possessions in India but somehow through diffusion the very fabric of metropolitan culture and polity.

The solution was sought, as it was to the problems of poverty and slavery, in the enlightened languages of moral philosophy and political economy.[37] Thus from the 1730s the providential spirit of conquest and the pursuit of military glory were displaced in Britain by an ethos that emphasized the mutual interdependence of commerce, Protestantism, maritime power and liberty.[38] This was none other than a British national identity, in the process of being forged from components of a culture reaching back to the sixteenth century. Liberty was enshrined in the invented tradition of an ancient English constitution manifest in a system of law that guaranteed rights for all of its subjects. This was underwritten by a Protestantism that set Britain apart from those European powers seen to be suffering under Catholic oppression. In the eighteenth century, the notion of an elect nation was displaced by one that increasingly embraced Britain's wider role as a rising commercial and naval power.[39] Here the influence of political economy was telling. In India, for example, board members of the East India Company constantly turned to the writings of the new breed of political economists for guidance. During the crisis of 1771 when faced with financial chaos they approached the leading economist, James Steuart, to report on the situation.[40] And despite the hostility of Adam Smith to the monopoly of the Company, the directors were prepared to ask him to participate in an inquiry into administrative malpractices. These instances were symptomatic of a general acceptance that commerce under the guiding hand of political economy should temper the influence of paternalism and evangelism in the economic affairs of the Company.

Ostensibly uniting the interests of Irish unionists, Glasgow merchants, Caribbean planters and officials in the thirteen colonies with those of the British state, this ethos provided an integrated empire within which individual rights and private property were secured. *Imperium* was unitary; *Dominium* divided.[41] Such a conception of empire found ready acceptance throughout the British Atlantic world as the various constituencies came to think of themselves as members of a single community – the 'British empire' – pursuing their commercial interests in a just and peaceful manner. Significantly, it also came to command in Britain during the 1740s a genuinely popular following. 'Rule, Britannia' dates from this time.

This *Imperium*, however, contained the seeds of its own destruction, for the political principles exported to the American colonies, particularly those governing rights, property and the common good, were readily appropriated against metropolitan authority. The rebellion of the thirteen colonies pushed these principles to the limit and then fractured them.[42] With their cession, and the revolutionary challenges that ensued, the dominant rhetoric of empire took on more authoritarian and hierarchical dimensions. Crown, Church and Constitution were appointed as its guardians; in their names new instruments of coercion and control were implemented that expressed and fostered an institutionalized ethos of racial superiority.[43]

From the putative crisis in the imperial state emerged a new empire. Although we must caution against crudely drawn boundaries, the second British empire was geo-politically and ideologically distinct. The turn to the East in a changed world order was accompanied by this new imperial ethos. That deriving from the 'medieval legacy of universalism', a presumed right of lordship, or from the pan-Atlantic *Imperium*, had no relevance to the role of the British state in India and Africa. Rather, the imperial ideology that underpinned the 'aristocratic authoritarianism' or 'proconsular despotism' of the state[44] was articulated to a newly forged British nationalism;[45] together they charted the course of the state in re-establishing the empire, and defining its attitudes toward colonial subjects.

This study is an attempt to understand something of the nature of the process by examining the homologies that existed between discursive constructions of colonial subjects and the metropolitan poor during the long nineteenth century. To my mind there were unmistakable parallels in their chronologies and rhetoric, and in the agencies that were responsible. If this is the case, then it follows that the perceived problems around colonial expansion, slavery and poverty have to be recast within the dynamic relationship between metropolis and empire. But before we come to explore the evidence, it is necessary to think further about the claim made at the outset that the articulating principle for these concerns was that of progress. To do this I wish to consider the thinking that informed ideas of progress, and why certain peoples were seen as barriers to imperial modernity.

Progress and the human order

Lecturing at Swarthmore College in the troubled year of 1941, the redoubtable Arthur O. Lovejoy had good cause to reflect on the transformation he had witnessed in human thought. He cited with approval Max

Lerner's declaration that 'the rational, right-thinking man has as surely ceased to be considered the center of our intellectual system as the earth has ceased to be the center of our planetary system'.[46] This revolution, Lovejoy proceeded to explain, had its counterpart in the seventeenth and eighteenth centuries, for the writers of that age also were preoccupied with the attempt to understand the irrational in human nature and how it was linked to progress. That they lacked the rigour or analytical insights of their successors is not in doubt; that they were less penetrating in their analysis is.

Some appreciation of this revolution will, I believe, enable us to understand better the complex and dynamic relationship between conceptions of progress and human nature in the eighteenth century, and thereby the reasons why different constituencies were subject increasingly to processes of social, cultural and political exclusion. Conventionally, these processes have rightly been seen as integral to the development of modernity in its capitalist or imperialist guises.[47] Such perspectives, however, in defining progress as capitalist or as endemic to Western societies – with very different experiences of colonialism and capitalist modernization – beg rather more questions than they answer. The identity made at the outset, therefore, between the emergence in mid-eighteenth-century Britain of ideas of progress and the new-found confidence in commercial and imperial activity is not as secure as it might first appear. For while a sense of material improvement did undoubtedly contribute to the acceptance of progress, it cannot explain fully why, for example, progress was seen differently in England and Scotland, or indeed why belief in progress existed at all.[48] Historical pessimism, after all, was a powerful current in intellectual thought and survived to feed nineteenth-century visions of decline and degeneration.

Ascent of the belief in progress has variously been attached by scholars to advances in Christian conceptions of history, the secularization of thought in the arts and sciences, and changing views of human nature.[49] Rarely considered in this diverse body of work, however, is how a celebration of belief in progress structured conceptions of the human order. I wish, therefore, to revisit these broader themes, specifically the great chain of being and the stages theory of historical development, for it was these that came to define the contours of progress and to identify its most potent enemies.

Such is the status of the great chain of being that it is conventionally capitalized. Its lineages can be traced to ancient Greek philosophy, but its real significance dates from the Middle Ages when as a plan of the universe the conception came to be accepted without question by the majority of educated opinion.[50] This was to remain so until the ascent in the nineteenth century of evolutionary theory. The guiding principles were plenitude, continuity and linear gradation. Providence had created nature, it was contended, as an infinite number of beings ranging from the lowest forms to man. These beings were linked to one another in hierarchical order, differing from that immediately below and that immediately above by such minute gradation – the least possible degree of difference – that it was impossible to determine the point at which one ended and the other began.

Although details of the underlying principles were viewed differently, these mattered less than the social and political consequences that flowed from the scheme in its totality. Plenitude was proof of God's existence because it demonstrated his cosmic beneficence, but simultaneously it gave support to the curious notion that nature had been created for the use of mankind. This anthropocentrism was tempered, however, by the recognition that man's location in the chain was well below that of the supreme being. Locke, for example, was persuaded that there was a far greater number of species above us than below us, and Kant surmised that higher beings viewed a Newton as 'we view a Hottentot or an ape'.[51]

This 'ethics of prudent mediocrity' confirmed man's station and the immorality of pretensions higher or lower. Wisdom began with knowledge of one's limitations. To strive for intellectual achievements beyond the meagre capacity of man was to commit the sin of pride. To pursue innate animalistic tendencies was to become degenerate. Either act was a threat to the balance of a universal system in which all beings were allotted a place.[52] It was one short step to apply these arguments to the social and political spheres of human activity. Imperfections may exist, it was surmised, in forms of government, but since these resulted from weaknesses in human nature any attempt to transform society through political action challenged the divine order. Society was maintained through the same set of principles. God had appointed all to their particular station in life. Those in lower estates had just cause to claim respect and consideration from their superiors, but demands for equality were an affront to nature. It was a profoundly pessimistic and conservative vision.

It was possible, however, to derive an antithetical, optimistic vision from the principle of plenitude. Imperfections exist in the providential design because they are necessary to the perfection of the whole and this to the common good. The limitations of each species of being define its place in the great chain, and so it is futile to ask why none is endowed with greater talent. Any alteration threatens the integrity of the organic world and hence its happy ordering. This was the vision that impelled much of the work of natural scientists as they sought proof of the ways in which every creature was endowed with characteristics consistent with, indeed necessary to, the perfection of the whole. But such inquiry cleared the ground for an approach that directed attention less to final causes than to origins, and hence the problem of evolution.[53]

The idea of least possible gradation as static and fixed began to be challenged by philosophers and scientists anxious to explain the possibility of movement from one species to another. The belief that upward movement, even if possible, was to the cost of those occupying the next order, gave way to the notion that general progress was achievable. Biologists and geologists, increasingly aware of the evidence on plenitude, sought to explain gaps in the chain. Here the relationship between humans and apes took on a particular significance. Although physical similarities between the two species had long been recognized, no one was yet bold enough to suggest that humans were the descendants of apes; instead, connecting links were sought. Invariably, the 'savage races of Africa' were identified in intellectual, physical and moral terms as the most likely sources.[54] The temporalizing of the chain of being, therefore, while opening the window to progress, simultaneously codified potential barriers to it.

This was a distinct reversal to another influential current of thought in eighteenth-century Britain. Primitivism was an historical and ethical philosophy that from at least the fifth century BCE had dominated Western thought on the historical development of human society. At the heart of the philosophy was the belief that early human society displayed noble qualities that in the course of time had been corrupted by the march of civilization. Thus essential human qualities such as goodness, kindness and wisdom were found in primitive society; now evil, greed and pride prevailed.

Toward the close of the eighteenth century, the influence of primitivism reached its zenith. The explorations of North American Indian and South Sea Island societies in the second half of the century gave considerable impetus to the primitivist critique of advanced Western society. In extolling the virtues of the simple life of nature it ran as a powerful current against the degenerative tendencies of luxury and pride endemic to industrial civilization. Luxury was of particular concern. As a concept it was sufficiently imprecise to engage the interests of most of the important and many of the popular writers of the age, and to be used by them as a talisman to express fears about a diverse range of social and political pathologies.[55] Much of this was inherited from the ancients. Luxury had long been regarded as a fundamental evil from which others ensued, and it was seen to be virtually limitless as human desires multiplied. In its most potent form luxury was against nature for it threatened to undermine the providential order of the chain of being, or was confirmation of historical regression. And luxury was ubiquitous. It was found in the church, in Westminster, in aristocratic mansions, in merchants' houses, but most evidently among the people. As was so often the case when social concern was expressed, only others were seen as corruptible. Hence the plebeian rabble, prone to licentiousness, and damned by excessive consumption of tea and tobacco, were identified as the single most toxic threat to civilization. Unless checked by moral or legal restraint, tyranny and barbarism would ensue.

Luxury became a particularly powerful weapon in the hands of the political opposition. The extreme suspicion with which more radical elements in the eighteenth century viewed political authority derived in large part from their hatred of the enervating influence of luxury.[56] Leaders, upon whom the future of the state depended so heavily, were diverted from serving the common good by the selfish and vainglorious pursuit of property. Corrupt and unprincipled government was the result. Dr John Brown – one of the most astute and widely read critics – wrote at a time of personal and political crisis 'to throw just light on the peculiar causes of our calamitous situation'. Among the few remaining virtues, he argued, were the spirit of liberty, humanity and the civil administration of justice, but these were assailed by the spirit of commerce, which 'begets a kind of regulated selfishness', and engenders in the character and manner of our times a 'vain, luxurious, and selfish EFFEMINACY'.[57] And in a revealing passage, he politicizes the chain of being to suggest how corruption in high places leads to the dismantling of political order in the same way as ambition threatens the natural order:

> Thus the great chain of political self-interest was at length formed; and extended from the lowest cobbler in a borough, to the King's first minister. But a *chain of self-interest* is indeed no better than a *rope of sand*: There is no cement nor cohesion between the parts.[58]

Pride was further evidence of human corruption. Material advantages and intellectual superiority over other beings, it was argued, engendered artificial desires and false vanities that disrupted man's harmony with nature.[59] The contemporary passion for approbativeness, self-esteem and emulation exemplified unconscious and non-rational pride that had set humans apart in the chain of being, and on a path increasingly divergent from reason and virtue. Mandeville's *Fable of the Bees*, for example, one of the most virulent social critiques of the eighteenth century, can be thought of as a damning indictment of irrational motives. In tracing the connection between 'private vices' and 'public benefits', he singled out pride as the trait upon which morality seemed to depend.[60] Only by returning to the humility of primitive peoples was moral redemption possible.

The intellectual and moral thrust of this complex but unifiable discourse shifted dramatically in the second half of the eighteenth century. Primitivism entered into crisis when it appeared to have reached its apotheosis. Part of the problem was that the philosophy, like that of the great chain of being, was so fluid that it could be used to arrive at contrasting interpretations of progress. The putative record was consistent with doctrines of both the inevitable decline and the constancy of human nature once the original state of innocence had been lost.[61] For some it could provide a programme of progress by reversion to the original state of nature. At that moment when events in science, economics and philosophy moved against it with unprecedented vigour, primitivism collapsed under the weight of its immanent logical inconsistencies. By 1788 Joseph Priestley – hardly a conservative – could claim that 'Idleness, treachery and cruelty are predominant in all uncivilized countries; notwithstanding the boasts which the poets make of the *golden age* of mankind, before the creation of empires'.[62]

The ideological props of primitivism were also assailed. Strands of Augustan and Enlightenment thought began to question the deleterious effects imputed to luxury and pride. The sceptical Johnson claimed that since luxury could only ever reach the few, no civilization was ever damaged by it. To the contrary, the poor are strengthened by material gain. And Gibbon, conventionally seen in his classic study of the fall of the Roman empire as an arch-enemy of luxury, actually made a subtle distinction between different forms. In an imperfect society, he argued, luxury is an effective means of mitigating inequality; only when it is pervasive, as in Rome before its fall, does luxury become 'a secret and destructive poison'.[63] More vigorous and telling, however, was the reassessment launched by political economists. Integral to their critique of primitivist theories was the valorization of commerce as a progressive stage in human development. Far from acting as a destructive influence on development, the desire for luxury, manifest in material improvement, was now seen as one of its principal motor forces. Ferguson, Millar and in particular Adam Smith argued cogently that commercial progress required the unfettered pursuit of material interest. The prospect of material gain, therefore, encouraged Protestant virtues and enhanced social stability.

In a similar vein, the dissembling influence of pride was rethought. Pride in its various manifestations came increasingly to be viewed as *the* inspiration for virtuous action and progress. Hume based his theory of moral judgement on the premise that the desire for self-esteem derives from approbativeness, and encourages virtuous behaviour since people are driven to act in ways that appear to others praiseworthy. Affection not rationality thus controls human volition. Smith also recognized the power of approbativeness, and conversely that of disapprobation and disapproval. Humans are endowed with a desire to please, and any feelings of self-love must be subordinated to the desire for admiration from others. This genuine human need for prestige fosters also a desire for material possession – an argument that in the *Theory of Moral Sentiments* came to be erected as the theology of commercialism.[64] Ownership of private property, he stated, was based on the need for emulation and honour; 'there is no other conceivable incentive to the accumulation of wealth'.[65]

This transformation in thinking on degenerative tendencies was framed by wider concerns of Enlightenment thinkers to valorize commercial society as the logical culmination of a distinct trajectory of historical change.[66] The publication of Locke's *Two Treatises on Government* in 1690 had opened the path for a stages theory of development. His discussion of the historical origins of property challenged ancient and scriptural accounts by suggesting that the more primitive modes of subsistence were not coexistent in the earliest ages of Asia and Europe, but rather were evidence of progress over time.[67] It was a path, initially, that few eighteenth-century writers were willing to follow. Mandeville, Hutcheson and Montesquieu all thought of stages in societal development, but their treatment of economic factors was fragmented and lacked coherence. With political economy, however, the stages theory of development reached maturity. Seminal thinkers such as Smith, Turgot and Quesnay constructed an overarching and teleological scheme of socio-economic progress through distinct and successive stages – defined essentially by their mode of subsistence – which embraced at one pole primitive societies witnessed in America and the South Pacific, and at the other advanced commercial economies. Thus the economy, like history, was seen to work to certain laws, the study of which could be pursued through comparisons of the division of labour, commodity exchange and accumulation of capital in different forms of society.[68]

The geo-politics of development derived from the work of the sixteenth-century political theorist Jean Bodin, who had reinterpreted the course of human history by identifying three crucial periods, each dominated by the peoples of a distinct region of the globe. The first two millennia had been dominated by the so-called Orientals (Babylonians, Persians and Egyptians), not because of their productive power, but because of their unrivalled hold over religion, philosophy and mathematics. Mediterranean peoples (Greeks and Romans) dominated the next two millennia because of their politics and practical knowledge, to be displaced by Northern peoples (Europeans) through their skills in warfare and mechanical inventions, and their ability to advance the scientific and philosophical work of the ancients.[69] Incommensurable though this geo-politics was with a stages theory of development, from the 1760s elements of the two theories were combined imaginatively to give even greater weight to the teleology of the West's ascent.

It was at this moment that Western civilization was invented.[70] A somewhat awkward synthesis of ideas on intellectual, artistic and scientific ability, socio-economic and political progress, historical narrative and geo-politics, it served to consolidate the self-identity of the West, in part and increasingly by the exclusion *both* of subordinates and of non-Western peoples as lower others. This transformation in thinking about the human order thus had a profound impact on the ways in which its various constituencies were viewed. To appreciate this issue more fully we need to consider the history of conceptions of difference from the time of the Renaissance when the other first entered into the European imagination as an object of concern.

Until the sixteenth century, the relationship between European and other was framed by a Christian cosmography that inherited medieval forms of classification.[71] Within this, savages were defined principally in terms of the religion they lacked, that is, as pagan, heathen or monstrous disciples of the devil. The 'discovery' of the Americas by Columbus and the tradition of travel and exploration that followed created a revolution in the geographical imagination. No longer could the world be seen in Ptolemaic terms as a relatively small island, centred on Jerusalem and surrounded by limitless and unknowable expanses of water; instead, it was recognized as a land surface forming a continuous whole, contiguous with but not bounded by oceans.

This integrity posed new challenges. The Christian subject may still be held to occupy the centre of the new geographical order, but he is brought forcefully into a relationship with peoples occupying the newly discovered spaces. The extraordinary period of exploration following Columbus emphasized the point. Travel accounts based on more reliable empirical observation displaced the medieval fantastic and monstrous by asserting the essential humanness of other peoples, and the necessity of bringing them into the European conceptions of the human order. To deny their humanity was to depart fundamentally from contemporary theological orthodoxy based on Genesis and the teaching of Moses that humankind possessed an essential unity, and that there was nothing in the colour of a person's skin that could suggest otherwise. An urgent question thus arose: if Indians – both of the Americas and the East (rediscovered by Vasco Da Gama in 1498) – are beyond the Judeo-Christian world, but nonetheless the brothers and sisters of Europeans, then how can they be located?

The answer was to be sought and found in the great chain of being. In a double movement of exclusion and incorporation, the savage was subordinated to the European as an ignorant and uncivilized non-Christian, but one capable of conversion. It was primarily through the lens of Christianity, then, that knowledge of the manners and customs of alien peoples was sought, not to understand and explain, but as a means of incorporating them into the European order. In the course of the eighteenth century, as the idea of progress took hold, so a spatially ordered hierarchy became a temporal one:

With the Renaissance revival of historiography, with the decline of degenerationism as a philosophy of history, with the insistence of the 'moderns' on their superiority over the 'ancients', with the idea of cultural progress, the hierarchy of being had to be converted from a spatial arrangement of forms into an historical, developmental, or evolutionary series.[72]

Contemporary savagery thus came increasingly to be identified with ancient stages of other cultures. At first sight this appeared an unlikely and implausible move. Evidence suggested few similarities between ancient societies and those of African or Indian natives. Nor could it be argued convincingly that savage cultures displayed any degree of uniformity. And yet by this identification contemporary native societies were condemned as degraded, and savages occupied the places previously reserved for human monsters. An order of contemporary difference was transformed into a 'genealogical scale of development'; the other, previously situated by ignorance spatially *beyond* Europe, was now defined by historical evolution *before* Europe.[73]

Progress and its antitheses

Just as the invention of European civilization demanded a temporalization of non-European others, so its future was to be secured by identification – and hence control – of the most potent threats to its progress. Having explored the intellectual origins of Western slavery and abolition,[74] David Brion Davis stood back to reflect on the value of recomposing their entire history 'around the theme of changing conceptions of progress'.[75] The result was a study that charted the momentous transformation from a consciousness of slavery as progressive to that of abolition as progressive. Since the first incursions of European traders into Africa during the fifteenth century, he argues, modern slavery was seen as a progressive force for change. The slave trade was driven not by adventurers, but by European merchants and financiers operating at the very heart of Western modernization. Black slavery, therefore, was absolutely integral to the growth of capitalism. Furthermore, enslavers justified their endeavours, even derived satisfaction from them, in the knowledge that enslavement liberated Africans from primitive paganism and ignorance. In the second half of the eighteenth century new conceptions of progress compelled influential sections of religious, manufacturing and political opinion to press for the abolition of the trade and emancipation of slaves. Britain was the focus of their activities, and since the country was fast emerging as the great commercial centre of the world, anti-slavery came to be articulated with modern progress, slavery with historical regression.

Conceptions of progress have also framed scholarly interpretations of the experience of slavery. Working within a stages theory of development, writers as diverse as Adam Smith, Karl Marx, August Comte and certain Christian abolitionists viewed slavery as an early but necessary phase in societal evolution. In previous eras it had enhanced productivity by enforcing labour discipline; indeed, all the great phases of imperial expansion had been accompanied by the enslavement of captives on previously unprecedented scales. By the eighteenth century, however, slavery was perceived by theorists of the stages theory of development as a wasteful and historically anachronistic form of labour. More recently, Eric Williams argued in his brilliantly polemical *Capitalism and Slavery* that black slavery financed the industrial revolution until it was recognized to hinder further expansion, at which point it was abolished.[76]

For eighteenth-century theorists of progress, slavery represented an all-too-immediate problem, for while offering validation of societal development it forced recognition of the human costs. Thus the vision of the New World which provided the focus for so much of their thinking was increasingly clouded by records of the suffering inflicted on the native populations and transported slaves, upon whose labour the miracle had depended. The pernicious consequences of the slave trade as an obstacle to progress entered forcefully onto the agenda of 'progressive' thinkers, appearing not only in conventional tracts, sermons and treatises, but also in the imaginative literature of late eighteenth-century Britain.[77]

To understand the nature of this profound transformation we would need to examine in depth its moral, economic and political dimensions. Instead, I wish to consider aspects that touch more directly on the putative connections between anti-slavery sentiment and concern over poverty and colonialism. If connections existed they did so because they were framed by the interests of an emergent capitalist world order. To acknowledge this is not necessarily to fall prey to a crude reductionism. The rise of abolition sentiment, for example, as Brion Davis has so cogently demonstrated, cannot be seen unproblematically as serving the interests of an industrial bourgeoisie, not least because as a class they fiercely resisted moves to end the slave trade. He concludes:

> The decision [in 1833] to free 780,000 colonial slaves and compensate their owners was not the result of some Machiavellian design to disguise an ulterior goal. It was the response of a conservative government, representing a defensive aristocracy, to the competing claims that reformers and planters voiced against a backdrop of economic crisis and potential revolution.[78]

Mutatis mutandis, similar arguments can be made for the period leading up to the abolition of the slave trade itself in 1806. What, however, were the claims made by reformers in this period, and how can they be linked to other moral and political concerns? From ancient times various millennialist sects had provided the only concerted opposition to slavery.

From a primitivist belief in the essential goodness of humankind, they sought a life free from sin and human exploitation in all of its forms, and anticipated an age when man would be emancipated from servitude. Persecuted by religious and political authorities, these sectarians were eventually driven into the wilderness, but something of their teaching survived among Quakers, providing their impulse against modern slavery. Their pursuit of human perfectibility and a life free from sin found practical realization through the considerable institutional and economic power they wielded. The decision in the mid eighteenth century to abandon all links with the slave trade, however, was predicated on complex developments in the culture of British Protestantism that promoted anti-slavery sentiment:

1 The place of servitude in the natural order was questioned by social philosophers who were encouraged by the dictates of reason to think anew about the putative certainties of the chain of being.
2 A sensibility of benevolence emerged in reaction to the apocalyptic visions of Calvin and Hobbes that stressed human goodness and perfectibility. Slaves, as innocents and victims, invoked particular compassion in the quest to rid the world of sin.
3 Evangelical currents within Anglicanism and Nonconformity held all to account for personal responsibility, thereby alerting people to the dangers of moral complacency, and marking the peculiar significance of genuine conversion.
4 Primitivism conferred positive images on slaves as inherently virtuous and sensitive, simultaneously serving to counterbalance patterns of prejudice that had previously isolated them from sympathy and identification.[79]

The intellectual and cultural landscape of abolitionism was defined initially by a convergence of these shifts in consciousness, but their influence was mediated by a complex relationship with the more secular belief system of the Enlightenment. The highly ambiguous stance that many Enlightenment thinkers took on the question of slavery suggested that anti-slavery sentiment did not follow automatically from their defence of natural rights. The truth was that thinkers considered to be part of the Enlightenment traversed the political spectrum. Thus the fierce denunciations of slavery in the writings of, say, Rousseau and Abbe Raynal have to be set against the conservative leanings of Hume and Montesquieu.

Clear also is the extent to which Enlightenment thought drew upon visions of the social order that had traditionally been the province of religious orthodoxy, with perhaps surprisingly 'unprogressive' consequences. Gordon Turnbull, who in writing a vindication of slave owners drew inspiration from Hume and Montesquieu, used the chain of being with as much effect as had the most conservative clerics in defending the social order:

> NEGRO slavery appears, then, to be, as far as reason can judge, one of those indispensable and necessary links, in the great chain of causes and events, which cannot and indeed ought not to be broken; or, in other words, a *part* of the stupendous, admirable, and perfect *whole*, which, if taken away, would leave a chasm, not [to] be filled up by all the wit or wisdom of erring and presumptuous man.[80]

More representative of the dilemmas of enlightened thought was the figure of Edmund Burke. Burke found it difficult to reconcile a belief in the sanctity of the natural order with the horrors of slavery. 'If the African trade could be considered with regard to itself only, and as a single object, I should think the utter abolition to be on the whole more advisable than any scheme of regulation and reform', he wrote to Henry Dundas in 1792, prefacing his *Sketch of a Negro Code*.[81] Immediate abolition, however, would be an affront to social equilibrium. His solution, consistent with evolution over time, was gradualism:

> I [am] of the opinion ... that a gradual abolition of slavery in the West Indies ought to go hand in hand with anything which should be done with regard to its supply from the coast of Africa.... It is not that my plan does not lead to the extinction of the slave trade, but it is through a very slow progress, the chief effect of which is to be operated in our own plantations, by rendering ... all foreign supply unnecessary. It was my wish, whilst slavery continued, and the consequent commerce, to take such measures as to civilize the coast of Africa by the trade, which now renders it more barbarous, and to lead by degrees to a more reputable, and, possibly, a more profitable connection with it, than we maintain at present.[82]

Strictures against immediate abolition, especially were it to be of a violent nature, were pervasive even among the most radical elements of enlightened opinion.[83] Thus few were willing to abandon entirely the conservative implications of the chain of being. Raynal's belief in human progress, for example, failed to prevent him adopting a gradualist approach to abolition similar to Burke's, except that freedom from slavery was planned through discrete phases rather than simply encouraged to grow organically.

For the more pessimistic, the spectre of moral decay stalked. Luxury and the unrestrained pursuit of wealth that had brought the Iberian empire down now threatened those European slave-trading nations that had destroyed Amerindians and had turned to Africa.[84] This pessimism, however, was increasingly challenged in principle by the belief that the desire for gain was essential to civilization. The task for philosophers after Mandeville was to find a middle ground. They sought it in Turgot's stages theory of societal evolution, and from its seductive teleology of progress found reassurance that regressive tendencies would be overwhelmed by the laws of development. None found it more so than Adam Smith, who in defining an identity between morality and utility launched a scathing attack on slavery. Slavery, according to Smith, was a crime against utility and humanity since it threw people into dehumanizing, corrupting and wasteful forms of labour; abolition would unblock the restriction and pave the way to future progress through untrammelled operation of the commercial market.

Finally, anti-slavery sentiment was fostered by an increased sensitivity in the latter half of the eighteenth century to its antithesis, namely, liberty. English notions of a common good based on order, hierarchy and monarchy were dismantled by the American revolution. For Americans freed from British rule, these notions were obsolete, and they set about constructing a society organized around the principles of equality, consent and respect.[85] In England, on the other hand, the common good survived more or less intact, only then to be assailed by strands of radical opinion imbued with the example of America and ready to struggle for alternatives. At the centre of the struggle were those Nonconformists and latitudinarian Anglicans who were in the vanguard of abolition. That many saw these causes as one was due to their profound belief in liberty of thought, and in the critical role that the moral, rational and freely inquiring citizen had to play in constructing a new community. This natural right to freedom found 'slavery' in all its forms a violation of natural rights that had to be eradicated.[86] Figures such as Granville Sharp and Richard Price who inhabited this moral universe were instrumental in laying down and campaigning for its precepts. Sharp, for example, secured the notable Mansfield judgement of 1772 whereby black slaves were free the moment they stepped on British soil. This victory, however, was seen merely as a prelude to the universalization of the right to freedom across the empire, even if imperial unity was compromised in the process.[87] From this complex and shifting intellectual landscape, marked by a certain convergence of religious, social, economic and political currents, arose a sense that slavery 'might symbolize all the forces that threatened the true destiny of man'.[88]

Slavery, however, was not the only matter of intense concern in late eighteenth-century Britain. As we have seen, poverty and colonial expansion were also perceived as barriers to progress, and the ways in which these were articulated and defined as such bore striking similarities to the discursive construction of slavery. Given that the same agencies were responsible, and that they drew upon common intellectual resources and vocabularies, this can come as no surprise. Political economy provided the most compelling framework within which connections could be identified and developed. Smith's aim was to remove those artificial restrictions and practices that hampered the free play of the market and hence of the realization of individual self-interest. On these grounds he justified the abolition of slavery as well as the removal of the poor laws and the settlement laws.[89] The rise of anti-slavery sentiment, therefore, was accompanied by a transformation in attitudes toward poor relief and labour discipline, heralding what many have subsequently perceived as a harsher and less sympathetic sensitivity to the poor. And those who were most vigorous in the denunciation of traditional paternalism – Pitt, Burke, Frederick Eden, John Townsend, Bentham and Malthus – also opposed the slave trade, even though they were determined to distinguish between slavery and poverty as problems requiring urgent attention.[90]

Evangelicals provided the clearest evidence of a concern – realized in practical action – that embraced the plight of slaves and the poor. The massive intervention by evangelical organizations into the lives of the London poor was launched, significantly, in the aftermath of the abolition of slavery, but its lineages can be traced to the late eighteenth century.[91] Members of the Clapham Sect who were in the vanguard of the abolition movement provided the focus. Thus a group around Wilberforce, including Thomas Bernard, Matthew Martin and Patrick Colquhoun, established in 1796 the Society for Bettering the Condition and Increasing the Comforts of the Poor. Its professed aim was to examine 'everything that concerns the happiness of the poor' so that

> in proportion as we can multiply domestic comforts, in the same degree we may hope to promote the cause of morality and virtue.... Let us give effect to that master spring of action, on which equally depends the prosperity of individuals and empire – THE DESIRE IMPLANTED IN THE HUMAN BREAST OF BETTERING ITS CONDITION.[92]

Here was an ethos of progress that owed much to the influence of Smith, but at the same time it was one that attempted to overcome the divergence already apparent in political economy between moral and material sentiment. The poor, it was argued, needed active encouragement to improve themselves through self-help, industry and frugality. For those who could not work, the harsh deterrence of the poor law was inappropriate. If genuine cases of distress were revealed through the systematic gathering of reliable information, then liberal scales of relief and instruction could be made available which would promote self-sufficiency and bring a permanent improvement.[93] Under such circumstances the poor would be rescued from moral degeneration, and evangelicals sleep easy in the knowledge that they had sought sanctification through good work. As Thomas Chalmers, who was to lay the theoretical foundation for evangelical work in the nineteenth-century metropolis, wrote: 'I should count the salvation of a single soul of more value than the deliverance of a whole empire from pauperism'.[94]

What is revealing about this statement is less its evident exaggeration than the fact that Chalmers thought fit to make reference to empire in a discussion of pauperism. For the matter of empire was of heightened concern to evangelicals in the late eighteenth century; indeed, in certain crucial respects their endeavours overseas predated and prefigured those in the domestic urban context. The chronology of missionary activity is instructive. Prior to the close of the eighteenth century, a variety of organizations had been established to undertake the work of Christianity abroad, although only in the widest possible sense could these be seen as missionary. The Society for Promoting Christian Knowledge was formed in 1699, ostensibly to publish religious works, but later provided limited financial support for missionary work in South India. And the Society for Propagation of the Gospel in Foreign Parts, formed in 1701, supported chaplains to expatriate communities abroad. Missionary work with indigenous peoples was rarely pursued, except on the personal initiative of individual priests,[95] until the 1790s when evangelical impulses within Nonconformity and Anglicanism gave birth to the Baptist Missionary Society (1792), the London Missionary Society (1795) and the Church Missionary Society (1799).

Relationships between evangelicalism and the imperial 'project' are too complex to allow ready generalization.[96] It is clear, however, that in the case of India missionary activity was viewed with rather more sympathy by the East India Company than is conventionally thought. Charles Grant, for example, was a director of the Company and a leading advocate of state intervention in the religious affairs of India. His object to plant English culture in Indian soil determined the agendas of most British evangelicals and officials from the late eighteenth century.[97] Furthermore, he knew members of the Clapham Sect, including Wilberforce, with whom he attempted during the 1793 debate on the renewal of the Company's charter to introduce a clause requiring it to finance missionary activity.

Imperial progress on the fronts of slavery, poverty and colonialism was conceptualized by agents operating across their narrowly defined boundaries using an intellectual and linguistic repertoire forged from the transformation in human consciousness that occurred late in the eighteenth century. Structural barriers were perceived, but these tended to assume less significance than the threats posed by the persistence of paupers and colonial subjects. How these threats were constructed discursively in the long nineteenth century as a means of understanding and hence controlling them is what I wish to address in the following chapters.

Notes

1 An extensive literature now covers these issues, but see especially C.A. Bayly, *Imperial Meridian. The British Empire and the World, 1780–1830*, London, Longman, 1989; John Brewer, *The Sinews of Power. War, Money and the English State, 1688–1783*, London, Unwin Hyman, 1989; Linda Colley, *Britons. Forging the Nation, 1707–1837*, London, Pimlico, 1994; and Kathleen Wilson, *A Sense of the People. Politics, Culture and Imperialism in England, 1715–1785*, Cambridge, Cambridge University Press, 1998.

2 The definition is that of David Spadafora, *The Idea of Progress in Eighteenth-Century Britain*, New Haven, Yale University Press, 1990, p. 6. I am indebted to him for what follows on religious thought.

3 *Ibid.*, p. 19.

4 Spadafora does seem to anticipate such criticism: 'Compared to the forms of ideas [in the arts and sciences and in religion], doctrines of economic and political progress, considered on their own, were not nearly as common.... [T]he belief in progress in the political and social realms was necessarily an integral part of the notions of general progress' (*ibid.*, p. 12). As I hope to demonstrate, this was not always the case.

5 This whole question is examined with exemplary scholarship by Mary Poovey, *A History of the Modern Fact. Problems of Knowledge in the Sciences of Wealth and Society*, Chicago, University of Chicago Press, 1998.

6 *Ibid.*, p. 174.

7 The best account of this remains Michael McKeon, *The Origins of the English Novel*, Baltimore, The Johns Hopkins University Press, 1987.

8 This telling phrase is from Gertrude Himmelfarb, *The Idea of Poverty. England in the Early Industrial Age*, London, Faber, 1984, p. 18.

9 *Ibid.*, p. 3. For other discussions, see J.R. Poynter, *Society and Pauperism. English Ideas on Poor Relief, 1795–1834*, London, Routledge, 1969; R. H. Tawney, *Religion and the Rise of Capitalism*, London, Pelican, 1948 [1926]; S. Woolf, *The Poor in Western Europe in the Eighteenth and Nineteenth Centuries*, London, Methuen, 1986.

10 Tawney, *Religion and the Rise of Capitalism*, p. 114.

11 For an authoritative survey of the eighteenth century, paying due regard to moral and economic concern, see Richard Sheldon, 'The politics of bread in eighteenth-century England', unpublished PhD thesis, University of Birmingham, 2000.

12 Poynter, *Society and Pauperism*, p. 21.

13 Daniel Defoe, *Giving Alms No Charity, and Employing the Poor a Grievance to the Nation*, London, 1704, cited in Himmelfarb, *The Idea of Poverty*, p. 26.

14 Bernard Mandeville, *The Fable of the Bees. Private Vices, Public Benefits*, London, Roberts, 1714, cited in Himmelfarb, *The Idea of Poverty*, p. 28. The sense of shock witnessed on its publication was created less by Mandeville's attack on the poor than by the uncomfortable recognition that his vehemence was directed also to the rich who were responsible for the great villainies.

15 Thomas Alcock, *Observations on the Defects of the Poor Laws ...*, London, Baldwin, 1752, cited in Poynter, *Society and Pauperism*, p. 30.

16 Himmelfarb, *The Idea of Poverty*, pp. 50–63.

17 The provision of relief under other aspects of the poor law, on the other hand, was supported by Smith. This may have been a move prompted by the moral philosopher rather than the political economist, but it singled Smith out at a time when the putative evils of the poor law system were viewed with heightened anxiety elsewhere.

18 A.L. Beier, *Masterless Men. The Vagrancy Problem in England, 1560–1640*, London, Methuen, 1985.

19 Christopher Hill, *Liberty against the Law. Some Seventeenth-Century Controversies*, London, Allen Lane, 1996; N. Rogers, 'Policing the poor in eighteenth-century London: the vagrancy laws and their administration', *Histoire Sociale–Social History*, 24:43, 1991, pp. 127–47.

20 Beier, *Masterless Men*, p. 132.

21 John Marriott, 'The spatiality of poverty in eighteenth-century London', in Tim

Hitchcock and Heather Shore (eds), *The Streets of London*, London, Rivers Oram, 2003.

22 For most of what follows I have relied heavily on the monumental work of David Brion Davis, in particular *The Problem of Slavery in Western Culture*, New York, Oxford University Press, 1988 [1966], and *Slavery and Human Progress*, New York, Oxford University Press, 1984.

23 Brion Davis, *The Problem of Slavery in Western Culture*, pp. 118–21.

24 *Ibid.*, p. 336.

25 Brion Davis, *Slavery and Human Progress*, pp. 382–90.

26 *Ibid.*, p. 388.

27 Brion Davis, *The Problem of Slavery in Western Culture*, pp. 433–4.

28 Clare Midgely, *Woman Against Slavery. The British Campaign, 1780–1870*, London, Routledge, 1992.

29 Take, for example, Anthony Trollope's travel account *The West Indies and the Spanish Main*, London, Chapman and Hall, 1859, which had such a decisive impact on post-abolition thought. Slavery, he argued, had led to a forced encounter of black people with a superior race, leading inevitably to progress. Emancipation, however, had provided former slaves with freedom from work, rather than a continued desire for progress. Left to themselves, they would regress into the barbarism from which enslavement had rescued them (Catherine Hall, *Civilising Subjects. Metropole and Colony in the English Imagination, 1830–1867*, London, Polity, 2002, p. 217).

30 Patrick O'Brien, 'Inseparable connections: trade, economy, fiscal state, and the expansion of empire, 1688–1815', in P.J. Marshall (ed.), *The Oxford History of the British Empire. Vol. II. The Eighteenth Century*, Oxford, Oxford University Press, 1998.

31 Brewer, *The Sinews of Power*, p. 175.

32 Bayly, *Imperial Meridian*, p. 2.

33 Anthony Pagden, *Lords of all the World. Ideologies of Empire in Spain, Britain and France, c.1500–c.1800*, New Haven, Yale University Press, 1995, p. 25.

34 A useful edition with an introduction by Anthony Pagden has recently appeared: Bartolome de Las Casas, *A Short Account of the Destruction of the Indies*, London, Penguin, 1992.

35 Pagden, *Lords of All the World*, p. 6.

36 David Hume, 'Of the study of history' (1741), cited in David Armitage, *The Ideological Origins of the British Empire*, Cambridge, Cambridge University Press, 1999, p. 191.

37 Unsurprisingly, the language was that of some of the most strident critics of empire, notably Condorcet, Hume, Diderot, Raynal and Smith (Pagden, *Lords of All the World*, p. 160). That this language was used to perpetuate European imperialism, albeit in a different guise, is another example of the ambiguous legacy of the Enlightenment, criticized so forcefully by postcolonial writings.

38 Armitage, *The Ideological Origins of the British Empire*, p. 8.

39 Jack P. Greene, 'Empire and identity from the Glorious Revolution to the American Revolution', in Marshall (ed.), *The Oxford History of the British Empire. Vol. II*, p. 214.

40 S. Ambirajan, *Classical Political Economy and British Policy in India*, Cambridge, Cambridge University Press, 1978, p. 2. Ambirajan makes a persuasive case for the influence of political economy on imperial policy in India, but adds the necessary caveat that 'it is extremely difficult to determine whether the arguments based on economic ideas were aids to reach a particular decision or were mere ancillary arguments used to buttress policies already adopted as a result of other non-doctrinal reasons' (p. 18).

41 *Ibid.*, p. 175.

42 For a fascinating discussion of the changing political rhetoric of state and empire in the eighteenth century, see Peter Miller, *Defining the Common Good. Empire, Religion and Philosophy in Eighteenth-Century Britain*, Cambridge, Cambridge University Press, 1994.

43 Bayly, *Imperial Meridian*, p. 108.

44 The terms are respectively those of Armitage, *The Ideological Origins of the British*

Empire, and Bayly, *Imperial Meridian.*
45 Pagden, *Lords of All the World*, p. 9.
46 Arthur O. Lovejoy, *Reflections on Human Nature*, Baltimore, The Johns Hopkins Press, 1961, p. 22.
47 For a recent cogent and accessible survey, see Kenan Malik, *The Meaning of Race. Race, History and Culture in Western Society*, Basingstoke, Macmillan, 1996.
48 Spadafora, *The Idea of Progress*, p. 331.
49 These seemingly disparate intellectual developments have been summarily dismissed by Spadafora as 'too vast to rest comfortably on the usually slender supporting evidence on which they rest' (*The Idea of Progress*, p. 321). Instead, he elects to focus on narrower doctrines of progress that commanded the attention of most of the seminal thinkers in Britain both before and after 1750. The triumph of the modern over ancients in the arts and sciences, the pliability of human nature, particularly in the recognition of the critical role of nurture, the influence of linguistic development, and improvement in religious knowledge, he claims, dominated the writings of people as diverse as David Hume, Lord Kames, Richard Price, Adam Smith, Joseph Priestley and William Robertson. While not wishing to question the fine detail of these arguments, it seems to me that the narrow focus is too limiting. The neglect of doctrines of political and economic progress, of broader traditions of Enlightenment thought, and of more popular manifestations in prose and poetry severely circumscribes an appreciation of the impact of progress on British thought. Most significantly for this study, it provides no insight into how conceptions of progress were linked to the rigidification of class and racial hierarchies in the late eighteenth century.
50 Arthur O. Lovejoy, *The Great Chain of Being. A Study of the History of an Idea*, Cambridge, Harvard University Press, 1961, p. 59. Although based on lectures given at Harvard University in 1933, the book remains the most lucid and thorough exploration of the idea.
51 *Ibid.*, pp. 190, 194.
52 *Ibid.*, p. 200.
53 Lois Whitney, *Primitivism and the Idea of Progress in English Literature of the Eighteenth Century*, Baltimore, The Johns Hopkins University Press, 1934, p. 142.
54 Lovejoy, *The Great Chain of Being*, p. 234.
55 For studies of this concept, see John Sekora, *Luxury. The Concept in Western Thought, Eden to Smollett*, Baltimore, The Johns Hopkins University Press, 1977, and Christopher Berry, *The Idea of Luxury. A Conceptual and Historical Investigation*, Cambridge, Cambridge University Press, 1994. Although Sekora's claim that luxury was 'the single most significant social and political idea of eighteenth-century England' (p. 9) overstates the case, this is not to deny its considerable importance. Among the writers who considered luxury were Mandeville, Addison, Defoe, Pope, Swift, Fielding, Hume, Johnson, Gibbon, Wesley and Adam Smith (p. 2).
56 Berry, *The Idea of Luxury*, p. xx.
57 John Brown, *Estimate of the Manners and Principles of the Times*, Dublin, Faulkener, Hoey and Exshaw, 1758, pp. 16, 20.
58 *Ibid.*, p. 111.
59 Lovejoy, *Reflections on Human Nature*, p. 16.
60 *Ibid.*, pp. 170–3.
61 Arthur O. Lovejoy, 'Foreword', in Whitney, *Primitivism and the Idea of Progress*, p. xii.
62 Cited in *ibid.*, p. 179.
63 Sekora, *Luxury*, p. 103.
64 Posterity has unfairly regarded Smith as the dour patron saint of *laissez-faire*, but this tends to neglect the fact that he was a moral philosopher of some note. His *Theory of Moral Sentiments* is described by Lovejoy as 'the most original and systematic eighteenth-century inquiry concerning the motivations of human behaviour' (*Reflections on Human Nature*, p. 190).
65 Cited in Lovejoy, *Reflections on Human Nature*, p. 215.
66 Ronald Meek, *Social Science and the Ignoble Savage*, Cambridge, Cambridge University Press, 1976, p. 6.

67 *Ibid.*, p. 22.
68 *Ibid.*, pp. 220–1.
69 *Ibid.*, p. 33.
70 Thomas C. Patterson, *Inventing Western Civilization*, New York, Monthly Review Press, 1997.
71 In what follows I have brought together the useful but conflicting perspectives found in Margaret Hodgen, *Early Anthropology in the Sixteenth and Seventeenth Centuries*, Philadelphia, University of Pennsylvania Press, 1964, and Bernard McGrane, *Beyond Anthropology. Society and the Other*, New York, Columbia University Press, 1989, overall tending to favour the more dynamic approach of the former.
72 Hodgen, *Early Anthropology*, pp. 389–90.
73 McGrane, *Beyond Anthropology*, p. 94.
74 Brion Davis, *The Problem of Slavery in Western Culture*, and *The Problem of Slavery in the Age of Revolution, 1770–1823*, Ithaca, Cornell University Press, 1975.
75 Brion Davis, *Slavery and Human Progress*, p. xix.
76 *Ibid.*, p. xiv.
77 For a collection of primary texts from the Romantic age, which does indicate usefully the extent to which the problem of slavery entered into the cultural fabric of British life, see Peter Kitson and Debbie Lee (eds), *Slavery, Abolition and Emancipation. Writings in the British Romantic Period*, 6 vols, London, Pickering and Chatto, 1999.
78 Brion Davis, *Slavery and Human Progress*, p. 222.
79 Brion Davis, *The Problem of Slavery in the Age of Revolution*, pp. 44–8.
80 Gordon Turnbull, *An Apology for Negro Slavery; or, the West-Indian Planters Vindicated from the Charge of Inhumanity*, London, 1786, cited in Brion Davis, *The Problem of Slavery in Western Culture*, p. 392.
81 Edmund Burke, 'A Letter to the Right Hon. Henry Dundas, one of His Majesty's Principal Secretaries of State. With the Sketch of a Negro Code', in *The Works and Writings of the Right Hon. Edmund Burke*, 12 vols, London, John Nimmo, 1899 [1792], Vol. VI, p. 257.
82 *Ibid.*, p. 259.
83 Brion Davis, *The Problem of Slavery in Western Culture*, p. 399.
84 *Ibid.*, p. 423.
85 Miller, *Defining the Common Good*, p. 16. These principles, of course, did not apply to native Indians or slaves.
86 It has to be remembered that slavery as a term was commonly used to describe all forms of servitude and bondage. This lack of discrimination was to have dire consequences for abolitionists since they often found themselves opposed by otherwise radical elements who argued that the 'white slaves' in British mines and factories had to be freed before the black slaves on plantations.
87 Miller, *Defining the Common Good*, p. 293.
88 Brion Davis, *The Problem of Slavery in Western Culture*, p. 445.
89 Brion Davis, *The Problem of Slavery in the Age of Revolution*, p. 353.
90 *Ibid.*, p. 358.
91 See my Introduction to John Marriott and Masaie Matsumura (eds), *The Metropolitan Poor. Semi-Factual Accounts, 1795–1910*, 6 vols, London, Pickering and Chatto, 1999.
92 *Report of the Society*, I (1798), cited in J.R. Poynter, *Society and Pauperism. English Ideas on Poor Relief, 1795–1834*, London, Routledge, 1969, p. 91.
93 *Ibid.*, p. 96.
94 Chalmers to John Brown, 1819, cited in Boyd Hilton, *The Age of Atonement. The Influence of Evangelicalism on Social and Economic Thought*, Oxford, Clarendon Press, 1988, p. 88.
95 Andrew Porter, 'Religion, missionary enthusiasm, and empire', in Andrew Porter (ed.), *The Oxford History of the British Empire. Vol. III. The Nineteenth Century*, Oxford, Oxford University Press, 1999, p. 228.
96 See, for example, T. Thomas, 'Foreign missions and missionaries in Victorian Britain', in J. Wolffe (ed.), *Religion in Victorian Britain. Vol. V. Culture and Empire*, Manchester, Manchester University Press, 1997, and Chapter 4 below.

97 Ainslie Embree, 'Christianity and the state in Victorian India: confrontation and collaboration', in R.W. Davis and R.J. Helmstadter (eds), *Religion and Irreligion in Victorian Society*, London, Routledge, 1992, p. 157.

CHAPTER TWO

Desarts of Africa or Arabia

The needy villains' gen'ral home

As a first stage in the exploration of progress and its antitheses I wish to focus on the problem of metropolitan poverty. We now have a reasonably secure understanding of its structural underpinnings in the modern era. Dorothy George's *London Life in the Eighteenth Century*, written some seventy-six years ago, remains unsurpassed as an account of the socio-economic conditions of the poorer classes.[1] More recently, Gareth Stedman Jones has described influentially the locus of the casual poor in the late nineteenth-century metropolis, while more quantitative approaches have been used by Leonard Schwarz to explore economic fluctuations in the metropolitan economy up to 1850, and by David Green to assess the impact of economic change on poverty from 1790 to 1870.[2]

And yet we have a rather imprecise and highly selective grasp of how the poor were actively constructed as an object of concern. Recently scholarly work on the discursive landscape of the nineteenth-century metropolitan poor has identified epistemological shifts, thought variously as from pauperism to poverty, rationalist hedonism to social Darwinism, individual to societal, demoralization to degeneration.[3] As abstract typologies expressing elite concerns around citizenship, poverty, political order and a range of social pathologies they are useful, but their selectivity masks real complexities and impedes a broader appreciation of the ways in which the metropolitan poor came to occupy an extraordinary centrality in the bourgeois imagination. To achieve this we need to go beyond government reports compiled by people well removed from their object of inquiry, and beyond fiction, which for most of the nineteenth century did not address the poor.[4] Rather, semi-factual accounts written by urban travellers and evangelicals exerted *the* formative influence on how the poor were perceived among all sections of Victorian society, not least because they could lay claim to privileged access to the cultural and physical environment inhabited by the poor. These writers lived amongst, conversed with and moved around the metropolitan poor to produce an impressive range of tracts, articles and books that were widely disseminated and read. The more popular accounts went through many editions. They appeared in different forms, were plagiarized, and were frequently cited in parliament, in some instances prompting legislative reform. They displayed an acute sensitivity to the moral and political concerns of the time – concerns that they in turn effectively shaped.[5]

The metropolitan poor, I wish to argue, were 'discovered' through their discursive creation as an object of concern and inquiry. This appropriation and subsequent reworkings were neither incidental nor insignificant. Upon them was erected the entire edifice of Victorian social and moral reform directed at the amelioration of poverty and its consequences. And these matters reached beyond the domestic, for much of the reform has to be seen within the context of the British imperial formation. The racialization of the poor, for example, which began in mid century and intensified during the 1860s and 1880s, was in terms of its chronology, narrative and rhetoric so similar to constructions of colonial others that they can be seen as shared and mutually reinforcing responses to deep anxieties about the future of the imperial race. To understand fully the distinctive nature of the moral universe that embraced the metropolitan poor, it is necessary to trace its lineages.

The literary expression of the metropolis has a complex history.[6] London emerged as a major urban centre in the nation's life from the early fifteenth century. Herein was concentrated an absolutist state wielding the power of an aristocracy whose origins could be traced to an old feudal order but which was now under increasing threat from a nascent mercantilist and industrial bourgeoisie, and from a migrant and dispossessed population of apprentices, casual labourers and vagrants drawn to the suburbs of London by the opportunities offered for gainful – but not necessarily productive – employment. The dissembling processes created by this urbanization could not be encompassed by the neo-feudal literary modes of church and court; instead there emerged a rich, transgressive literature which sought to articulate tensions within the new moral and spatial landscapes.

In the years from 1580 to 1620, London witnessed an extraordinary literary renaissance. Located in a period of transition between a late medieval order and an ascendant mercantilism, a large and diverse body of ballads, chapbooks, canting verse, pamphlets and plays was published which, in expressing discrepancies between traditional and new, elite and popular, court and urban, embodied secular images of the changing metropolitan landscape. Its most notable exponents were John Awdeley, Thomas Nashe, Robert Greene and Thomas Dekker. In this rogue literature, ethical alternatives were offered to traditional authority through 'an endorsement of mobility, a cultivation of bohemianism and aggressive individuality, a new sense of "crisis" and temporality geared to the rhythms of economic exchange, and a tendency to naturalize the frightening sense of change associated with London'.[7]

Remote from patronage and establishment, subject to the vicissitudes of the publishing market, the liminal status of these authors made possible experiential modes of inquiry into previously unexplored areas of London life. Marginalized and subordinate realms associated with the street were brought centre stage and hence revealed. The preferred mode was travelogue and repentance. With an authority derived from dissolute lives, these writers 'discovered' the criminal underworld of Tudor London. The series of popular beggar books, canting lexicons and cony-catching pamphlets not only elaborated taxonomies of villainy and trickery – even giving voice to the rogues themselves – but by extension exposed the fraudulent nature of all those associated with the marketplace.[8] Descent into the underworld becomes an act of personal and public renewal.

The reception of such literature in large part depended upon its ability to articulate and offer reassuringly practical resolutions to the host of moral and physical tensions that beset the metropolis. Pamphlets sold at a time when novel urban pathologies such as crime, vagrancy, disease and acquisitiveness entered forcefully into the bourgeois psychic universe. Their readers – for the most part members of an educated elite – may have looked with disfavour on imaginative literature, but this did not prevent them from enjoying it. Justification could always be found that such literature lifted the spirit, or was improving because it provided reliable evidence on the villainy that prevailed.[9] The genre, however, was relatively short-lived. By the early seventeenth century the cohesion of neo-feudal metropolitan culture was under threat from the destabilizing decline in power of its guilds and the exclusion of merchants from spheres of influence exercised by the Stuart court.[10] Cony-catching pamphlets continued in revised forms but entered into irreversible decline since they were no longer able to provide visions of the urban appropriate to a more modern but narrowly vocal mentality.

London was in the process of reinventing itself through its literary culture as *the* site of mercantilist endeavour. Caroline plays, for example, celebrated bourgeois virtue and social harmony, while poetry contributed to the formation of an elite literary order that culminated in the eighteenth-century Augustan. The result was an urban literature which although heterogeneous cohered around the unified and dominant vision of an ascendant bourgeoisie. Subversive elements persisted, but these were either incorporated into the 'polite and innovative accomplishments of later urbane writers',[11] or assumed by literary hacks who lacked the ability to sustain alternative visions and hence challenge this dominance. Ned Ward's *London Spy* (1698) inherited little of Dekker's grasp of the complex plurality of London life.

The heterogeneity of this vision resulted from the diverse attempts sought by the eighteenth-century metropolitan bourgeoisie to grasp London's totality as a precondition to the modernization of its streets, public spaces and built environment.[12] The opportunity radically to rebuild the capital along planned and rational lines after the great fire of 1666 was squandered. Major thoroughfares were widened and large numbers of houses and public buildings reconstructed, but the medieval palimpsest was preserved, and much of the capital's public space remained irregular, haphazard and dirty. This lack of vital space for citizens to meet, converse and relax in a secure and congenial environment hampered the constitution of new publics of privatized individuals. In response, conceptions of the space were transformed, and in the course of the eighteenth century legal, parochial and literary authorities attempted to know and hence civilize its streets. This project, in large part fuelled by a desire to identify public space as a bourgeois sphere, has been seen as integral to metropolitan modernity.[13]

It was against this backdrop that urban improvement gathered momentum. Plans were outlined by John Spranger in 1754 which heralded a cultural geography of Westminster appropriate to its status as the locus of an ascendant commercial and imperial power:

> In all well-governed Countries, the first Care of the Governors hath been to make the Intercourse of the Inhabitants, as well as of Foreigners, sojourning in the Country, safe, easy and commodious, by open, free and regular *Highways*. This is more especially incumbent on *Trading* Nations, as, without a free and safe Intercourse between Place and Place by Land as well as by water, *trade* cannot subsist, much less flourish.[14]

He proposed that authority be invested in commissioners, elected by local ratepayers to make by-laws, raise funds through the rates and punish offenders. The resultant Act, 2 Geo. III cap. 21, provided Westminster with the power and finances to take control out of the hands of local bodies, and adopt systematic programmes of improvement, thereby guaranteeing an unprecedented uniformity in paving and street lighting.

Within this ethos of improvement a homology existed between moral and topographical visions. Public markets, buildings, thoroughfares, theatres, and places of entertainment and consumption were identified as the sites of bourgeois urbanity most in need of attention as a means of ameliorating the unseemly chaos of much metropolitan life. When sensibilities of progress gathered momentum in the course of the eighteenth century, they were framed in terms of the physical rather than the human environment. Improvement was therefore predicated on a detailed knowledge of metropolitan topography; cartographers, surveyors, travel writers and poets applied themselves to the task of mapping the streets of the city, so opening them up to the bourgeois travellers. In this period London's expansive physical body became known. John Strype's edition of Stow's *Survey of London* appeared in 1720. The product of nearly twenty years' labour, it was, however, such a massive expansion of the original text by so much obsessive detail that Stow's personal stamp was almost entirely lost.[15] Strype mapped London's topography through descriptive travelogues, interrupted by historical detours into churches, monuments, dignitaries and charities. But the intimate details of individual wards revealed little more than their physical streetscapes.

This was a venture made possible by the active involvement of commercial and political interests. The mayor and court of the City of London, to whom Strype dedicated the work, offered practical and financial support from the outset, and the list of subscribers included attorneys, goldsmiths, merchants and gentlemen. Most significant, however, were booksellers and printers, who numbered forty-three out of a total of 272. The control of cultural production was passing from the hands of personal patronage to the local state and the metropolitan market. These interests, augmented by the City, influential figures such as Horace Walpole, government offices and academic institutions numbering among four hundred subscribers, were also evident in the publication of John Rocque's great maps of London. Published in 1746 as twenty-four imperial sheets making a map measuring thirteen by six and a half feet, they represented the first systematic cartographical survey of London since 1682.[16] The map, drawn with an intricacy and precision previously unknown, was intended both as a reliable guide to the 'street traveller' and an accurate record of London's world status as a commercial and imperial centre. In the event its form rendered it difficult to use, and it remained, like Strype's survey, little more than an ordered inventory of names and shapes without interpretation.

Something of a transition was heralded by the publication in 1766 of the Rev. John Entick's weighty and detailed record of the metropolis.[17] Combining history, sociology and topography, Entick attempted for the first time a totalizing vision of the labyrinthine complexity of spaces of London previously beyond the purview of detached observers such as Strype. In this, he drew upon earlier surveys, particularly of Stow, but simultaneously anticipated the later survey of Charles Booth by over a hundred years:

> *Grub-Street*, as far as *Sun-Alley*, is in Cripplegate-Ward; but it is not either well-built, nor inhabited better than *Moor-Lane*. Nevertheless, it contains a

number of courts and alleys, as, *Lins-Alley, Honey-Suckle Court*, well built; *Fleur de lis Court, Little Bell-Alley, Flying horse-Court, Oakley-Court, Butler's Alley, Crosskeys Court, Great Bell Alley*; all very mean.[18]

These surveys opened up Westminster and the City to the bourgeois pedestrian and traveller; all they now needed were clearly visible street names:

> Whereas, were but the names of Streets cut on white Stones, the Letters blacken'd, and set up at every Corner, the Greatest strangers might, with the assistance of a small pocket Map, find his Way to any Part of these contiguous Cities and their extended Liberties.[19]

The attempt to know London's complex physical totality was accompanied by changes in the literary appropriation of metropolitan space. The London of Daniel Defoe was akin to that of Strype and Rocque. Evident in his *Tour thro' the Whole Island of Great Britain* and novels such as *Moll Flanders*, it was one of a featureless, formless and two-dimensional inventory of street names and buildings, conveying a sense only of an anonymous and ceaseless traffic.[20] More significant over time was the topography that came to be revealed in the writings of Augustan satirists. Pope, Gay, Swift and Hogarth provided dense maps of the city and its inhabitants that were not only reliable guides to its intimate topography, but simultaneously gazetteers of a distinct cultural geography in which the infested courts, alleys and markets became symbolic sites of a sombre regime of dullness. Their moral symbolism, therefore, was not located in some vague, Miltonic pandemonium, but on the congested physical landscape of London.[21]

As a result of these various impulses, in the latter half of the eighteenth century London streets became straighter, better paved, better lit, better known, more closely surveyed, cleaner – in short, more civilized and modern. Thus constituted, they in themselves formed an urban space fit for bourgeois intercourse and conviviality, but also a communications infrastructure opening up the new sites of relaxation – parks, shops, coffee houses and theatres – to a wider public.[22] There remained, however, a continued threat to this modernization. Streets could be cleansed and straightened by the determined removal of physical detritus; human forms proved rather more stubborn. Beggars, vagabonds, and criminals of various descriptions found in the capital favourable sites for their trades, and as long as they contested its streets and found refuge in its innermost sanctuaries, bourgeois public space was never likely to be secured, modernized or cleansed.

And yet here was a constituency that remained remote from the inquiring gaze of urban explorers. The self-confident and celebratory guides that later took the bourgeois traveller around the most notable features of the commercial, social and built environment of the metropolis adopted a panoramic vision in which London's grandeur, history and monumentality emphasized the imperial, stately and symmetrical. *Leigh's New Picture of London*, for example, first published around 1815 and reissued many times subsequently, provided a view of the infrastructure of metropolitan government, commerce, medicine and religion.[23] Less authoritative guides to historic buildings appeared,[24] as did the more didactic.[25] Here was an ordered city, emptied entirely of the untidy and inconvenient presence of people.[26] Displaced and seemingly inaccessible in the literary appropriation of the metropolis was any knowledge of its underworld. For all this attention to accurate detail, the topographical imagery of eighteenth-century writers tended toward a featureless and two-dimensional inventory of streets and their inhabitants in which slum courts and alleys were symbolic sites of moral depravity. Given the instinct to reveal overarching moral patterns in pursuit of a vision of an ordered and harmonious metropolis, there was a certain inevitability to their failure to grasp its lowly forms. For this we need to turn to alternative literary genres.

Tricks of the town

The establishment toward the end of the seventeenth century of new economic and political settlements based on an ascendant bourgeois order rendered obsolete the transgressive urban literature of Greene, Nashe and Dekker, as a consequence of which it fragmented and declined. The radical potential in revealing complex interconnections among diverse 'criminal' activities in all sections of metropolitan life failed to materialize. Instead, rogue literature degenerated into tediously reworked taxonomies of criminal plurality encompassed within fictional narratives of the travelogue. *The Country Gentleman's Vade-Mecum; or, His Companion for the Town* effectively set the agenda. Published in 1699 to draw on the popularity of Ward's *London Spy*, it comprised a series of letters written by a gentleman now wise in the ways of city life to a friend in the country in an effort to dissuade him from coming to London.[27] It lacked the sensationalism of Ward, and had little success, but seeds were sown of a genre that lasted well into the nineteenth century.[28] There followed *A Trip through London* (1728), *A Trip through the Town* (1735), *A Ramble through London* (1738), *A Trip from St James's to the Exchange* (1744), a revised edition of *The Country Gentleman's Vade-Mecum* retitled as *The Tricks of the Town Laid Open* (1747), and then dozens of pamphlets on the same theme, most of which were shameless plagiarisms of the originals.[29]

Flat and unimaginative though this genre was, these moral baedeckers[30] do provide clues to the nature of contemporary concern about the threat from dissembling processes, in particular the poor inhabiting unknown and inaccessible spaces:

> The Town of London is a kind of large forest of *Wild-Beasts* where most of us range about at a venture, and are equally savage and mutually destructive one of another: ... The strange *Hurries* and *Impertinences*, the busy *Scrambling* and *Underminings*; and what is worse, the monstrous *Villainies, Cheats* and *Impostures* in it.... [A gentleman] complained of the great number of *Robberies* and *Riots*, that were daily committed within the Bills of Mortality to the great scandal of the Christian Religion, and the Honour of the Nation, and the great trouble it gave the *Magistrates*, for that he had been *Committing* and *Binding over* all the Morning.[31]

The passage was reproduced word for word in subsequent versions and used to good effect by Henry Fielding in his *Enquiry into the Recent Increase in Robberies* (1751) (see later). The untamed forest thus became a familiar trope to capture a sense of threat experienced at a time when the metropolitan streetscape began to be surveyed for the first time.[32] Beggars were singled out as a source of particular concern:

> Turning out of *Covent-Garden* to go to the *Strand* I was accosted by several Beggars, maim'd, lame and lazy. As Pity is so often by our selves and in our own Cases mistaken for Charity, so it assumes the Shape and borrows the very name of it; a *Beggar* asks you to exert that Virtue for *Jesus Christs sake*, but all the while this great Design is to raise your pity ... People not used to great Cities, being thus attacked on all sides, are commonly forced to yield, and cannot help giving something, tho' they can hardly spare it themselves.[33]

These sentiments were those of a metropolitan bourgeoisie forced to contemplate the logical inconsistencies of its moral universe by a seeming antithesis. Beggars were a challenge not because they constituted a serious material threat but because they were able to touch directly the moral and aesthetic sensibilities of a metropolitan elite *in public*:

> When sores are very bad, or seen otherwise afflicting in an extraordinary manner, and the Beggar can bear to have them exposed to the cold air, it is very shocking to some People; 'tis a shame they cry such Sights shou'd be suffer'd: the main reason is, it touches their Pity *feelingly*, at the same time they are resolv'd, either because they are covetous, or count it an idle Expense, to give nothing, which makes them more uneasy. They turn their Eyes, and where the Cries are dismal, some would willingly stop their Ears, mend their Pace, and be very angry in their Hearts, that Beggars shou'd be about Streets.[34]

It was a peculiarly modern challenge (one which many of us still find familiar and uncomfortable) whose symbolic importance seemed to gain force as London emerged as a great commercial and imperial centre. The threat posed by beggars to bourgeois space was transcoded to the nation.

Take, for example, Joshua Gee's *The Trade and Navigation of Great Britain Considered*, first published in 1729, and reprinted many times subsequently. This was a substantial thesis on the 'mighty consequence' of trade, and the threat posed to 'vast riches' by the 'want of due regard and attention'. It contained thirty-four chapters describing in detail Britain's trade with various countries around the world, and outlining proposals for increasing its share, most notably by 'enlarging the plantation trade' since it was the 'one great cause of enriching this nation'. Among them, however, was a chapter entitled 'Proposals for better regulating and employing the poor'. This seeming incongruity makes sense only when the location of the poor within empire is understood:

> But not withstanding we have so many excellent Laws, great numbers of sturdy beggars, loose and vagrant Persons infest the Nation; but no place more than in the city of London and parts adjacent. If any Person is born with any defect or deformity, or maimed by fire, or any other casualty, or by any inveterate distemper, which renders them miserable Objects, their way is open to London; where they have free Liberty of shewing their nauseous sights to terrify People, and force them to give money to get rid of them; and those vagrants have, for many years past, removed out of several parts of the three kingdoms, and taken their stations in this Metropolis, to the interruption of Conversations and Business.[35]

The consequence, Gee argued, drawing on contemporary concern about luxury, was 'very pernicious; for what they get by begging, is consumed commonly in ale-houses, gin shops, etc.'. The solution was mercantilist: 'The first and greatest [remedy] will be in finding effectual ways for employing our Poor, and putting all the hands to work, either at Home, or in the *Plantations*, who cannot support themselves'.[36]

The vast torrent of luxury

It was in Henry Fielding's *An Enquiry into the Causes of the Late Increase of Robbers* (1751), however, that we can see the most determined attempt to think through the relationships among metropolitan poverty, street crime and the progress of the nation.[37] Written at a time of heightened anxiety about the future of the nation, it was a work of awkward synthesis rather than originality, but while replete with conceptual confusion it had the merit of articulating the complex range of contemporary concern. Descriptions of the poor, for example, drew upon familiar rhetoric aired in debates on the poor law and in rogue literature. And the identification of 'expensive diversions', 'drunkenness' and 'gaming' as the sources of crime reflected sentiments repeated constantly in literature, courts, churches and parliament on the corrosive influence of luxury. Overall, Fielding's approach to the nature, rights and impact of the poor was informed strongly by conventional economic, religious and legal thought.[38]

Using a familiar taxonomy he divided the poor into those 'unable to work', 'able and willing to work', and 'able to work, but not willing'.[39] Beggars, most of whom were recruited from the first two classes, were not of particular concern. If in England 'should be found more Beggars, more distress and miserable objects than are to be seen thro-out all the States of Europe', this was owing to the virtuous humanity of 'all men of Property', who are 'so forward to relieve the Appearance of Distress in their Fellow-creatures' that they fail to appreciate that they are encouraging a nuisance.[40] More threatening were the vagabonds, who were unwilling to work, preferring to find their way to London where they could thieve while avoiding detection:

> Whoever indeed considers the Cities of *London* and *Westminster*, with the late vast Addition of their Suburbs; the great irregularity of their Buildings, the immense Number of Lanes, Alleys, Courts and Bye-places; must think, that, had they been intended for the very Purpose of Concealment, they could scarce have been better contrived. Upon such a View, the whole appears as a vast Wood or Forest, in which a Thief may harbour with as great Security, as wild Beasts do in the Desarts of *Africa* or *Arabia*. For by *wandering* from one Part to another, and often shifting his quarters, he may almost avoid the Possibility of being discovered.[41]

A lengthy diversion into Anglo-Saxon mythology followed in which Fielding celebrated the ancient constitution introduced by Alfred to 'prevent the Concealment of Thieves and Robbers' in the immediate aftermath of the state of licentiousness and rapine brought by Danish invaders. The intimate powers that surveillance made possible, however, had been undermined by free movement of the poor about the country. Legislation subsequently introduced to deal with the problem by enforcing settlement and employment had proved ineffective because of undue expense and administration, as a result of which criminal activity flourished, particularly on the streets of London.

As a reforming magistrate who encountered directly those unfortunates who were unable to avoid 'discovery', Fielding displayed a predictable tendency to criminalize the streets, and in so doing redefined the criminal geography of the metropolis. Of equal significance, however, was the extent to which he drew upon mercantilist thought and contemporary concern about luxury in elaborating the causes of crime and proposals for its amelioration. Citing freely the orthodoxies of William Petty, Josiah Child and Charles D'Avenant, Fielding displayed a guarded enthusiasm for the benefits of colonial trade, 'by which the Grandeur and Power of the Nation is carried to a Pitch that it could never otherwise have reached'.[42]

Such trade was of advantage to Britain so long as a favourable balance of trade be maintained and emigration create more employment in home manufactures. Under these circumstances the costs of production had to be minimized. The lives of the industrious poor should be frugal, sparse and settled, while the reserve army of the idle and criminal be converted into productive labour. From the darkness of 1751, however, Fielding – somewhat contradictorily – saw only dysfunction. Trade produces riches, which in turn promote luxury, with inevitable consequences:

> Nothing hath wrought such an Alteration in this Order of People, as the Introduction of Trade. This hath indeed given a new Face to the whole Nation, hath in great measure subverted the former State of Affairs, and hath almost totally changed the Manners, Customs, and Habits of the People, more especially of the lower Sort. The Narrowness of their Fortune is changed into Wealth; the Simplicity of their Manners changed into Craft, their Frugality into Luxury, their Humility into Pride, and their Subjugation into Equality.... I think that the vast Torrent of Luxury which the late Years hath poured itself into this Nation, hath greatly contributed to produce among many others, the Mischief I here complain of.[43]

Luxury is not, therefore, a 'casual Evil', but a threat to the empire. Drawing upon Middleton's *Life of Cicero*, Fielding makes the inevitable comparisons with Rome. Like this once 'Mistress of the World, the Seat of Arts, Empire and Glory', Britain risks running the same course 'from virtuous Industry to Wealth; from Wealth to Luxury; from Luxury to and Impatience of Discipline and Corruption of Morals', thus sliding into a state of 'Sloth, Ignorance and Poverty; enslaved to the most cruel, as well as to the most contemptible Tyrants, *Superstition and Religious Imposture*'.[44]

In analysing the causes of London crime, the consequences of allowing thieves to find refuge in the private and gothic haunts of London's congested slums, and the seeming ineffectiveness of public executions in deterring crimes against property, Fielding revealed that the most intense fear in the minds of eighteenth-century London's property owners arose not from the petty activities of villains and rogues described in rogue literature, but from the threat posed by the violent excesses of murderers, highwaymen and footpads. The ordering of criminal and poor space in the metropolis was, however, complex and dynamic. It was intimately related to perceived distinctions between criminal and pauper activity, and their structural underpinnings. 'The nature and importance of illegality were in part defined by its social location', argues McMullan,[45] but the process was reciprocal – space was also powerfully formed by its criminalization. Criminal enclaves persisted in the bourgeois imagination as proximate antitheses of its own space in the City and Westminster, but at particular moments of economic depression, bourgeois space itself was seen as threatened by incursions from the only too visible presence of beggars.

We understand little of this dynamic. What is apparent is that much of the writing on metropolitan poverty and crime during the eighteenth century was consciously or otherwise an attempt to think through this spatial reordering. Inevitably, the previous era of metropolitan history had a formative influence. In the period from 1550 to 1700 distinct criminal enclaves emerged with a powerful sense of territorial independence that persisted until the mid nineteenth century.[46] Thus the Clink and the Mint in Southwark, Whitefriars and Alsatia at the City's south-eastern boundary, Spitalfields and Whitechapel, and the Newgate–Cripplegate area entered into popular imagination as congested zones of criminal activity. Here were defensible spaces where thieves, prostitutes, cheats and beggars found refuge from the law and public surveillance. The complex networks of alleys, lanes and stairs made pursuit difficult, and it was rendered even more so by strategies of mutual protection adopted by their inhabitants to discourage intruders.

This unknowability contrasted sharply with the only too visible presence of beggars on the main thoroughfares. Stationary beggars adopted strategies that relied on distinct appropriations of space.[47] Sites offering privileged access to pedestrian and carriage traffic were occupied and jealously guarded. Thus the Royal Exchange, St Paul's, the Strand and Charing Cross were favoured. Here beggars could prey upon the sensibilities of large numbers of passers-by without undue risk of apprehension under the vagrant laws. The least mobile had to claim their pitch early in the morning; over time they became familiar figures in the metropolitan streetscape.[48]

Beggars and petty thieves were perceived as less of a threat than hardened professional criminals such as thieves, footpads and highwaymen. Beggars may have jostled and disgusted bourgeois pedestrians, but they rarely posed a danger to personal and material well-being. And draconian as the vagrancy laws were, they could hardly compare with the murderous judicial regime created by the litany of capital statutes introduced at the beginning of the century under which minor acts of theft commanded the death penalty. For the most part, beggars were seen as an inconvenient and unpleasant presence on metropolitan streets.

At particular moments, however, when their numbers increased dramatically, more serious concern was expressed in the literature. The extent of begging was determined by the state of the labour market. It was linked, therefore, to the trade cycle, and if it were possible accurately to chart the course of trade, correlations could be made between economic recessions and concern over begging. The eighteenth-century picture, however, was complicated by the frequent interruptions of imperial wars.[49]

Although the effect of war depended upon the particular stage in the trade cycle when it broke out, what is not in doubt is the impact that the cease of hostilities had on unemployment. As war ended, tens of thousands of ex-soldiers and sailors were dumped on the streets to survive as best they could; many did so through begging and crime. Some 157,000 men were discharged in 1713–14 (War of the Spanish Succession), 79,000 in 1749–50 (War of the Austrian Succession), 155,000 in 1764–65 (Seven Years War), 160,000 in 1784–85 (American War of Independence), and 350,000 after 1815 (Napoleonic Wars). Unsurprisingly, these were the moments of the most intense anxiety about the state of metropolitan streets, when the putative links between begging and crime were stated most forcefully.

The distinction between roguery and villainy was also evident in popular literature. Rogues were rascals, generally without malice, who lived and worked on the peripheries of the criminal underworld. From the seventeenth century, their culture was described in the picaresque literature of jest books, canting verses and lexicons, travelogues and biographies. In this literature had appeared the first attempts to know the underworld of early modern London, but during the eighteenth century the genre created by Greene and Harman degenerated into tedious formulae. Previous works were pirated, canting lexicons repeated with little variation. Similar trajectories were apparent in fictional and dramatic representations. Richard Brome's *A Jovial Crew* and John Gay's *The Beggar's Opera* have long been recognized as among the most popular and significant plays about roguery. In seeming to celebrate the comparative freedom of beggars from the economic and moral restraint of the time, they touched on a range of contemporary concerns.[50] But these concerns were not around beggars. First staged during the extreme tensions of 1641, *A Jovial Crew* used a familiar narrative of redemption to expose the hazardous and circumscribed liberty of anyone denied property and political rights in an arbitrary and savage regime. And *The Beggar's Opera*, performed in the aftermath of the bloody regime heralded by the introduction of the Black Act and the troubled economic climate created by the South Sea Bubble fiasco, used a London gang of highwaymen and thieves (not beggars) to expose the hypocrisy and corruption of upper-class rule embodied in the Walpole regime.

Rogue fiction in the remainder of the eighteenth century possessed little of this critical capacity. Cibber Colley's production of *The Beggar's Wedding* (1729), *The Beggar's Pantomime* (1736) and the revival of a traditional tale in *The Blind Beggar of Bethnal Green* (1741) were examples of fanciful celebrations of the putative exoticism and gaiety of outlaw life.[51] All these were eclipsed, however, by the extraordinary success of *An Apology for the Life of Bampfylde-Moore Carew*, first published in 1745 and republished in a considerable variety of editions until well into the nineteenth century.[52] It recounted the story 'taken from the mouth' of Carew, the son of a Devonshire gentleman, who toured Britain and North America in the company of beggars, whose culture the book claimed to reveal. Like most other rogue literature of the eighteenth century, however, it was a clumsy compilation of extracts from other publications, including Dekker's *Belman of London* (1608), Harman, Fielding's *Tom Jones* and canting dictionaries. Its success, concluded Chandler, 'was disproportionate to its merit'.[53]

This literature stood in sharp contrast to an alternative genre of rogue literature, namely, criminal biography. Well over 2,000 pamphlets in this genre appeared between the late seventeenth century when fears first found expression and the late eighteenth century as anxiety receded. Narrating the lives of criminals, most of whom were located within London, they were read enthusiastically by or to virtually all sections of the population. The socio-poetics of this literature suggests that by providing mythical resolutions to crime and retribution it mitigated the fears of the propertied who felt threatened and of the dispensers of justice who pondered on its effectiveness.[54] Ostensibly describing in lurid detail the careers and dying confessions of convicted villains, the accounts were rather more than vicarious sources of sensation for the reader. They rendered criminal activity fictional, strange, unfamiliar and hence distant. Thus disturbing questions about criminal lives were sweetened by frivolous and inchoate detail, making them more palatable for an audience anxious that crimes against property were 'too often at the margins of consciousness, and too ready to intrude'.[55]

In the second half of the eighteenth century, as their social and political salience weakened, so criminal biographies became rare. By the 1740s petty criminals attracted little attention; by the 1770s, even highwaymen were forgotten. It was as if a closure had been forced on attempts to gain access to or even register the presence of the criminal poor in the metropolis. Thus, in spite of numerous topographical and literary surveys that attempted to confer order on the criminalized spaces of the metropolis, by the end of the eighteenth century it was apparent that its underworld remained remote and inaccessible.

The extensive literature on the metropolitan poor, vague and imprecise thought it may have been in identifying the boundaries between its various constituencies, did help to promote change in the latter half of the eighteenth century.[56] After 1750, and in particular during 1780–1820, the violent and brutal excesses of metropolitan life gradually diminished. Contemporary observers such as John Fielding and Francis Place noted the transformation in manners among the populace as lives became cleaner, healthier and less precarious.[57] These improvements, according to Dorothy George, were engendered by reforms in the administration of justice, pioneered by the Fieldings. Henry supplanted the corruption of trading justices by a public and disinterested magistracy, which was developed by his half-brother John into a reforming institution, laying the foundation for a permanent police force, and confronting the toll taken by gin on the London poor. Simultaneously, local government was rationalized. Vestries, still existing as a complex patchwork of overlapping authorities, obtained enabling legislation to regulate the poor more effectively. Rates were levied to clean and light the streets, to establish watch committees, and generally to set parish affairs on a more efficient and financially sound footing.[58] Some escaping the net of these reforms found a champion in Jonas Hanway, who, concerned that the high mortality rates among children of the metropolitan poor threatened the very existence of the nation, set about saving them by establishing foundling hospitals, and campaigning for the abolition of climbing boys and the worst abuses of the apprenticeship system.[59]

Significant also were shifts in the moral universe of the poor law. For the century following the fall of the Stuarts, perspectives on poverty had hardened. Quite apart from the demonization of beggars and vagrants, those forced legitimately to seek relief were viewed as personally inadequate and subjected to harsh disciplinary regimes. Toward the end of the eighteenth century attitudes softened. Poverty began to be seen as less of a crime, and more of an unfortunate consequence of trade depression and low wages.[60] Tracts were published to expose the undue hardships suffered under the poor law,[61] in response to which the 1783 Gilbert Act was introduced. In ending parochial administration of relief in most areas of the country, it signalled a more humane and sympathetic approach to the poor.[62] In general, levels of poor relief increased in this period.

Important as these changes may have been to the life chances of the poor, the impact of underlying improvements in the metropolitan economy has been neglected. The protracted and deep depression that afflicted London from 1726 began to lift in the 1750s and from then until the turn of the century expansion, as measured by a variety of indicators such as foreign trade, building and coal imports, was healthy and sustained. Population change mirrored this pattern, with a period of stagnation or even decline up to 1750 followed by growth of some 50 per cent by 1800. Any assessment, however, of the effect of these movements on income levels is troublesome, not least because of the diversity in life chances. Overall, it appears that while the 1760s and 1770s were made difficult by international conflicts, the years following 1784 were good.[63]

It may seem surprising that amidst this climate of improvement expressions of foreboding gathered strength, becoming particularly strident after 1815. The paradox has been explained by a mounting concern with the putative destruction wrought by luxury, and with the decline in subordination.[64] In the figure of the relatively well fed artisan these conflicting sentiments could be articulated together to construct an image of moral deterioration threatening the nation.[65] But these fears cannot explain adequately the transformation in attitudes toward the metropolitan poor that occurred in the crisis decade of the 1790s, largely under the influence of Patrick Colquhoun. Moving freely in influential political and commercial circles, mixing with leading evangelicals, utilitarians, and other social reformers, he was able best to articulate the range of contemporary concerns around metropolitan poverty and define aspects of an agenda that was profoundly to shape nineteenth-century perspectives on the metropolitan poor. Before considering this, however, it is necessary briefly to consider how India had entered into the British imagination.

India in European cosmography

The argument that India came to be better known to the British in the late eighteenth century is a seductive one. Recognition of the potential of imperial conquest heightened European rivalry, and impelled projects to investigate the topography, people, culture and history of the subcontinent; the actuality of conquest provided unprecedented opportunities for so doing. As a consequence, in the years following Clive's crucial victory at Plassey in 1757 the number of publications on India increased dramatically.[66]

It is an argument, however, that has to be treated with a degree of caution, not least because it tends to understate the contribution made by early travel writings on India. From the extraordinary life work of Donald Lach we gain a measure of the extent and diversity of European views of Asia during 1500–1800, and the impact that these changing knowledges had on European artistic and intellectual endeavour.[67] More recently, Joan-Pau Rubies has revealed the significance of writings by European travellers to India during the fifteenth and sixteenth centuries.[68] In contrast to Lach's copious Asia in the Making of Europe, and to the pioneering work of Margaret Hodgen on early modern ethnology,[69] Rubies focuses on the question of how travel literature structured moral and political thought, and so contributed to the transition from the theological epistemology of medieval European culture to the historical and philosophical concerns of the nascent Enlightenment. It was not merely that this literature dispelled notions of the fantastic and monstrous by an elaboration of human diversity, but that by forcing recognition of cultural difference it radically challenged prevailing orthodoxies on the human order.

Situated as it was in European cosmography in a peculiar and troublesome relationship to Chinese civilization and the New World, and possessing its own ancient culture, India presented a particular challenge. In confronting it, Portuguese, Spanish and Italian travellers wrote accounts that were not, of course, the product of innocent observation, but were framed by what Stuart Schwartz has termed implicit understandings.[70] Travellers drew upon a body of common knowledge that was rarely elaborated, but at the same time was open to revision as knowledge accumulated. Nor were these accounts simply the outcome of a putative 'orientalist' project, for perceptions were influenced by dialogue with indigenous peoples, and by the practical interests that guided the authors' travels. Accounts of early travels to the few coastal areas that were known sought answers to questions determined for the most part by the commercial concerns of merchants and soldiers. Lacking training in theology, law or the humanities, and the erudition to undertake comparative analysis, these travellers attempted to make sense of India's diversity through detailed empirical observation. Recourse was frequently had to pejorative stereotypes of 'black and inferior natives'; what prevailed, however, was a profound sense of the difficulty of providing a unified and coherent image. Furthermore, many of these accounts remained unpublished or were, in the pursuit of Iberian imperial ambitions, restricted; as such they were marginal to the development of European cosmography.

In England, knowledge of India was sketchy, unreliable and largely mythical. Until the latter stages of the sixteenth century, merchants and priests demonstrated little interest in challenging Portuguese dominance better to exploit trade with India or to convert its population. Without first-hand accounts of travellers, prevailing wisdom was based exclusively on translations of medieval cosmographies and travel books. The exotic, monstrous and fabulous found in Sir John Mandeville's *Travels* were still taken seriously by geographers.[71] This ignorance was compounded by restrictions on the printing and book trades imposed by authorities fearful of sedition and heresy. Translations of foreign works on overseas travel were forbidden; even Mandeville suffered, for while four editions had appeared between 1498 and 1510, no other was published until 1568.[72]

Toward the late sixteenth century Jesuit missionaries in India laid the foundations for an epistemological transformation. Working with a sophisticated interpretative framework that made possible comparisons among non-European peoples, they published accounts that attempted increasingly to locate India within a wider comparative field. Descriptions of its topography and economy were displaced if not superseded by ethnographic and historical narratives – part of the shift from the spatial to the temporal that defined the course of early ethnology, and on the basis of which India was positioned hierarchically between Africa and Europe.[73] By this time, however, Portugal's hold on trade with India had begun to weaken, and its monopoly was challenged with some success by Dutch commercial initiatives. Encouraged, English merchants embarked on ventures to determine the feasibility of a north-east passage to China and India. Jesuit and merchant travellers began to record their observations, and the East entered symbolically into England's burgeoning literary domain. England's relationship with Asia underwent a profound transformation.

It was through the writings of Father Thomas Stephens, Ralph Fitch, Thomas Coriat, Edward Terry and other travellers of the late sixteenth and early seventeenth centuries that England 'discovered' India, and finally put to rest Mandeville's ghost. Although most of these travellers acted at the behest of commerce – focused after 1600 in the activities of the East India Company – their accounts cannot be reduced simply to crude reflections of those interests. Nor were they written to be read exclusively by Company functionaries. When in 1625 Samuel Purchas published his anthology of travel writings, he offered 'for [those] which cannot travell farre ... a World of Travellers to their domestike entertainment, easie to be spared from their Smoke, cup, and Butter-flie vanities ... and to entertain them in a better Schoole to better purposes'.[74] No incongruity may have been felt in providing reliable information on trade and topography, pseudo-ethnological knowledge and tales of wonder, but in meeting such demands the accounts drew contradictorily upon observation and medieval fantasy to produce diverse and unstable narratives.

The Jesuit Thomas Stephens was arguably the first Englishman known to have lived in and written about India.[75] Arriving there in 1579, he wrote to his father, setting the tone for subsequent accounts. The long letter provided valuable information on maritime routes around Madagascar, the fauna of the southern seas, and first impressions of the Indians. 'The people be tawny', he declared, effectively locating them in the great chain of being, 'but not disfigured in their lips and noses, as the Moors and Kaffirs of Ethiopia.'[76] Stephens is remembered best, however, as an English pioneer in the study of Indian languages, and the founder of Christian literature in Goa. After nearly forty years in India he completed in 1614 the *Christian Purana*, an account of the Old and New Testaments in Marathi intended to reveal through comparison with Hindu *Puranas* the idolatrous and heathen nature of Hinduism. It was still in popular use in the twentieth century.[77]

Unsurprisingly, accounts of merchant travellers provided the most reliable information on the commercial potential of India at the beginning of the seventeenth century. In their various ways, Ralph Fitch, Thomas Coriat, Thomas Roe, Edward Terry, Henry Lord and others mapped out favourable terrain for exploitation by an ascendant mercantile elite. They noted places where precious metals and stones, spices, foodstuffs and other commodities could be found, recorded routes and journey times between ports and cities, and described the types of trade conducted.[78] In pursuit of commercial concessions many were drawn to the Mughal court where they were dazzled by its wealth, exoticism and grandeur, and mystified by what they saw as the capriciousness of Jehangir, Shah Jehan and Aurangzib.

Of greater interest here are observations on the social and cultural practices of the Indians encountered. Constant references to the veracity of first-hand observation were included to validate their authenticity to an intended readership, but amidst the detail what emerges from these writings is a sense of the struggle to describe and comprehend the seemingly incomprehensible. Meticulous some accounts may have been, but these travellers viewed India through the lens of earlier narratives found in epic stories, the Bible, classical tales and medieval travelogues; in so doing they laid the foundation for the poetics of a nascent geographical and ethnological consciousness.[79] Thus, to interpret the mystery and marvel of India they turned to familiar tropes of otherness, structured almost exclusively by a Christian cosmography. Coriat, for example, described that most spectacular of Hindu festivals, the Kumb Mela, in terms that would have had meaning for his readers:

> I expect an excellent opportunity ... to goe to the famous River Ganges, whereof about foure hundred thousand people go hither ... to bathe in the River, and to sacrifice a world of gold in the same River ... and doing other notable strange Ceremonies most worth of obseruation, such a notable spectacle it is, that in no part of all Asia ... [is] the like to be seen; this show doe they make once euery yeere, coming hither from places almost thousand miles off, and honour their Riuer as their God, Creator, Sauior; superstition and impeity most abominable ... these brutish Ethnickes, that are aliens.[80]

From these various accounts emerged a stock repertoire of customs and traits that came to define Indianness for European readers. Nakedness, child marriage, sati, idolatry, Brahmanism, thuggee and sacrifice in particular seemed to outrage European sensibilities, as a result of which they featured prominently in a collective consciousness which remained intact for at least the next two hundred years. The examples proliferate. Fitch noted that in spite of the abundance of cotton cloth, the people of Sonargaon in East Bengal 'goe with a little cloth before them, and all the rest of their bodies is naked'.[81] In other parts of India, notable contemporary travellers such as the Italians Ludovico Di Varthema and Pietro Della Valle and the Dutch Jan Huygen van Linschoten made virtually identical observations.[82] Sati was singled out by William Methold, Edward Terry, Francois Bernier, Henry Lord and Nicholas Withington. The last captured graphically the lot of condemned widows:

> [I]f any one of them purpose to burn, and (after Ceremonies done) bee brought to the Fyer, and these feelinge the scorching Heate, leape out of the Fyre, her

Father and Mother will take her and bynde her, and throwe her into the Fyre, and burne her per force.[83]

Forraigne sects

Reliable though many of the observations were, at best they were superficial with no real understanding of Indian culture. Not until the publication in 1630 of Lord's *A Display of Two Forraigne Sects in the East Indies* was there a serious attempt to interpret Hindu and Parsi religious practices by consulting with Indian pundits. Replete with error, prejudice and confusion it may have been, but Lord's study of ancient mythology and the origins of caste was notable, later commanding the attention and praise of William Jones.[84] It was also published in France and Holland, and formed the basis of numerous commentaries on these religions by better-known travellers such as Thomas Herbert and Francois Bernier.

The existence of common tropes in these early accounts derives in part from the extensive textual borrowing that took place among writers of the time. Most travellers were familiar with earlier narratives and plagiarized them freely. Fitch, for example, relied so heavily on Cesare Federici's account of a journey to India twenty years earlier, that he reproduces not only empirical detail, but style and language.[85] This pan-European outlook was encouraged by the general availability of travel literature. Indeed, it seems likely that in the early modern period, translations of foreign accounts had the greatest influence on English readers. The fanciful imagination of Mandeville continued to exert its presence, but toward the end of the sixteenth century the exploits of contemporary European travellers began to appear.[86] Largely under the guidance of Richard Eden, Richard Willes and Richard Hakluyt, collections of foreign travel literature were published which were designed to encourage English merchants to take advantage of the opportunities offered by the East for commercial and imperial exploitation.[87] Eden's *A Treatyse of the Newe India* appeared in 1553, subsequently to be revised and expanded in Willes's *The History of Trauayle in the West and East Indies* (1577). More important, however, were the translations of Juan de Mendoza's *History of China* (1588), Cesare Federici's *The Voyage and Travaile of M.C. Federici* (1588), John van Linschoten's *His Discours of Voyages into ye East and West Indies* (1598) and anonymous accounts of the first two Dutch voyages to India (1598 and 1599).

Accounts of the early English travellers were less well known.[88] Coriat (1613) and Lord (1630) were among the very few successful in having their accounts published. Most of the original manuscripts of travelogues appeared for the first time in the second edition of Hakluyt's *Principall Navigations* (1598–1600) or in Purchas's *Pilgrimes* (1625), and then in abridged forms. A letter of Thomas Stephens and the accounts of Ralph Fitch, John Mildenhall, William Hawkins, William Finch, Nicholas Withington and Edward Terry were all published in one of these collections; it was not until the nineteenth century that most of these were published in their own right.

But the availability of travel accounts was a necessary rather than sufficient condition; other factors were involved. Few authors strove for originality. Their aim was to provide reliable and comprehensive information, and if this meant recourse to accounts of places visited by previous travellers then it was available as a ready and convenient option.[89] In turn, this borrowing was predicated on and promoted cultural assumptions about India from which certain European perspectives emerged on its peoples, customs and topography that informed the strategic repertoire of imperial discourses during the late eighteenth and early nineteenth centuries.

For the remainder of the seventeenth century little of originality appeared. The best known – Herbert's *A Relation of Some Yeares Travaile, Begunne Anno 1626* – appeared in 1634. It contained first-hand descriptions of coastal areas, but much of the information on Indian cultural practices derived from earlier studies.[90] Only with the publication of Robert Knox's *An Historical Relation of Ceylon* in 1681 and John Ovington's *A Voyage to Surat* in 1696 were significant new areas of the Indian subcontinent opened to the public gaze. Anthologies, however, again proved the most popular. *A Collection of Voyages and Travels* was the result of the labours of the London booksellers Awnsham and John Churchill. It was first published as four volumes in 1704, and contained numerous travel writings of the seventeenth century. The volumes were reprinted in 1732, supplemented by two others. Contemporaneously, John Harris edited *Navigantium atque Itinerantium Bibiotheca, or, A Compleat Collection of Voyages and Travels*. Originally, it was little more than a compendium of accounts previously published in Hakluyt and Purchas, but in the 1740s it was revised and enlarged by John Campbell. Determined to promote British commercial activity and overcome what he considered to be the indolent attitude displayed toward discovery, Campbell claimed to have drawn upon more than 600 volumes.[91] And in 1743 the bookseller Thomas Astley issued in instalments his ambitious *A New General Collection of Voyages and Travels*. It was essentially a compendium of what Astley considered to be the most reliable accounts. Attracting over a thousand subscribers, amongst whom were large numbers of merchants and brokers rather than clergymen, it provided evidence of the critical role of booksellers in promoting this literature, and of the growing attention it commanded in commercial circles. For those who could not afford the costly collections, even when published in instalments, popular periodicals provided an alternative source of information. The *Gentle-*

man's *Magazine*, the *London Magazine*, and later the *Monthly Review* and the *Critical Review* contained regular reviews of travel books, and long serial articles on foreign regions which freely included extensive extracts from previously published materials.[92]

Important though these anthologies were in meeting the need for information, they remained compendia of earlier accounts and thereby contributed only limited knowledge of the contemporary world. Those requiring up-to-date knowledge of India were poorly served. Anthologies included few relevant accounts of India, and original travelogues were conspicuous by their absence.[93] That of Captain Alexander Hamilton,[94] published in 1727, seemed sensitive to the problem, for at the outset he is anxious to claim legitimacy on the basis of the veracity of first-hand observation:

> You will find [this account] more particular, correct and extensive, than any of the kind, at least, of any that I ever saw.... I'll not acknowledge mistakes of taken before Map-travellers, or who have only the Sanction of other Mens Journals, or Memoirs to qualify them.... [A]lthough some amuse the World with large and florid Descriptions of countries they never saw used, yet, since their Stock of Knowledge is all on Tick, the want of being Eye and Ear-witnesses very much depreciates their accounts.[95]

To illustrate the point Hamilton refers to the 'ingenious Observations and Remarks' published by a 'reverend Gentleman' in 1690. He 'received a great deal of Applause, and many Encomiums', and yet

> his greatest Travels were in Maps, and the Knowledge he had of the Countries ... was the Accounts he gathered from common Report; and perhaps, those Reports came successively to him by Second or Third Hands; for, to my certain Knowledge, there were none then at Surat or Bombay that could furnish him with any tolerable Accounts of some Countries that he describes.[96]

None of these strictures, however, prevented Hamilton from reproducing a familiar miscellany of history, topography, trade and religion, or from indulging in condemnations of the strange and exotic. Ascetics were singled out for opprobrium:

> There is another Sort called *Jougies*, who practise great Austerities and Mortifications. They contemn world Riches, and go naked, except for a Bit of Cloth about their Loyns, and some deny themselves even that, delighting in Nastiness and an holy Obscenity, with a great Shew of Sanctity.... I have seen a sanctified Rascal of seven foot high, and his limbs well proportioned, with a large Turband of his own Hair wreathed about his Head, and his body bedaub'd with Ashes and Water, sitting quite naked under the Shade of a Tree, with a *Pudenda* like an Ass, and a Hole bored through his Prepuce, with a large Gold Ring fixed in the Hole. This Fellow was much revered by numbers of young married women, who, prostrating themselves before the

living *Priapus*, and taking him devoutly in their Hands, kiss him, whilst his bawdy Owner strokes their silly Heads, muttering some filthy Prayers for their Prolification.[97]

The absence of significant new travel accounts hampered British knowledge of India, as did the paucity and unreliability of information on those few territories under control of the British gleaned from functionaries of the East India Company. There was simply no 'body of "colonial knowledge", but, instead, a congeries of technical commercial information and impressions drawn from diplomatic discourse with Indian states'.[98] Indeed, it seems likely that in the first half of the eighteenth century knowledge of India and understanding of its culture declined: into the gap flowed familiar tropes of orientalist fantasy.

These faltering attempts in early travel literature to know London and India displayed sharp contrasts. Evidence of dialogue between the genres is scant. What prevails, however, is a continued sense of epistemological insecurity which in the course of the eighteenth century actually heightened. The absence of significant new inquiry that could have drawn productively on previous work created a vacuum which was filled by tropes of criminal and orientalist fantasy. The crisis in confidence attendant on the collapse of the first British empire and the outbreak of the French Revolution impelled new modes of observation. If a unitary field of knowledge was created between metropolis and India it was surely at this moment.

Notes

1   M. Dorothy George, *London Life in the Eighteenth Century*, London, Peregrine, 1966 [1925].
2   Gareth Stedman Jones, *Outcast London. A Study in the Relationship between Classes in Victorian Society*, Oxford, Clarendon Press, 1971; Leonard Schwarz, *London in the Age of Industrialisation. Entrepreneurs, Labour Force and Living Conditions, 1700–1850*, Cambridge, Cambridge University Press, 1992; David R. Green, *From Artisans to Paupers. Economic Change and Poverty in London, 1790–1870*, London, Scolar Press, 1995.
3   Jose Harris, 'Between civic virtue and social Darwinism: the concept to the residuum', in David Englander and Rosemary O'Day (eds), *Retrieved Riches*, London, Scolar Press, 1995; Gertrude Himmelfarb, *The Idea of Poverty. England in the Early Industrial Age*, London, Faber, 1981; Stedman Jones, *Outcast London*; Karel Williams, *From Pauperism to Poverty*, London, Routledge, 1981.
4   Peter Keating, *The Working Class in Victorian Fiction*, London, Routledge, 1971.
5   I have recently edited two extensive collections of this material: see John Marriott and Masaie Matsumura (eds), *The Metropolitan Poor. Semi-Factual Accounts, 1790–1910*, 6 vols, London, Pickering and Chatto, 1999; John Marriott (ed.), *Unknown London. Early Modernist Visions of the Metropolis*, 6 vols, London, Pickering and Chatto, 2000.
6   I have explored this in my Introduction to Marriott (ed.), *Unknown London*.
7   Lawrence Manley, *Literature and Culture in Early Modern London*, Cambridge, Cambridge University Press, 1995, p. 20.
8   F.W. Chandler, *The Literature of Roguery*, London, Constable, 1907.

9   Richard Altick, *The English Common Reader. A Social History of the Mass Reading Public, 1800–1900*, Columbus, Ohio State University Press, 1998.
10 Manley, *Literature and Culture in Early Modern London*, p. 369.
11 *Ibid.*, p. 519.
12 John Marriott, 'The spatiality of the poor in eighteenth-century London', in Tim Hitchcock and Heather Shore (eds), *The Streets of London*, London, Rivers Oram, 2003.
13 Miles Ogborn, *Spaces of Modernity. London's Geographies, 1680–1780*, New York, The Guilford Press, 1998; Richard Sennett, *The Fall of Public Man*, London, Faber, 1986.
14 John Spranger, *A Proposal or Plan for an Act of Parliament for the Better Paving, Cleansing and Lighting of the Streets, Lanes, Courts and Alleys ... within the Several Parishes of the City and Liberty of Westminster*, London, 1754.
15 Charles Kingsford, *John Stow. A Survey of London. Reprinted from the Text of 1603*, Oxford, Clarendon Press, 1971, p. xlii.
16 Ogborn, *Spaces of Modernity*, pp. 30–1.
17 John Entick, *A New and Accurate History and Survey of London, Westminster and Southwark, and places adjacent ...*, 4 vols, London, Dilly, 1766.
18 *Ibid.*, Vol. IV, p. 132.
19 Spranger, *A Proposal or Plan for an Act of Parliament*, Preface.
20 Max Byrd, *London Transformed. Images of the City in the Eighteenth Century*, New Haven, Yale University Press, 1978, pp. 12–13.
21 Pat Rogers, *Hacks and Dunces. Pope, Swift and Grub Street*, London, Methuen, 1972, pp. 2–9.
22 Sennett, *The Fall of Public Man*, p. 17.
23 Anon., *Leigh's New Picture of London, or, A View of the Political, Religious, Medical, Literary, Municipal, Commercial, and Moral State of the British Metropolis*, London, Leigh, 1816.
24 W. Hutton, *A Journey to London, Comprising a Description of the Most Interesting Objects of Curiosity to a Visitor of the Metropolis*, London, Nichols, 1818.
25 T. Williams, *The Insane World; or, A Week in London*, London, Westley, 1820.
26 Deborah Nord, *Walking the Victorian Streets. Women, Representation, and the City*, Ithaca, Cornell University Press, 1995.
27 Anon., *The Country Gentleman's Vade-Mecum; or, His Companion for the Town. In Eighteen Letters, from a Gentleman to his Friend in the Country, wherein he Passionately Dissuades him against coming to London*, London, 1699.
28 R. Strauss (ed.), *Tricks of the Town*, London, Chapman and Hall, 1927.
29 Anon., *A Trip through London*, London, 1728; Anon., *A Trip through the Town, containing Observations on the Humours and Manners of the Age*, London, 1735; Anon., *A Ramble through London; or, A Trip from Whitehall to Whitechapel*, London, 1738; Anon., *A Trip from St James's to the Exchange. With Remarks Serious and Diverting on the Manners, Customs, and Amusements of the Inhabitants of London and Westminster*, London, Withers, 1744; Anon., *The Tricks of the Town Laid Open; or, A Companion for Country Gentlemen. Being the Substance of Seventeen Letters from a Gentleman at London to his Friend in the Country, to Disswade him from Coming to Town*, London, Slater, 1747.
30 This felicitous term is borrowed from Byrd, *London Transformed*.
31 Anon., *A Trip through London*, pp. 113, 122.
32 Byrd (*London Transformed*, p. 25) suggests that images of forests and labyrinths invoked not only adventure, but also alienation and anonymity at a time when the scale and pace of metropolitan growth seemed beyond comprehension. Their pervasiveness, however, derived from a versatility in conjuring up a range of discourses, including an antithetical unknown (no doubt with Freudian undertones), and images of imperial expansion.
33 Anon., *A Trip from St James's to the Royal Exchange*, p. 12.
34 *Ibid.*, pp. 12–13.
35 Joshua Gee, *The Trade and Navigation of Great Britain Considered*, London, 1729,

pp. 8–9.

36   *Ibid.*, p. 36.

37   Henry Fielding, *An Enquiry into the Causes of the Late Increase of Robbers, etc., with some Proposals for Remedying this Growing Evil*, London, Millar, 1751. The work has been republished with useful commentary in M.R. Zirker (ed.), *An Enquiry into the Causes of the Late Increase in Robbers, and Related Writings*, Oxford, Clarendon Press, 1988.

38   Fielding, *An Enquiry*, p. lxiii.

39   *Ibid.*, p. 65.

40   *Ibid.*, p. 38.

41   *Ibid.*, p. 116.

42   *Ibid.*, p. xxiv.

43   *Ibid.*, pp. xi, 3.

44   *Ibid.*, p. xxxi.

45   J.L. McMullan, *The Canting Crew. London's Criminal Underworld, 1550–1700*, New Jersey, Rutgers University Press, 1984, p. 55.

46   *Ibid.*; F. McLynn, *Crime and Punishment in Eighteenth-Century England*, London, Routledge, 1989.

47   These should be distinguished from itinerant domestic beggars and the beggarly self-employed, who were less numerous and perceived to be rather less of a problem. For a discussion of these issues, see Tim Hitchcock, 'Beggar-man, thief: the publicity of poverty in early eighteenth-century London', unpublished paper, 1998.

48   Some of these were portrayed in an outstanding collection of contemporary engravings in J. Smith, *Vagabondiana; or, Anecdotes of Mendicant Wanderers through the Streets of London, with Portraits of the Most Remarkable*, London, Chatto and Windus, 1817.

49   Schwarz, *London in the Age of Industrialization*, pp. 90–9.

50   Christoper Hill, *Liberty Against the Law. Some Seventeenth-Century Controversies*, London, Allen Lane, 1996.

51   Cibber Colley, *The Beggar's Wedding. A New Opera. As it is acted at the Theatre in Dublin*, London, Knapton, 1729; R. Dodsley, *The Blind Beggar of Bethnal Green*, London, 1741.

52   C.H. Wilkinson, *The King of the Beggars. Bampfylde-Moore Carew*, Oxford, Clarendon Press, 1931.

53   Chandler, *The Literature of Roguery*, p. 168.

54   L.B. Faller, *Turned to Account. The Forms and Functions of Criminal Biography in Late Seventeenth- and Early Eighteenth-Century England*, Cambridge, Cambridge University Press, 1987.

55   *Ibid.*, p. 175.

56   It would be interesting to trace the links between this reforming zeal and the moral endeavour to humanize London. Between the apocalyptic visions of Defoe and Blake, poets and writers such as Pope, Johnson, Boswell and Wordsworth attempted to bring the metropolis within the scale of human imagination. Through anthropomorphic projections, they revealed a struggle to control the vital energies that brought together and sustained the city in the latter half of the eighteenth century. For tentative glimpses into these matters, see Byrd, *London Transformed*, and M.H. Abrams, *Natural Supernaturalism. Tradition and Revolution in Romantic Literature*, New York, Norton, 1971.

57   This is an argument found in Dorothy George's *London Life in the Eighteenth Century*. It is one, however, that has to be treated with some caution. The evidence submitted to the select committees on mendicity and vagrancy, and on the police in the metropolis, for example, much of which addressed the question of change over the previous decades, was rather more ambivalent. While many of the witnesses pointed to improvement, others testified that conditions had deteriorated sharply – a reflection of the continued lack of knowledge about London poverty (*Minutes of Evidence Taken before the Select Committee Appointed by the House of Commons to Inquire into the State of Mendicity and Vagrancy in the Metropolis and its Neighbourhood*, London, Sherwood, Neely and Jones, 1815; *Minutes of Evidence Taken before the*

Select Committee Appointed by the House of Commons to Inquire into the State of the Police of the Metropolis, London, Sherwood, Neely and Jones, 1816). I touch on the evidence later (pp. 71, 75).

58 George, *London Life*, pp. 18–23.

59 Jonas Hanway, *An Earnest Appeal for Mercy to the Children of the Poor, particularly those belonging to the Parishes within the Bills of Mortality*, London, Dodsley, 1766.

60 Dorothy Marshall, *The English Poor in the Eighteenth Century. A Study in Social and Administrative History*, London, Routledge, 1969.

61 See, for example, James Massie, *Considerations relating to the poor*, London, 1758; and J. Scott, *Observations on the state of the parochial and vagrant poor*, London, 1773.

62 The Gilbert Act was not applied to London parishes. Indeed it was not until the 1867 Metropolitan Poor Law Act that all of London was brought under the centralized authority of the Poor Law Board. This exceptionalism lends weight to the suggestion that the administration of the poor laws was perceived principally as a problem of rural areas; the metropolis had a different poor to contend with.

63 Such brief arguments do scant justice to the sophisticated case, backed up with ample statistics, made by Schwarz, *London in the Age of Industrialization*.

64 Luxury was not the sort of conspicuous consumption we now associate with the term. For Fielding, it referred to undesirable expenditure among the labouring poor on alcohol and gambling; for others, consumption of tea, sugar and white bread was considered a luxury.

65 George, *London Life*, pp. 27–33.

66 Peter J. Marshall (ed.), *The British Discovery of Hinduism in the Eighteenth Century*, Cambridge, Cambridge University Press, 1970, p. 2.

67 Donald F. Lach, *Asia in the Making of Europe. Vol. I. The Century of Discovery*, Chicago, University of Chicago Press, 1965; *Asia in the Making of Europe. Vol. II. A Century of Wonder*, Chicago, University of Chicago Press, 1977; Donald F. Lach and Edwin J. Van Kley, *Asia in the Making of Europe. Vol. III. A Century of Advance*, Chicago, University of Chicago Press, 1993. The original intent was to publish two books on each of the three centuries. Inevitably, the project expanded, as a result of which the 1500s attracted two, the 1600s three, and the 1700s four.

68 J.P. Rubies, *Travel and Ethnology in the Renaissance. South India through European Eyes, 1250–1625*, Cambridge, Cambridge University Press, 2000; 'New worlds and Renaissance ethnology', *History and Anthropology*, 6 (1993), pp. 157–97; 'Instructions for travellers: teaching the eye to see', *History and Anthropology*, 9 (1996), pp. 139–90.

69 Margaret Hodgen, *Early Anthropology in the Sixteenth and Seventeenth Centuries*, Philadelphia, University of Pennsylvania Press, 1964; see also my discussion of Hodgen in Chapter 4.

70 S.B. Schwartz (ed.), *Implicit Understandings. Observing, Reporting and Reflecting on the Encounters between Europeans and Other Peoples in the Early Modern Era*, Cambridge, Cambridge University Press, 1994.

71 There remains doubt over the existence of Mandeville. *Travels*, first published in 1356, was a compilation of earlier travel writings – particularly those of Odoric and John de Carpini – which he infused with a vivid literary imagination. It was written for a popular audience, and was widely translated into a variety of European languages.

72 Lach, *Asia in the Making of Europe. Vol. II*, p. 362.

73 See my later discussion, p. 77.

74 Samuel Purchas, *Hakluytus Posthumous, or Purchas His Pilgrimes: Containing a History of the World in Sea Voyages and Lande Travells by Englishmen and others*, Glasgow, MacLehose 1905 [1625], p. xliv, cited in Jyotsna Singh, *Colonial Narratives/Cultural Dialogues. 'Discoveries' of India in the Language of Colonialism*, London, Routledge, 1996, p. 20.

75 Ram Chandra Prasad, *Early English Travellers in India. A Study in the Travel Literature of the Elizabethan and Jacobean Periods with Particular Reference to India*, Delhi, Motilal Banarsidass, 1980.

76 Cited in C. Raymond Beazley, *Voyages and Travels*, Oxford, Clarendon Press, 1903, p. 175.
77 Prasad, *Early English Travellers*, p. 20.
78 For useful summaries see Prasad, *Early English Travellers*, and Lach and Van Kley, *Asia in the Making of Europe. Vol. III*, pp. 547–97, 601–837.
79 For an interesting discussion of this, with particular reference to the writings of Coriate and Roe, see Singh, *Colonial Narratives/Cultural Dialogues*, Chapter 1.
80 Thomas Coriat, *Mr. Thomas Coriat to his Friends in England sendeth Greeting*, 1618, cited in Singh, *Colonial Narratives/Cultural Dialogues*, pp. 22–3.
81 Richard Hakluyt, *Principall Navigations*, 1599, p. 258, cited in Prasad, *Early English Travellers*, pp. 52–3.
82 *Ibid.*, p. 53.
83 Purchas included an abridged version of Withington's narrative in his *Pilgrimes*; the complete text was later incorporated as an appendix to Anon., *A Journey over Land, from the Gulf of Honduras to the Great South Sea Performed by John Cockburn, and Five Other Englishmen, &c.*, 1734, p. 315, cited in Prasad, *Early English Travellers*, p. 259.
84 Prasad, *Early English Travellers*, p. 316.
85 See an interesting comparison between the two descriptions of the same part of the itinerary in *ibid.*, pp. 39–42.
86 This trend was, of course, not confined to England. By the end of the seventeenth century most of the important travel literature was available in the major European languages.
87 Lach, *Asia in the Making of Europe. Vol. I*, pp. 208–15; Lach and Van Kley, *Asia in the Making of Europe. Vol. III*, pp. 547–9.
88 Lach notes that the initial dominance over travel writings on India exercised by the Iberians was challenged by the Dutch after 1630, and by the French after 1680 (*Asia in the Making of Europe. Vol. III*, pp. 590–1). This is nicely illustrated by the popularity of individual publications. Using information on the numbers of editions, he suggests that among the most popular travel books of the seventeenth century were Le Maire and Schouten's circumnavigation (1617) and Bontekoe's *Journael* (1646), both of which were published in thirty-eight editions. Compared with writings on the Far East, those on India do not feature that strongly. Only Bernier's travels (1670–71) and Tavernier's account (1676–77) are included among the best-sellers. No English books appear.
89 Rubies, *Travel and Ethnology*, p. 105.
90 Lach and Van Kley, *Asia in the Making of Europe. Vol. III*, pp. 571–2.
91 Peter J. Marshall and G. Williams, *The Great Map of Mankind. British Perceptions of the World in the Age of Enlightenment*, London, Dent, 1982, pp. 48–9.
92 *Ibid.*, pp. 52–3.
93 In their surveys of colonial narratives of India, Jyotsna Singh and A. Chatterjee include none from the first half of the eighteenth century. Their coverage is far from comprehensive, but that no travel account of India from this period is thought worth mentioning is significant (Singh, *Colonial Narratives/Cultural Dialogues*, and A. Chatterjee, *Representations of India, 1740–1840. The Creation of India in the Colonial Imagination*, Basingstoke, Macmillan, 1998).
94 Alexander Hamilton, *A New Account of the East Indies ... from the Year 1688 to 1723*, Edinburgh, Mosman, 1727.
95 *Ibid.*, pp. xii–xiii.
96 *Ibid.*, p. xiv.
97 *Ibid.*, p. 152.
98 C.A. Bayly, *Empire and Information. Intelligence Gathering and Social Communication in India, 1780–1870*, Cambridge, Cambridge University Press, 1996, p. 44.

CHAPTER THREE

The intimate connexion

Discovery of the metropolitan residuum

Patrick Colquhoun, like the Fieldings, was a London magistrate. Having made a fortune as a young man in North America, and established himself as a leading figure among Glaswegian merchants, he migrated to London in 1792, where with the patronage of Henry Dundas he was appointed as the first stipendiary magistrate at the Finsbury Square Office.[1] Utilitarianism mediated by Christian philanthropic sentiment and fears of the consequences of the French Revolution inspired him to write a variety of tracts on ale-houses, education and diets for the poor, the practical application of which was realized in the organization of soup kitchens to alleviate destitute silk weavers in Shoreditch, and in the promotion of the Society for Bettering the Condition and Increasing the Comforts of the Poor. In 1795 appeared the work for which Colquhoun is best remembered. *A Treatise on the Police of the Metropolis* has generally been regarded as laying the foundation for the establishment of the Marine Police Office at Wapping in 1798 and the Metropolitan Police in 1829. Arguably of greater historical significance, however, was its influence on perceptions of the poor, for in this and the subsequent *A Treatise on the Commerce and Police of the River Thames* (1800) and *A Treatise on Indigence* (1806) Colquhoun effectively redefined the poor as a predatory presence, organized in confederacies that operated within a moral economy to defend customary rights of access to moveable property.[2]

Using novel and sophisticated techniques of statistical inquiry, he estimated (often overestimated) the value of public and private property annually plundered in the metropolis:

1. Small Thefts £710,000
2. Thefts upon the Rivers and Quays 500,000
3. Thefts in the Dock-Yards, &c. on the Thames 300,000
4. Burglaries, Highway-Robberies, &c. 220,000

5. Coining base Money 200,000
6. Forging Bills, Swindling, &c. 170,000
   Total £2,100,000[3]

'This sum', Colquhoun added, 'will, no doubt, astonish the Reader, at first view; and may even go very far to stagger his belief; but when the vast extent of the trade and commerce of London is considered ... it will cease to be a matter of surprize, that under an incorrect system of police and deficient laws, the depredations are estimated so high.'

This classification was significant in a number of respects. *A Treatise on the Police* broke with the long tradition of perceiving the metropolitan poor as a bizarre collection of beggars and vagrants with criminal propensities. It did this by effectively remapping their moral, political and spatial boundaries. First, Colquhoun dismissed mendicity as a source of large-scale criminal activity. His conception of criminal plunder was based exclusively on commerce and empire. He displaced elaborate taxonomies of petty street crime by conceptions of a criminal culture inscribed firmly within the sinews of capitalism and imperialism. Small theft was committed by 'servants, chimney-sweepers, dustmen, porters, apprentices, journeymen, stable boys, itinerant Jews, and others' from 'houses, shops, foundries, workshops, ... every other place where property is deposited'. More significant, however, was large-scale theft from riverside trade by various 'nautical Vagabonds' employed in the docks and on the river, or simply by those 'lurking about for plunder', which over time had reached levels 'to the great injury of the Community':

> By degrees, probably ... little distinction was made in illicit transactions between the *Adventure of the Individual, and the Property of the Merchant or Consignee of the Cargo....* The mind thus reconciled to the action, the offence screened by impunity, and apparently screened by custom, the habits of pillage increased: others seduced by the force of example, and stimulated by motives of avarice, soon pursued the same course of Criminality, while the want of apposite Laws, and the means of carrying into execution those that existed, gave an extensive range to Delinquency. New Converts to the System of Iniquity were rapidly made. The mass of Labourers on the River became gradually contaminated. – A similar class upon the Quays, and in the Warehouses, caught the infection, and the evil expanded as Commerce increased.[4]

This was not an exotic culture of finely delineated rogues, but an endemic, predatory and organized international underclass whose presence threatened the future of the nation. Over time, custom and practice, combined with the opportunity to pursue criminal activities without restraint, had perpetuated the evil. The establishment of the Marine Police Office had done much to eliminate these practices and reduce incidences of plunder.

A more lasting solution, however, had to address the wider malaise not of poverty, but of indigence. Here Colquhoun reveals his debt to eighteenth-century discourses around poverty and progress:

> *Poverty* is ... a most necessary and indispensable ingredient in society, without which nations and communities could not exist in a state of civilization. It is the lot of man – it is the source of *wealth*, since without poverty there would be *no labour*, and without *labour* there could be *no riches*, no *refinement*, no *comfort*, and no *benefit* to those who may be possessed of wealth – inasmuch as without a large proportion of poverty surplus labour could never be rendered productive in procuring either the conveniences or luxuries of life. *Indigence*, therefore, and not *poverty*, is the evil.[5]

The means must be found of preventing the poor from descending into indigence. Provision of the basic necessities is an urgent priority: 'There is no subject connected with political economy so difficult or important to the nation at large', Colquhoun argued, 'as the proper management of that branch of internal police which applies to those members of the body politic whose indigence exposed them to the miseries incident to the want of *shelter, food*, and *clothing*.'[6] Such want renders poverty 'worse in a state of civilization than in savage life'. Without this, the nation will continue to be afflicted by the criminal poor 'rendered noxious, offensive, and even dangerous, in consequence of depraved morals and criminal turpitude'.[7]

Second, this underworld, created by commercial and imperial activity, was located not in the City or Westminster but in the riverside areas of East London. Colquhoun effectively 'discovered' the casual residuum, simultaneously opening up East London to inquiry as the centre of gravity shifted to the dockland areas of Wapping and Limehouse. His endeavours, backed financially by the West India Merchants Committee, were initially directed to the establishment of Marine Police Station at Wapping, some thirty years before the Metropolitan Police force was eventually formed. In attempting to reveal this area of criminal activity, however, Colquhoun effectively criminalized large parts of the East End by linking casual labourers in the docks to an extensive and highly organized network of receivers and dealers in stolen property. Sugar, for example, was disposed of as follows:

> There are several Public Houses in the neighbourhood of Thames-street, to which the Journeymen Coopers resort with their Boards of Sugar. – In these receptacles a kind of market is held, where the small Grocers attend, and by means of fictitious Bills of Parcels cover the stolen Property to their respective houses.... The parties who form this criminal confederacy, are said to be great adepts in eluding Justice. – They have established a principle with regard to judicial oaths, affecting the security or tending to the acquittal of their companions in iniquity.[8]

Concern was heightened by the belief that this criminal underworld was organized. Although fears had occasionally surfaced in the eighteenth century that itinerant vagrants roamed the countryside in gangs, few believed metropolitan beggars and thieves formed themselves into confederacies. For the most part such crime was seen to be petty and individualistic.[9] River plunder, on the other hand, was a complex operation that depended for its success upon cooperation. Colquhoun estimated, for example, that each day more than ten hundredweight of sugar was taken from West India ships by lumpers and their associates:

> These aquatic labourers are for the most part in connection with the journeymen Coopers and Watermen, who are supposed to share in the plunder. They generally go on shore three times a day, and being *in a body together*, it is difficult, and sometimes not very safe, for a Trinity or Police Officer to attempt to search or to secure even one of them.[10]

Third, Colquhoun revealed this underworld through rational inquiry. His use of detailed statistics and reports was from the outset recognized as a departure:

> [T]he author has submitted to the consideration of the reader, a variety of *evils* of great magnitude, with other specific details; which are not to be found in books, and which, of course, have never been laid before the public through the medium of the press. It may naturally be expected that such an accumulation of delinquency, systematically detailed, and placed in so prominent a point of view, must excite a considerable degree of astonishment in the minds of those readers who have not been familiar with subjects of this nature.[11]

This found an audience among a reading public anxious to know better the complex totality of social and spatial relationships in the metropolis. History tends to remember Colquhoun as the founding spirit of the Metropolitan Police, but his influence on nineteenth-century discourses of poverty and crime was of equal significance. Frequent references were made to his data in the writings of evangelicals and urban travellers. More obliquely, the trope of the casual residuum, concentrated in the East End, was to frame much of the thinking on the spatiality of poverty for the remainder of the century.

Not that concern around begging and vagrancy entirely evaporated. At the close of the Napoleonic Wars, when beggars seemed again to swarm the streets of London, the government appointed committees of inquiry into the state of mendicity and vagrancy (1815) and the state of the police (1816) in the metropolis. Much of the evidence submitted on the extent of mendicity, recommendations for its suppression, and the effectiveness of the law and its officers, was so contradictory that it was virtually impossible to build a coherent and reliable picture. What did emerge, however, was a sense of the extent to which beggars continued effectively to order space. William Gurney, minister of the Free Chapel, St Giles, spoke of beggars' ability to claim walks as a 'sort of property' – a claim made possible by the 'humanity of the population; people cannot bear to pass by distress without relieving it'.[12] And Sampson Stephenson, iron founder in Seven Dials, described the ways in which groups of beggars quartered the town into sections and divisions, 'and they go one part one way, another part another'.[13]

Gothic heaps of stone

Colquhoun thus 'discovered' the casual residuum in East London, and to an extent East London itself. As London developed to the east, its manufacturing centre of gravity shifted from the older areas of silk weaving in Whitechapel and Spitalfields to the dockland areas of Wapping and Limehouse. And yet East London remained little known. In 1783 J. Ralph surveyed London. Noting the 'celebrity of the Metropolis of the British Empire, and that natural wish which the intelligent among its inhabitants must have to be acquainted with the remarkable things it contains', he began by exploring the built environment of its 'remotest extremity':

> As there were no attempts, till lately, ever made to erect any building which might adorn it at all, there was the more necessity to be particularly careful that the first design of this nature should not miscarry; and yet the four churches which have been built at Limehouse, Ratcliffe, Horsleydown, and Spital Fields, though they all have the advantage of ground which can be desired, are not to be looked at without displeasure. They are merely Gothic heaps of stone without form or order, and meet with the contempt from the best and worst tastes alike.[14]

Colquhoun developed this anthropomorphism precisely by elaborating the 'form and order' of these 'Gothic heaps of stone'. Property plundered in the metropolis was classified in ways that would have been familiar to Fielding. The values lost through small thefts committed by 'servants, chimney-sweepers, dustmen, porters, apprentices, journeymen, stable boys, itinerant Jews, and others', burglaries, highway robberies, counterfeiting and forgery were all estimated. But the real object of concern was riverside plunder. Thefts upon the river and quays, and in the dockyards of East London, were subjected to detailed statistical inquiry, as a result of which casual labourers, concentrated around the riverside areas, and the large variety of dealers in the vicinity supported by their activities came to be identified as the new criminal underworld. The theoretical status of this residuum was consolidated by classifications of poverty. Colquhoun's delineation of the poor into the useful, vagrant, indigent, aged and infirm, and infant was hardly original, but he conferred on it a dynamic sense of change. Boundaries were recognized to be mobile; under particular circumstances, the useful poor, for example, could descend into the indigent poor to be relieved through public funds, or into the vagrant poor to be the peculiar object of the 'national police'.

The metropolitan poor were thus reconstituted as an international and criminalized underclass at the vortex of commercial and imperial endeavour. Colquhoun acted for and articulated the interests of a mercantile elite who not only initiated the investigation of river plunder but also subsequently financed the Marine Police Office at Wapping. He had the ear of those West India merchants and politicians who had played a prominent role in establishing the Atlantic system and who at a time of political and economic uncertainty now felt threatened by the unfettered activities of their labour forces.

It would be mistaken, however, to view figures like Colquhoun solely as zealous persecutors of the poor. His avowed aim was to prevent rather than punish criminal propensities by leading the poor into 'the paths of honest industry'. For those unable to work, adequate provision had to be made through the 'benevolence of the Publick', equalization of rates, soup kitchens, savings banks, and reform of the poor laws. As the political crisis passed, and the Marine Police Office survived[15] (to the evident satisfaction of the West India merchants, who witnessed a dramatic fall in losses and with renewed confidence embarked on plans to build the West India docks), so Colquhoun continued to campaign for a metropolitan-wide police force, wrote books on the problems of redundant labour and immersed himself in charitable pursuits. In this he confronted and revealed some of the complexities in contemporary thinking about metropolitan poverty, for Colquhoun moved in evangelical, utilitarian and legal circles, and evidently saw no incongruity in so doing.

The Society for Bettering the Condition and Increasing the Comforts of the Poor was founded in 1796 by a group of evangelicals under the leadership of Sir Thomas Bernard. Bernard had a history of involvement in the humanitarian campaigns of Jonas Hanway, and with the help of Wilberforce was able to recruit a highly influential committee that included the king as patron, bishops, MPs and Colquhoun.[16] Although based in London, the Society had a national focus, evidenced in the undue attention given in its reports to the administration of the poor law. In its 1799 report *Information for Overseers*, a spinning school, a parish windmill, stewed ox head and whitewash were offered as advice.[17] These could hardly be construed as solutions to metropolitan problems. And yet we can detect in the reports a faltering elaboration of an evangelical moral and practical universe that was to have a profound impact on the metropolis for much of the nineteenth century. The overarching ethos was of a passionate moral paternalism rather than material paternalism.[18] Public relief and rigorous discipline of the poor were discouraged; instead 'that master spring of action, on which equally depends the prosperity of individuals and empires – THE DESIRE IMPLANTED IN THE HUMAN BREAST OF BETTERING ITS CONDITION' was raised as the guiding principle to action.[19] Moral regeneration of the poor through self-help, industry, frugality, purity and the suppression of vice was the ideal to be pursued.

All this was predicated on an unabashed empiricism. Information on the education, health and general condition of the poor, together with successful schemes of improvement, was sought from a large variety of sources and then repackaged and disseminated widely as the practical basis to action. Significantly, in the metropolitan context mendicity attracted the attention of the Society. On the instigation of Bernard, and with the support of the government under the sanction of Lords Pelham and Portland, Matthew Martin undertook in 1796 an inquiry into London beggars.[20] Two thousand cases were examined by Martin and his assistants. But the task proved overwhelming. Six years later he was forced to write an open letter to Pelham expressing regret for failing to produce the report:

> [T]he complicated nature and extent of the misery, which has been the subject of my research, and the consequent difficulties which ... I have encountered in my endeavours to reduce my observations to such a form, as to explain the matter with a suitable degree of perspicacity and force, may, I hope, plead my excuse.[21]

In spite of this perceived failure, the statistical data on the metropolitan poor were significant. Whereas Colquhoun had produced impressive tables to strengthen his arguments, much of his information was based on estimates, some of them wildly exaggerated. Martin's figures, however, were the first to be gathered using recognizably modern techniques of surveying, and it is retrospectively perhaps of little surprise that he was defeated by the sheer unknowability of the problem they uncovered.

Others in the movement were beginning to appreciate the importance of obtaining first-hand knowledge of the poor. In 1799 John Venn established a local branch of the Society for Bettering the Condition of the Poor in Clapham. The parish was divided into eight districts where the poor were regularly visited.[22] And in 1812, against a backdrop of unremitting and widespread destitution amongst silk weavers, the Association for the Relief of the Industrious Poor of Spitalfields and its Neighbourhood was established. The inspiration was the evangelical and former overseer Thomas Buxton, who later claimed in a speech made at the Egyptian Hall in

1816 that the association was necessary because 'private charity found itself perplexed, confused and baffled by the variety of applicants, and hardly knew which was right, the partiality which would elect some, to the exclusion of others – or that impartiality which would give but a crumb to each'.[23] Over a hundred volunteers helped to undertake a survey during which every street was visited regularly. The system was immediately recognized to have distinct advantages for 'the poor are seen at their own houses, the truth of their tale is ascertained; we are not so much exposed to deception'. In the eleven weeks preceding November 1816, 8,460 visits were made. Buxton paid generous tribute to Colquhoun for his role in bringing the plight of Spitalfields to the attention of the Privy Council: 'The unwearied exertions that this indefatigable magistrate persevered in … can only be sufficiently appreciated by those to whom they are fully known:- his name will long be revered by many in this parish, and when they cease to respect it, they will cease to exist'.[24]

Concern about poverty and crime intensified toward the end of the Napoleonic Wars when thousands of demobilized soldiers and sailors were reduced to begging on the streets of London. The select committees established to investigate mendicity and vagrancy (1815) and the state of policing in the metropolis (1816) reflected both renewed anxiety and the continued failure to grasp fully the complexities of the problems. The evidence taken before the Committee on Mendicity were republished commercially in the

> hope of drawing attention of the public to a subject, involving considerations of the highest importance to the community, from its connection with the morals and the welfare of the lowest classes in society. Mendicity, wherever it prevails, and in proportion to its extent, is a great evil, which calls for the most serious attention of the legislative and executive powers.[25]

Among the variety of magistrates, reformers, police and poor law officials who appeared there was little agreement on the extent of mendicity, its causes or potential solutions. Faced with this, the Committee confessed it could not 'refrain from a smile on perusing some of the evidence', in particular the conundrums of Conant and the metaphysical distinctions of Colquhoun', and declined to 'express any opinion as to the measures it may be fit for Parliament to adopt'.[26] The Police Committee was no more successful. The evidence submitted on crime and the enforcement of law was replete with contradiction, and the Committee for the most part seemed content to record caustic comments on it. No recommendations were forthcoming.

From the close of the eighteenth century, therefore, the metropolitan poor were viewed with heightened concern as a threat to commercial and imperial interests. At the moment when London emerged as a great centre of world trade, empire, law and government, built upon an extensive Atlantic system and with an avowed determination to exploit massively its links with the East, here was a constituency located at the very core which presented a barrier to progress. For the poor defied these modernizing impulses. They remained on the streets, effectively resistant to all attempts to cleanse and hence secure sites of bourgeois public space. And as a picaresque and international residuum drawn in increasing numbers to dock and riverside areas, they were a canker at the heart of commercial prosperity.

Late eighteenth-century travel in India

If a unitary field was created between metropolis and India it was not done so instantaneously. The emergence of significant bodies of knowledge in the late eighteenth century followed a period of relative inactivity when little new was learnt about the diversity of either metropolitan culture or that of native Indians. Even during the climate of enthusiasm for information, however, we must be cautious in identifying putative links. The investigative modalities instigated by the East India Company, for example, were no doubt driven by rational impulses of an Enlightenment epistemology, but their aims were distinctive. Three projects stood out.[27] William Jones sought to codify the Indian legal system, and in so doing 'discovered' India's ancient past; Thomas Munro laid the foundations for the administration of land settlements; and James Rennell mapped India. Although each relied on knowledges and methodologies that had been developed in the West, there was no obvious reference to metropolitan concerns. Thus Rennell's *Memoir of a Map of Hindustan* may have first appeared in the aftermath of the detailed mapping of London by cartographers such as John Rocque and John Entick, and may have expressed the same desire to gain authority over unknown space, but the outcome was very different. Neither topographical maps of London nor Ordnance surveys contributed to the project of mapping India.[28]

Attempts to locate India historically similarly drew upon implicit understandings and served to consolidate Company administration. Alexander Dow's *History of Hindostan* (1768) and Robert Orme's *A History of the Military Transactions of the British Nation in Indostan* (1763) inhabited teleological narratives celebrating the advantages of British rule, particularly over the tyranny of the Mughal empire. Neither contributed to contemporary knowledge of India. More significant was William Robertson's *An Historical Disquisition concerning the Knowledge which the Ancients had of India* (1791). This was a serious study, written by a noted historian[29] who, although he had never visited India, was familiar with the latest work:

Major Rennell's Memoir for illustrating his Map of Indostan ... suggested to me the idea of examining ... into the knowledge which the ancients had of India, and of considering what is certain, what is obscure, and what is fabulous, in the accounts of that country which they have handed down to us.... I have consulted with persevering industry, the works of all the authors I could procure, who have given an account of India.[30]

Robertson, like Jones upon whom he relied for much of his knowledge of Indian literature, admired much in ancient Indian culture. '[T]he wisdom of the East (an expression which is to be understood as a description of their extraordinary progress in science and arts)', he claimed, was early celebrated by the inspired 'ancient Heathen writers'.[31] In the modern age, however, European thought had surpassed the ancients. 'Proud in their superior attainments', but with 'proper sentiments concerning the people of India', Europeans now had a moral duty to bring Indians to the same level of civilization.[32]

Important though this body of work was in framing British responses to India in the late eighteenth century, it remained the province of elites in terms not only of the object of inquiry but also of the inquirers and audience. The culture described was that of the Brahmin intellectual and religious elite; no attempt was made to understand popular Hinduism or Indian culture more widely.[33] And although works such as Dow's sold well, most reached few readers beyond Company functionaries and interested middle-class observers of Indian affairs. The reading public turned to travel narratives.

We have already examined the contribution of travel writings to the early knowledge of India. The growing body of recent scholarly work on the genre suggests strongly that in the modern colonial era this contribution showed no signs of diminishing.[34] Travel and travel writing were deeply implicated in Western modernity. The earlier displacement of a Christian cosmography by secularized frames of reference was further developed in the post-Enlightenment era by a more sophisticated geographical and ethnological consciousness. Complex taxonomies of colonial spaces emerged that facilitated differentiation not only among, say, Europe, India, America and Africa, but also regions with distinct topographies and cultures.[35] Thus were promoted influential currents of thought around primitivism and orientalism that both problematized and provided mythical solutions to questions about the right path to civilization.[36] Unsurprisingly, the European emerged as triumphant.

In a comprehensive literary survey of British travel writings on India, Ketaki Dyson has pointed to similar currents. Accounts were erratic, diverse and inconsistent but in broad terms can be understood only in the context of intellectual concerns. Eighteenth-century attitudes toward India, therefore, were broadly shaped by Enlightenment thought.[37] As the century closed, this outlook was displaced increasingly by evangelicalism and a radical utilitarianism, in the course of which the sympathetic conservatism of orientalism yielded to a more aggressive project intent on dragging India into the civilized and modern world. This shift was accompanied by changes in the modes of literary expression as an eighteenth-century sensibility was gradually superseded by Romanticism.[38]

The renewed interest in travel accounts attendant upon Britain's colonization of India in the latter half of the eighteenth century displays a faltering struggle to comprehend its land and peoples. The artist William Hodges was an accomplished traveller by the time he reached India in 1780. He had previously painted scenes of Europe, and, as a draughtsman on Cook's second voyage, produced a series on New Zealand. Under the patronage of Warren Hastings, his journey to India aimed to record initial impressions in a series of drawings as a means of providing information on aspects neglected by orientalists:

> The intimate connexion which has so long subsisted between this country and the continent of India, naturally renders every Englishman deeply interested in all that relates to a quarter of the globe which has been the theatre of scenes highly important to his country.... It is only a matter of surprize, that, of a country so nearly allied to us, so little should be known. The public is, indeed, greatly indebted to the learned labours of gentlemen who have resided there, for the information which they have afforded concerning the Laws and the Religion of the Hindoo tribes; as well as for correct and well digested details of the transactions of the Mogul government. But of the face of the country, of its art, and natural productions, little has been said.[39]

Hodges's artistic imagination responds with unalloyed wonder and pleasure to the novel sights he encounters but reveals little beyond the immediate sense of the visual. Using classical referents to make sense of his first sight of India, he contemplates that the English settlement at Madras resembled a Grecian city at the time of Alexander:

> The clear, blue, cloudless sky, the polished white buildings, the bright sandy beach, and the dark green sea, present a combination totally new to the eye of an Englishman, just arrived from London, who, accustomed to the sight of rolling masses of clouds floating in a damp atmosphere, cannot but contemplate the difference with delight.[40]

In an act that became of singular importance to the appropriation of the remote in the late eighteenth century,[41] landscapes and people were also seen primarily in visual terms. Such sights as travelling family groups or Muslim women attending the tombs of relatives at night are described as picturesque, while the flat landscape by the expansive Ganges provides a sublime prospect of 'inexpressible grandeur'. Other landscapes are compared to England.

The hard-headed George Forster, a clerk in the employ of the East India Company, viewed such narratives with a degree of scepticism. 'Travellers stand accused', he stated, 'of adopting a figurative and loose style of description.'[42] His journey may include places 'removed from the eye of European observation', but he could reassure the public that the work 'has no tendency to discolour or misrepresent truth'. Relying on disguise and a fluency in the 'Mahometan language', Forster travelled widely. His observations on diverse aspects of Indian culture augmented a linguistic repertoire that was to become familiar. Hindus were of an 'inert disposition', facilitating the rise to power of inept rulers, often with ruinous consequences. And Kashmiris were dismissed as a body of men 'impregnated with the principles of vice'. It would be wrong, however, to view Forster as a crude racial caricaturist; his assessments were replete with ambiguity. Indian women, for example, no matter how uneducated and subordinated in a patriarchal society, possessed extraordinary vocal imagination and stamina:

> In the exercise of the tongue a female of Hindostan hath few equals; and if she hath ever followed a camp, I would pronounce her invincible on any ground in Europe. An English woman, educated at our most noted seminaries, and skilled in all the various compasses of debate, will, perhaps, ... maintain the contest for an hour, which then terminates in blows and victory. But an Indian dame, improved by a few campaigns, has been known to wage a colloquial war, without introducing one manual effort, for the space of three successive days; sleeping and eating at reasonable intervals. There is a fertility of imagination, a power of expression, inherent in the mind, and vocal ability, of an Asiatic, particularly a female one, which cannot be engendered in the cold head of an European.[43]

Forster was also interested in the Sikhs, whose nascent political presence and distinctiveness were registered in the British imagination for the first time. He begins by describing their warlike character. This 'new and extraordinary people' are a

> turbulent people, and possess a haughtiness of deportment which ... peculiarly marks their character.... From the spirit of independence so invariably infused amongst them, their mutual jealousy, and a rapacious roving temper, the Sicques at this day are seldom seen cooperating in national concert.[44]

But then in a remarkable passage he proceeds to predict the rise of Sikh power under Ranjit Singh:

> Should any future cause call forth the combined efforts of the Sicques to maintain the existence of empire and religion, we may see some ambitious chief led on by his genius and success, and, absorbing the power of his associates, display, from the ruins of their commonwealth, the standard of

monarchy.... Under such a form of government, I have little hesitation in saying that the Sicques would be soon advanced to the first rank amongst the native princes of Hindostan; and would become a terror to the surrounding states.[45]

From the earliest years of the revival in travel writings on India women authors were prominent. As wives of Company functionaries and army officers many women played subsidiary roles in the business of empire. Endless days of boredom could be relieved by recording observations on their lives in India, published details of which found a ready audience in Britain. As such these travel writings can be situated within a longer tradition of autobiographical self-expression, particularly in the form of diaries. The more vexed question is whether or not there was a distinctly female mode of observation. Dyson claims that women were directed to distinct objects of inquiry. Because they had little access to the male preserves of administration, orientalist research and sport, women's journals were rich sources of information on Indian domestic life, rituals, fashion and food.[46] The contrasts, however, can be overstated. Many of the women were intrepid travellers who proved themselves capable of reaching the remotest regions of Indian topography and culture. In the case of the zenana – a subject of particular fascination to the British reading public – they had privileged access. And they were intensely curious about mythology, folklore and custom. Importantly, even if we can detect a gendered object of inquiry, it is difficult to support the argument that it was seen differently by women. 'There is no specifically female gaze', concludes Indira Ghose in her comprehensive survey of female travel writings on India, 'for the simple reason that gender is only one of a multiplicity of factors that determine identity.'[47]

Jemima Kindersley was married to an officer in the Bengal Artillery. She arrived in India in 1765 and stayed with him for four years. Her reaction to the first sighting of Indians reveals an outlook inflected more by race and class than gender:

> the first specimen I had of India rather surprised than pleased me; I could not be reconciled to the vast numbers of black people who flocked to the shore on my first arrival; although I must acknowledge, that they were so far from being terrible in their appearance, that at first sight I believed them all to be women, from the effeminacy both of their persons and dress, the long white jemmers and turbands appear so truly feminine to strangers. But the almost stark-nakedness of the lowest class is still more disgusting.[48]

Blackness and nakedness were familiar signifiers of otherness, but it would be incautious to interpret them as evidence of a blatant racial discourse. Elsewhere Mrs Kindersley resisted the thesis that black people were 'by nature inferior to white'.[49] Instead, inhabiting an Enlightenment sensibility heavily influenced by Montesquieu, she attributes Indians' indolence, stupidity and lack of development to climate, superstition and despotism:

> [I]n the cold season they have a fire made with a little straw in the middle of their huts, which smothers them with smoak; their minds, except what nature gave them, no more informed than the beasts which perish: no liberty, no property, subject to the tyranny of every superior. But what seems to complete their misery is, that whether pinched by cold, or enervated by heat, indolence equally prevails, to such a degree as seems to absorb every faculty; even immediate self-preservation scarcely rouses them from it.[50]

The strength and energy of some Indian labourers suggested that indolence was not a physical problem: 'although the climate is certainly extremely relaxing, it seems to impair their minds more than their bodies; to which indolence of spirit, a despotical government and its consequences has perhaps not a little contributed'.[51]

Early in the nineteenth century Captain Thomas Williamson, a resident of more than twenty years in Bengal, felt confident enough to write a compendium of useful information 'to promote the welfare, and to facilitate the progress of those young gentlemen who may ... be appointed to situations' in the East Indian Company.[52] He drew upon the state of contemporary knowledge. Among works cited are Brooke's *Gazetteer*, Dow's *History of Hindostan*, Fuller's *Apology for late Christian Missions to India*, Tennant's *Indian Recreations*, Lauderdale's *Government of India*, Orme's *History of the Military Transactions*, Robertson's *Disquisitions on Ancient India* and Wellesley's *History of the Mahratta War*. Books recommended for the traveller, on the other hand, are mostly on language and law, and include studies by notable orientalists such as Wilkins, Colebrooke and Jones. *The East India Vade-Mecum* was, however, more than simply a guide – it simultaneously aimed to promote a 'just conception of the characters of the natives', so removing those 'doubts, prejudices, and national opinions, which, if suffered to prevail, must occasion every object to be seen through a false medium'. In over a thousand pages of unbroken prose, Williamson provides instruction on a bewildering variety of topics from travel to India, coins and weights, classifications of servants, vaccination, heat, salt manufacture and slavery to dress, ornaments, snakes and styles of buildings.

The lengthiest section is devoted to servants. In a style redolent of eighteenth-century vade-mecums on the metropolis, Williamson details the histories, responsibilities and propensities of Indians whom the European is likely to encounter. Moonshies (linguists), for example, are 'generally influenced by motives wide from purity.... With very few exceptions, we find them extremely debauched, and unhealthy. With what venary, drinking, smoking, &c. nine out of ten of them exhale the most intolerable effluvia!'[53] The Sircar (book keeper) is a

> Genius whose whole study is to handle money ... and who contrives either to confuse acounts ... or to render them most expressively intelligible when such should suit his purpose. These rogues are pretty near the same as the Madras *debashes*: no compleater knaves are to be found in any part of the world.[54]

This seemingly exaggerated interest in servants was symptomatic of the general sense of unease felt by members of the eighteenth-century bourgeoisie. Servants transgressed the boundaries between the public and private space. They had access to possessions and, more importantly, information, as a result of which they were considered a threat, or at best treated with suspicion. In the colonial context, as Kate Teltscher has reminded us, this threat was intensified.[55] Servants outnumbered their masters, and as part of a wider network were able to subvert political, financial and cultural relationships. Deference and subservience could always be read as acts to disguise defiance. And yet Williamson refuses to accuse the 'natives of India' of being

> so debased, so immoral, or so vindictive, as they have been represented by many gentlemen, especially some divines who have lately returned from the East, and whose opinions breathe by no means the spirit of that sublime religion they would coerce the natives to adopt.... I think we have by far more to admire than to censure, in a race of people, who, notwithstanding some highly remarkable instances of depravity, may be classed among the most innocent, and most industrious, of worldly inhabitants!!!!![56]

The reference here to a harsher discourse on colonial subjects is significant, for by the turn of the century it was apparent that missionaries, particularly evangelicals, were beginning to intervene in the production of knowledge about India. Over time this intervention was to be of critical importance to the ways in which British people saw Indian people and culture.

Early evangelical activity

Missionary activity in India was transformed in the course of the eighteenth century. For the first seventy years French and Portuguese Jesuits continued to dominate the scene, and it was largely through their published accounts that the European imagination of India was formed. *Lettres Edifiantes et Curieuses*, for example, appeared in thirty-four volumes during 1702–76, effectively eclipsing secular narratives while displaying few of their uncertainties in representing Indian culture.[57] A

Danish Lutheran mission was established at Tranquebar in 1706. It was later adopted and partly financed by the Society for Promoting Christian Knowledge (SPCK), but remained small. British Protestant missionary activity in India can realistically be dated to the last decade of the eighteenth century. In 1792 the Particular-Baptist Society for Propagating the Gospel Among the Heathen (happily soon to be changed to the Baptist Missionary Society, BMS) was established, and within a year despatched William Carey to set up the first of its missions at Serampur. Three years later the interdenominational London Mission Society (LMS) was formed, followed in 1799 by the Church Missionary Society (CMS), largely under the inspiration of Anglicans who had broken adrift from the LMS.

Much scholarly work has been devoted to an explanation of this sudden rise in British missionary endeavour.[58] One broad camp links it to the simultaneous expansion of the British imperial state. According to this perspective, missionaries were agents in the spread of colonial power, not least as bearers of its underpinning values. The second views it as the product of profound theological changes in the eighteenth century. British evangelicalism first emerged in a domestic context; the development of its mission work overseas was integral to the project of spreading the word of Christ around the world, and operated independently of the pursuit of imperial ambitions. I cannot here adjudicate between these positions – to propose, as Susan Thorne has,[59] a synthesis, or to raise, as Andrew Porter has, the divergence between religious and imperial needs[60] – but it is necessary to examine some of the complex specificities of evangelicalism in India.

The spatial and temporal dimensions of missionary endeavour in the subcontinent were critical. The opening up of India after Plassey provided opportunities for missionaries as well as imperial entrepreneurs. The first mission was located at Serampur within easy reach of Calcutta. Only later did missionaries venture out into territories beyond the reach of the British Raj. And in certain important respects the moment was tied to imperial expansion. The transformation in missionary activity signalled first in the Caribbean and then in India has to be linked to the transition from the first to the second British empires at the end of the eighteenth century.[61] During this period the emphasis of colonial policy turned from securing British settlement to the governance of indigenous populations. When John Wesley and George Whitfield established evangelical missions in America it was to help remove the threat posed by the native Indian population. In India, missions were much more determinedly committed to the large-scale conversion of the indigenous population, and even if this civilizing mission was not always thought in terms of the maintenance of political and cultural authority, in practice that was how it tended to operate.

This transformation was impelled also by conceptions of progress that emerged toward the close of the eighteenth century. Two aspects in particular were significant. Missionary activity abroad in part represented a new vision of work among the dispossessed. Eighteenth-century philanthropy and the poor law had emphasized secular, material provision as a means of ameliorating distress and meeting the demands for productive labour. As critiques of poor relief and philanthropy mounted,[62] and as the demographic crisis eased, so attention turned to spiritual improvement. Evangelicals, preoccupied as they were by conversion and atonement, were eminently qualified to take up the cause. This shift from humanitarian to missionary philanthropy affected attitudes to the poor, but simultaneously directed attention to peoples colonized by the (re)orientation of Britain's imperial endeavours. Thus, although missionary activity was rarely blind to the material deprivations suffered by Indians, its emphasis was almost exclusively on the saving of their souls as a precondition of bringing them into the civilized world. And this promoted harsher and more rigid categorizations of the colonized.[63]

The first wave of missionary activity in India came at a time when expressions of the need for evangelization of its peoples were being voiced with increased concern. Under the rubric 'Go ye into all the world, and preach the gospel to every creature' (Mark XVI 15), Joseph White, Professor of Arabic at Oxford, preached before the university in 1784 on the duty of promoting the universal and progressive message of Christianity 'among our Mahometan and Gentoo Subjects in India'.[64] The decisive intervention, however, was made by Charles Grant. Grant travelled to India in 1768 as a private agent to Richard Beecher, a prominent servant of the East India Company.[65] Over time Grant established himself variously as a founder member of the Clapham Sect, a Director of the East India Company, a Member of Parliament, and until his death in 1823 the dominant voice on Indian affairs. His first years, however, were hardly auspicious. Like so many of his contemporaries, he gambled heavily and lived beyond his means, running up a debt of £20,000. These losses were compounded by the death from smallpox of his two children, convincing Grant that he had been singled out by God. He underwent a conversion of sorts, after which he lived a virtuous and hard-working life in pursuit of what he considered the best interests of the Company and the Indian people.[66]

Grant transformed attitudes to Company rule. In contrast to criticism of the Company launched by Adam Smith in the aftermath of the devastating Bengal famine of 1770, Grant had argued that the directors did all in their power to prevent suffering. By the time of Warren Hastings, Grant's opinion of Company rule had hardened. He blamed Hastings for a war of aggression against the Marathas which was not only unnecessary but threatened the security and prosperity of Bengal. During the subsequent impeachment proceedings he resisted a public demonstration of support for either side, and while continuing to defend the Company from undue state interference, recognized the merits of the 1784 India Act, seeing it as the culmination of reforms already set in motion by Company servants.[67] Increasingly, however, Grant was persuaded that moral reform in India was a precondition of political reform. In a letter to Thomas Raikes soon after the 1784 Act entered onto the statute book, he argued that although

> inquiries into the evils that afflict the people and the means of addressing them are now deservedly become a business of Government, yet I shall fear that all remedies will prove ineffectual which have no respect to the moral and intellectual state of the inhabitants.... I am not, as you may believe, for following the Mahomedan example of establishing opinions by the sword; but I certainly am for helping those poor people whose land we enjoy, who are now in effect subjects of Britain, to recover the almost lost life of nature, and to become acquainted with the truth and excellence of Revelation, with the improvements and the rights of man.[68]

By now Grant was beginning to think seriously about effective missionary work in India. A plan for an Indian mission had been communicated to him by Thomas Coke in 1783, and four years later Grant expressed his first thoughts in a paper entitled 'A Proposal for Establishing a Protestant Mission in Bengal and Behar', fourteen copies of which were distributed to influential contacts.[69] In the event it aroused only limited support in Anglican circles. We can detect in the Proposal, however, the elements of Grant's thoughts on the relationship between imperial administration and missionary endeavour that were to exercise such a significant influence on the establishment of the CMS and the agenda of subsequent debates. He begins by pointing out the neglect of such vital matters. 'Among all advantages accruing to Great Britain from the acquisition of Asiatic Territories', he argued, 'the power of introducing the Light of Truth among them, of making known to them the way of Everlasting Life, and the true source of source of temporal happiness, has hardly been mentioned.' It is evident, however, that in spite of Grant's interest in the spiritual welfare of Indians, the exigencies of rule were never far from his thoughts:

> [T]he People of these Provinces in their present state are far from being easily governed, if that term means any thing more than keeping them from Insurrection and Revolt.... [They] are universally and wholly corrupt, they are as depraved as they are blind, and as wretched as they are depraved, and to govern them and render them obedient and orderly upon right principles, is no easy Work. There has been much inquiry concerning the best system of managing the Country. It seems to us clear that no system which has not the Reformation of the morals of the People for its basis can be effective; for they

are lamentably destitute of those Principles of Honesty, Truth, and Justice which are necessary for the Well-being of Society. And to reconcile them to Foreign dominion like Ours, it seems equally clear that We and they ought to have some *strong common Principles*; at present they are united to us neither in Interest nor in Sentiment.[70]

The Proposal galvanized the support of Charles Simeon and William Wilberforce. Politicians and established churchmen, on the other hand, were less than enthusiastic. Pitt and Cornwallis, while not opposing missionary schemes, had no faith that they could be effective.[71] Without this support Grant's plan for government patronage of missionary work in India failed. Determined to learn from this lesson, he took the first propitious opportunity to elaborate on his thesis, this time for a political audience. Thus the initial draft of *Observations on the State of Society among the Asiatic Subjects of Great Britain* was addressed to Henry Dundas. It appeared during negotiations for the renewal of the Company's charter in 1792, and was intended to provide the basis for government policy. The negotiations for the renewal of the Company's charter provided a propitious moment. Over time and in its various manifestations the work was to become arguably the single most influential tract on missionary work in India.[72]

Observations is a hymn to the spiritual and rational progress of India, written at a time when its edifice seemed under threat from revolutionary currents. Indeed, so sensitive was Grant to these currents that he felt impelled from the outset to distance the novelty of his proposals:

> At a time when the wildest fanaticism in politics and philosophy is pursuing, with impious and inhuman success, the indiscriminate subversions of received principles and existing establishments, labours under peculiar disadvantages. Truth however, and reason, always the same, are not to be abandoned because they may sometimes be perverted and abused.[73]

His aim is 'to promote the peace and happiness of men, by pacific and rational means'. What precisely did this mean in the context of India? To answer this Grant reviews the recent history of British intervention. Although the Company has had success 'which the commercial history of the world affords no parallel', and demonstrated a 'laudable zeal for extending ... the knowledge of the Gospel to the Pagan tribes', it has neglected the welfare of 'our Asiatic subjects'.[74] In the early years of its activities, private European traders and native agents had abused their trust and power in the 'collection of revenues' and in the 'conduct of the courts of justice'. But as a result of reforms introduced in 1769, Company servants had been brought under restraint, and are now 'worthy of more confidence than transient adventurers, ignorant and barbarous, from the Upper Asia'.[75]

Having corrected abuses, and provided Hindu subjects with 'secure enjoyment of property', Grant inquired, 'does nothing further remain to be done?' He proceeds to identify in strikingly unambiguous arguments his vision for missionary work. Since the implementation of reform the Company has grown confident in its ability to maintain financial and political advantages. In areas, particularly Bengal, it is strong, and so long as Britain can retain superiority at sea, a challenge from European or Indian 'enemies' is unlikely. On the other hand,

> Hindostan is the region of revolutions. A few more successful turns in Benares on the part of so inferior a chief as Cheyte Sing, would have put all Bengal in commotion. We ought also to remember how much the authority of a handful of strangers depends on *opinion*. To reduce the sources of prejudice against us, and to multiply impressions favourable to us, by assimilating our subjects to our mode of thinking, and by making them happy, and teaching them to understand and value the principles of the people who confer happiness upon them, may be some of the surest means of preserving the footing we have acquired.[76]

If such a project is to succeed, Grant continues, the 'state of society and manners among the people of Hindostan ... becomes in the first place a special object of attention'. He launches into an extended critique of previous studies, particularly those of travel writers and orientalists whom he sees as remote from the grim realities of Indian life:[77]

> It has suited the views of some philosophers to represent that people as amicable and respectable; and a few late travellers have chosen rather to place some softer traits of their characters in an engaging light, than to give a just delineation of the whole.

For foreign residents and even the Indians themselves (presumably the only ones who can have real knowledge) the picture is very different:

> Of the Bengalee then, it is true most generally that they are destitute, to a wonderful degree, of those qualities which are requisite to the security and comfort of society. They want truth, honesty, and good faith, in an extreme, of which European society furnishes no example.... Want of veracity especially, is so habitual, that if a man has truth to defend, he will hardly fail to recur to falsehood for its support. In matters of interest, the use of lying seems so natural, that it gives no provocation, it is treated as an excusable indulgence, ... and the practice of cheating, pilfering, tricking and imposing, in the ordinary transactions of life are so common, that the Hindoos seem to regard them as they do natural evils, against which they will defend themselves as well as they can, but at which it will be idle to be angry.[78]

There follows a litany of traits. Cruelty, lack of benevolence and affection, gross laxity of behaviour and principle, indecency, licentiousness, malevolence and animosity are seen by Grant as characteristic of the Bengali people, although he is careful to add that his wish was not to 'excite detestation, but to engage compassion, and make it apparent, that what speculation may have ascribed to physical and unchangeable causes, springs from moral sources capable of correction'.[79] Grant's engagement with Enlightenment humanism, however, was rather more complex than this rider suggests. Nowhere is this more apparent than in his discussion of progress. He concurs with the argument in Robertson's *Historical Disquisition* that the 'original inhabitants of Hindostan' never existed in a 'savage state', but he remained sceptical of the optimistic excesses of the stages theory of development. True, a people can reach the 'highest stages of refinement' through a long process of internal improvement, and in countries like India the 'ideas of men seem to ripen ... with a quickness analogous to the rapidity of their vegetation'.[80] But progress has been mitigated by the debilitating influence of climate, despotic government, law, caste and mythology on the 'Hindoo character'. Under these circumstances the only cure of the darkness engulfing Indian society is 'the communication of our light and knowledge'. Of these, knowledge, as exemplified by English, printing, natural philosophy, agriculture and mechanics, is important, but 'undoubtedly the most important communication which the Hindoos could receive ... would be knowledge of our religion':[81]

> It is not asserted, that such effects would be immediate, or universal; but admitting them to be progressive, and partial only, yet how great would the change be, and how happy at length for the outward prosperity and internal peace or society among the Hindoos! Men would be restored to the use of their reason; all the advantages of happy soil, climate, and situation, would be observed and improved; the comforts and conveniences of life would be increased; the cultivation of the mind, and rational intercourse, valued; the people would rise in the scale of human beings.[82]

In addition, and in conclusion, Grant declares:

> [I]n communicating light, knowledge, and improvement, we shall obey the dictates of duty, of philanthropy, and of policy, we shall take the most rational means to remove inherent, great disorders, to attach the Hindoo people to ourselves, to ensure the safety of our possessions, to enhance continually their value to us, to raise a fair and desirable monument to the glory of this Country, and to encrease the happiness of the human race.[83]

Observations, like the Proposal, initially had a mixed reception. The taint of revolutionary fear from which Grant had attempted to distance himself proved too deep-seated. The king and Cornwallis thought that the scheme would interfere unduly with the established order in India.[84] Wilberforce, on the other hand, while nervous at the prospect of aggressive missionary activity of the sort set out in the Proposal, was reassured by the emphasis in *Observations* on education. His support heralded a commitment by the Clapham Sect to Indian reform that over time was to rival – even outstrip – its interests in abolition and poverty.[85] The Sect came to have only qualified success in realizing an ambition to have the Company sanction, indeed sponsor missionary activity, but it did establish the grounds upon which the case for British rule over the Indian people could be justified and maintained.

The conversion of heathens

There were, however, other influential currents of evangelical thought that in the short term were more decisive in promoting missionary activity. In the same year as Grant's *Observations* was written, the Baptist shoemaker William Carey published *An Enquiry into the Obligations of Christians to use Means for the Conversion of Heathens*. Modest in scope, it sought to demonstrate that in spite of the various attempts made since apostolic times to spread the gospel, a 'very considerable part of mankind are still involved in all the darkness of heathenism'.[86] These attempts continue, but they remain 'inconsiderable in comparison with what might be done if the whole body of Christians entered heartily into the spirit'. Carey counters the charge that missionary endeavour will meet with implacable resistance from the heathen by pointing to the example of traders, who in the pursuit of gain have shown it possible to 'insinuate themselves into the favour of the most barbarous clans, and uncultivated tribes'. And to those who object on the grounds that there are 'multitudes in our own nation ... who are as ignorant as the South-Sea savages', he declares that unlike those in foreign lands who have 'no Bible, no written language, no ministers, no good Civil government, nor any of those advantages which we have', we have the 'means of knowing the truth'.[87] Carey's vision, however, is an inclusive one. Quoting from Paul that there is 'no difference between the Jew and the Greek: for the same Lord over all, is rich unto all that call on him', he argues that of those that live in darkness, the majority are:

> poor, barbarous, naked pagans, as destitute of civilization, as they are of true religion.... Barbarous as these poor heathens are, they appear to be capable of knowledge as we are, and in many places, at least, have discovered uncommon genius and tractableness.[88]

Missionary work, in contrast, is exclusive, for Carey concludes by proposing the formation of a missionary society amongst the particular Baptist denominations. This was not out of any desire to restrict such activity to one denomination, but 'in the present divided state of Christendom, it would be more likely for good to be done by each denomination engaging separately in the work.... There is room enough for us all, without interfering with each other.'[89] Within a year the BMS was established; within a decade its mission at Serampur was busy in the work of preaching and translating the Bible into Indian languages.[90]

Too little attention has been paid to these contrasts in missionary visions, and yet they are crucial to an understanding of how different denominations understood and approached subjects thought in need of salvation. Part of the problem derives from the notorious imprecision of the term evangelicalism in defining the broad range of socio-religious thought brought to bear on the perceived problems of the poor and non-Christian peoples. Used conventionally to embrace the broad spectrum of belief from evangelical Arminianism to high Calvinism,[91] it masked important differences in attitudes toward predestination, millenarianism and rationalism leading to striking contrasts in approaches to material and spiritual pathologies.

The view that poverty and heathenism were the inevitable consequences of a spiritual want that could be cured only by evangelization shaped the thoughts and activities of succeeding generations of evangelicals working abroad and in the metropolis.[92] Although the position of individuals in the continuum between pre- and post-millenarianism determined the emphases given to the role of spiritual versus material imperatives, it was generally the former that prevailed. Thus no matter how intense was sympathy for the plight of poor families, and how much individuals contributed to private charities, the solution to destitution was sought through redemption by aggressive evangelical activity.

The real significance of evangelicals derived from their ability to integrate theology with policy at a time of perceived crisis in the fabric of the empire brought about by the recognition of the presence at its heart of an endemic poor and of colonized peoples untouched by civilizing influences. For in spite of differences in emphasis, they shared a belief in the fundamentals of evangelicalism as a theology, namely, original sin, atonement though Christ's crucifixion, regeneration through faith, and attainment of holiness, around which were constructed powerful narratives that determined policies toward the colonial and metropolitan poor, and shaped the spiritual autobiographies of missionaries, and the lengthy commentaries on the state of moral and physical depravity they encountered.

These narratives had historical antecedents in the spiritual autobiographies of sixteenth- and seventeenth-century preachers.[93] The human condition was a pilgrimage, the narrator an allegorical pilgrim who, following conversion, abandoned all to undertake an arduous spiritual journey through the world beset by the dangers of temptation and persecution in search of a promised land. There was no closure, however; the land proved beyond reach, condemning the pilgrim to ceaseless struggle. *An authentic narrative of some remarkable and interesting particulars in the life of ********, written by John Newton in 1764, is representative of this genre.*[94] Newton was a captain of a slave ship who, during a severe storm, experienced a powerful conversion, subsequently abandoning his life of 'wickedness' to become one of the foremost evangelical preachers of the eighteenth century. In the *Authentic narrative* evangelical selfhood derived largely from this Pauline conversion. Newton's career at sea became a Christian experience, in which Bunyanesque images of storms, routes of navigation, shipwrecks and the dangers from enemy ships were used to convey a sense of the ways in which the immanent meaning in past misdeeds is revealed teleologically by ultimate meaning after conversion. Thus a theology was constructed around the familiar predestinarian narrative of salvation: calling, justification through faith, sanctification in good work, and final glorification.[95]

Certain homologies existed between the narratives of spiritual autobiography and travel writing. The emergence of a concern among eighteenth-century travellers with historical veracity achieved through uncorrupted use of scientific observation promoted among evangelicals those private virtues of honesty and integrity that underpinned diligent observation and recording of 'truth'. But while for the traveller personal validation is sought through the 'attainment of the reader's conviction', atonement in spiritual autobiography is achieved introspectively by the revelation of divine grace.[96]

Tensions in evangelical theology and policy reached some sort of resolution in 1813 with the introduction of the pious clause into the Company's charter. The complex chain of events leading up to this have been described elsewhere.[97] Suffice it to say here that the shifting balance of forces among the Company, the British state, evangelical denominations and the Indian peoples have to be seen in the context of what often appeared as competing demands to secure imperial rule and to provide salvation to colonial subjects at a time of revolutionary and post-revolutionary struggle in France. But precisely how did evangelicals respond to events, in particular through changing perceptions of their relationships to India?

In the early days of British missionary activity Claudius Buchanan was appointed the Company chaplain to Bengal, and from this position he wrote influentially on the state of Christianity in India. He soon acquainted himself with the Serampur mission, and defended it against charges of Jacobinism levelled by many of his fellow Anglicans. Indeed, he helped with the work, and used his position to raise funds for translating the Bible into Indian languages. He was also instrumental in securing Carey's appointment as a lecturer in Bengali and Sanscrit at the newly established Fort William College. By the time Buchanan began to write on India, however, relationships with the Baptist missionaries had become soured following his attempt to take control of their translation work. Mindful of the suggestion of Dr Porteus, the Bishop of London, that the Anglican church should control the activities of missionary work in India, and Wellesley's determination to eradicate the influence of French republicanism,[98] Buchanan's *Memoir on the Expediency of an Ecclesiastical Establishment for British India* (1805) unsurprisingly owed rather more to Grant than Carey, even though many of the fears of 1793 had receded. 'Our extensive territorial triumph over our only formidable foe', he opened, 'seems to mark the present era, as that intended by Providence, for our taking into consideration the moral and religious state of our subjects in the East.'[99] His concern with the future of empire, however, stemmed less from the putative dangers attendant on attempts to convert Indians, than from the moral laxity of the British in India:[100]

> The French revolution has imposed on us the duty of using new means for extending and establishing Christian principles. Our territorial possessions in the East have been nearly doubled in extent, and thence arises the duty of cherishing the religion and morals of the increased number of our countrymen who occupy these possessions; as well as promoting the civilization of our native subjects by every rational means.[101]

That the *Memoir* was written essentially to promote Anglican supremacy in India suggests that this responsibility was to be assumed by the established church in formal alliance with the Company. There followed a rather contradictory assessment of the prospects of reaching Indian subjects. On the one hand, Buchanan argues:

> The natives of Hindostan are a Divided people. They have no common interest. To disseminate new principles among them is not difficult. They are less tenacious of opinion than of custom.... Our religion is therefore inculcated ... because its civilizing influence is certain and undeniable. We have *seen* that it has dispensed knowledge and happiness to every people, who have embraced it.... [I]t attaches the governed to their governors; and facilitates our intercourse with the natives.[102]

But this is mitigated with pessimism born out of an embryonic sense of racial separateness:

> You will sometimes hear it said that the Hindoos are a mild and passive people. They have apathy rather than mildness, their hebetude of mind is perhaps their chief negative virtue. They are a race of men of weak bodily frame, and have a mind conformed to it, timid and abject in the extreme.... The European who has long been resident in India looks on the civilization of the Hindoos with a hopeless eye. Despairing, therefore, of intellectual or

moral improvement, he is content with an obsequious spirit and manual service.[103]

Buchanan concludes with a familiar list of the 'sanguinary rites' prac-tised by Hindus including sati, swinging with hooks, drowning in the Ganges and sacrifice of children. Not content, in 'The Star in the East', a sermon preached at Bristol in 1809 for the benefit of the Society for Mis-sions to Africa and the East, he attempts to undermine the positive fea-tures of the intellectual heritage of ancient India by rewriting the histories of Christianity and Hinduism.[104] Drawing upon Wilford's *The History of the Introduction of the Christian Religion into India*, he proposes that Christianity appeared first in the East, thereby providing the inspiration for all religions. The presence in Vedic writings of doctrines including the trinity, incarnation, atonement and divine revelation proves this to be so. Our task in India, therefore, is to fulfil Christianity's destiny, not through the false creed of a Romish church sunk in the same darkness as Hindu-ism, but by the united efforts of Protestant evangelicals.

This task was hampered, however, by critical tensions at the heart of the evangelical vision that could not readily be resolved. First, uncertainty existed as to the precise means of realizing the Christian mission. Evangelicals embraced a teleological conception of progress. Buchanan, for example, posited a stages theory according to which the world develops historically through three eras – primitive Christianity, when Christ spread the gospel, the reformation, and finally the era of light, when the triumph of Christianity would inevitably result.[105] This theory of progress, however, was tempered by a recognition of the need for active evangelical intervention, particularly among those who seemed to defy its logic. Sec-ond, the relationship between evangelical and imperial missions was a troubled one. As we have seen, there were elements within Anglican evan-gelicalism that openly stressed the benefits of Christianity to imperial rule. But Grant and Buchanan were hostile to much of Company policy; in turn, influential directors such as Major John Scott Waring and Thomas Twining, who claimed to represent the majority, viewed missionary activ-ity as an undue interference in Indian culture, threatening the stability of the Indian empire.[106] If anything, the relationships between frontline dis-sent – with a professed commitment to the reform and education of Indi-ans – and the Company were even more strained. To mask these tensions, evangelical discourse hardened around a complex litany of Hindu cultural pathologies, descriptions of which were used to legitimate continued inter-vention. On the less than convincing precept that the 'untravelled writer … enters into the discussion free from all the trammels of party and preju-dice',[107] J.W. Cunningham chose to survey previous writings on Christian-ity in India. He selected quotations out of context from Jones, Orme,

Verelst, Holwell and most especially Buchanan to demonstrate a putative consensus on the degenerate, enervated and treacherous nature of Hindus, on the basis of which he opines that 'although the physical and political powers of the Hindus would be increased by the introduction of Christianity, no increase of their power to inquire would necessarily take place'.[108]

In the course of the protracted and heated debates leading up to the renewal of the Company's charter in 1813, the most effective voices were those advocating strengthened missionary activity. Grant, Buchanan and Wilberforce wrote widely and lobbied tirelessly; missionary societies and their supporters organized a massive campaign of petitioning.[109] The Charter Act passed through parliament by 89 votes to 36. It declared:

> [W]hereas it is the Duty of the Country to promote the interests and happiness of the native inhabitants of the British dominions in India, ... such measures ought to be adopted as may tend to the introduction among them of useful knowledge, and of religious and moral improvement, and in furtherance of the above objects, sufficient facilities ought to be afforded by law to persons desirous of going to and remaining in India, for the purpose of accomplishing those benevolent designs so long as the authority of the local governments respecting the intercourse of Europeans with the interior of the country be preserved, and the principles of the British government on which the natives of India have hitherto relied for the free exercise of their religion be inviolably maintained.[110]

Hailed by evangelicals as a victory, the Act was in fact a skilful compromise. It established the authority of the Anglican church in India, but allowed missionaries to enter, albeit under continued close scrutiny. More significantly, the arguments used to define Christian obligations in India which were enshrined in the Act, and the nature of the peoples to whom these obligations applied, became unquestioned assumptions in British opinion.[111] William Ward, a missionary at Serampur, undertook a comprehensive survey of Hindu society. Published in eight editions over 1811–22, his *A View of the History, Literature and Mythology of the Hindoos* came to represent the tenor of this new consensus. 'It must have been to accomplish some very important moral change in the Eastern world', he opens, 'that so vast an empire as is comprized in British India' should have been placed under the 'dominion of one of the smallest kingdoms of the civilized world'. He proceeds:

> This opinion, which is entertained unquestionably by every enlightened philanthropist, is greatly strengthened when we consider the long-degraded state of India, and of the immense and immensely populous regions around it; the moral enterprise of the age in which these countries have been given to us, and that Great Britain is the only country upon earth, from which the intel-

lectual and moral improvement of India could have been expected.... To form a just conception of the state of darkness in which so many minds are involved as are comprized in the heathen population of India, a person has need to become an inhabitant of the country, that he may read and see the productions of these minds, and witness the effects of the institutions they have formed, as displayed in the manners, customs, and circumstances of the inhabitants.[112]

In the four volumes that followed, Ward detailed at inordinate length this 'state of darkness'. From the writings of Grant, researches of the orientalists and what 'the author has been able to collect and condense relative to the civil state of the Hindoos, the reader will be able to perceive something very superior to mere Savage life, or to brutal uncontrolled tyranny'.[113] In the end, however, it is his exhaustive catalogue of pagan superstitions, idolatries and acts of extreme cruelty that prevailed to provide a vital source of information on Hindu worship.

Lata Mani has detected in the various editions a shift from a preoccupation with miscellany to a more rigorous and authoritative handling of information approximating to an ethnography. In the early editions Ward seemed to collect and randomly present curiosities of Hindu society, leaving the reader to synthesize the material and draw out its social and moral significance. The final edition, by contrast, contains claims that are 'confident, authoritative and totalizing'.[114] This she sees as evidence of the consolidation of evangelical discourse in the years following 1813. There is something in these arguments. Over time Ward did rework the material. Any shift, however, has to be seen in the context of a hardening of evangelical discourse, and, more importantly, the emergence of a new mode of observation attendant on the continued sense of epistemological insecurity. For the shift evident in Ward was symptomatic of a more general crisis in the production of knowledge about India, in response to which travel and evangelical writings moved toward more totalizing perspectives.

Notes

1   For a more detailed account of Colquhoun's life and contribution, see my article 'Policing the poor: social inquiry and the discovery of the residuum', *Rising East*, 3:1, 1999, pp. 23–47.

2   [Patrick Colquhoun], *A Treatise on the Police of the Metropolis, Explaining the Various Crimes ... which ... are felt as a Pressure upon the Community, and Suggesting Remedies for their Prevention. By a Magistrate*, London, Dilly, 1795; *A Treatise on the Commerce and Police of the River Thames: Containing an Historical Overview of the Trade of the Port of London; and Suggesting Means for Preventing the Depradations thereon, by a Legislative System of River Police, etc.*, London, Mawman, 1800; *A Treatise on Indigence; Exhibiting a General View of the National Resources for Productive Labour; with Propositions for Ameliorating the Condition of the Poor, etc.*, London, Mawman, 1806. The last greatly expanded on arguments that originally appeared in a tract, significantly entitled *The State of Indigence, and the Situation of the Casual*

Poor in the Metropolis, Explained ... with Suggestions Shewing the Necessity ... of an Establishment of Pauper Police, Immediately Applicable to the Casual Poor, etc., London, Baldwin, 1799. These texts were all revised in several subsequent editions.

3 [Colquhoun], *A Treatise on the Police*, p. 44.

4 Colquhoun, *A Treatise on the Commerce and Police of the River Thames*, p. 44.

5 Colquhoun, *A Treatise on Indigence*, pp. 7–8.

6 *Ibid.*, p. 5.

7 *Ibid.*, p. 36.

8 *Ibid.*, p. 79.

9 See F. McLynn, *Crime and Punishment in Eighteenth-Century England*, London, Routledge, 1989, p. 8, and Tim Hitchcock, 'The publicity of poverty in early eighteenth-century London', in J.F. Merritt (ed.), *Imagining Early Modern London. Perceptions and Portrayals of the City from Stowe to Strype, 1598–1720*, Cambridge, Cambridge University Press, 2001.

10 [Colquhoun], *A Treatise on the Police*, p. 57.

11 *Ibid.*, p. v.

12 *Minutes of Evidence Taken before the Select Committee Appointed by the House of Commons to Inquire into the State of Mendicity and Vagrancy in the Metropolis and its Neighbourhood*, London, Sherwood, Neely and Jones, 1815, p. 41.

13 *Ibid.*, p. 78.

14 John Ralph, *A Critical Review of the Public Buildings, Statues, and Ornaments, in and about London and Westminster*, London, Wallis, 1783, p. 4.

15 The early days were precarious. In October 1798 the station was besieged by a riotous assembly of coal heavers who dispersed only after Colquhoun read the riot act and one of the police officers opened fire, fatally wounding, it was rumoured, one of the leaders.

16 J.R. Poynter, *Society and Pauperism. English Ideas on Poor Relief, 1795–1834*, London, Routledge, 1969, pp. 91–8.

17 *Ibid.*, p. 97.

18 See the succinct and informative discussion in Boyd Hilton, *The Age of Atonement. The Influence of Evangelicalism on Social and Economic Thought, 1795–1865*, Oxford, Clarendon Press, 1988, pp. 98–100.

19 *Report*, I (1796), p. 12, cited in Poynter, *Society and Pauperism*, p. 92.

20 From the outset Portland, Secretary of State at the Home Department, had also been an enthusiastic supporter of Colquhoun's work.

21 Matthew Martin, *Letter to the Right Hon. Lord Pelham, on the State of Mendicity in the Metropolis*, London, Philanthropic Society, 1803, p. 3.

22 Poynter, *Society and Pauperism*, p. 98.

23 *Speech of T.F. Buxton, Esq. At the Egyptian Hall, 26 November 1816 on the Subject of the Distress in Spitalfields*, London, Phillips, 1816, p. 14.

24 *Ibid.*, p. 17.

25 *Minutes of Evidence Taken before the Select Committee ... into the State of Mendicity*, p. iii.

26 *Ibid.*, pp. iv, vi.

27 David Ludden, 'Orientalist empiricism: transformations of colonial knowledge', in Carol A. Breckenridge and Peter van der Veer (eds), *Orientalism and the Postcolonial Predicament. Perspectives on South Asia*, Philadelphia, University of Pennsylvania Press, 1993.

28 Matthew Edney, *Mapping and Empire. The Geographical Construction of British India, 1765–1843*, Chicago, University of Chicago Press, 1997, pp. 27–8.

29 Robertson was Principal of the University of Edinburgh and had written major histories of Scotland and America.

30 William Robertson, *An Historical Disquisition concerning the Knowledge which the Ancients had of India*, London, Cadell and Davies, 1817, pp. v–vi.

31 *Ibid.*, p. 197.

32 *Ibid.*, p. 286.

33 Peter J. Marshall (ed.), *The British Discovery of Hinduism in the Eighteenth Century*,

Cambridge, Cambridge University Press, 1970, p. 43.

34 See, for example, Ketaki Kushari Dyson, *A Various Universe. A Study of the Journals and Memoirs of British Men and Women in the Indian Subcontinent, 1765-1856*, Delhi, Oxford University Press, 1978; Charles Batten, *Pleasurable Instruction. Form and Convention in Eighteenth-Century Travel Writing*, Berkeley, University of California Press, 1978; Sara Mills, *Discourses of Difference. An Analysis of Women's Travel Writing and Colonialism*, London, Routledge, 1991; Dennis Porter, *Haunted Journeys. Desire and Transgression in European Travel Writing*, Princeton, University of Princeton Press, 1991; Mary Louise Pratt, *Imperial Eyes. Travel Writing and Transculturation*, London, Routledge, 1992; David Spurr, *The Rhetoric of Empire. Colonial Discourse in Journalism, Travel Writing and Imperial Administration*, Durham, Duke University Press, 1993; Tim Youngs, *Travellers in Africa. British Travelogues 1850-1900*, Manchester, Manchester University Press, 1994; Jyotsna Singh, *Colonial Narratives/Cultural Dialogues. Discoveries of India in the Language of Colonialism*, London, Routledge, 1996; David Miller and Peter Reill (eds), *Visions of Empire. Voyages, Botany and Representations of Nature*, Cambridge, Cambridge University Press, 1996; Indira Ghose, *Women Travellers in Colonial India. The Power of the Female Gaze*, Delhi, Oxford University Press, 1998; James Duncan and Derek Gregory (eds), *Writes of Passage. Reading Travel Writing*, London, Routledge, 1999; Tim Fulford and Peter Kitson (eds), *Travels, Explorations and Empires, 1770-1835*, 8 vols, London, Pickering and Chatto, 2002.

35 James Duncan and Derek Gregory, 'Introduction', in Duncan and Gregory (eds), *Writes of Passage*, pp. 5–6. Their argument that travel came also to embrace modernity because it was no longer a duty, but a pleasure in itself, increasingly undertaken as part of a 'quintessentially bourgeois experience', lacks conviction since it tends to privilege the eighteenth-century aristocratic grand tour as paradigmatic.

36 Henri Baudet, *Paradise on Earth. Some Thoughts on European Images of Non-European Man*, New Haven, Yale University Press, 1965, p. 55.

37 Dyson, *A Various Universe*, p. 19.

38 *Ibid.*, p. 123. More recent scholarship has tended to substantiate this prescient but undeveloped thesis – see, for example, Tim Fulford and Peter Kitson (eds), *Romanticism and Colonialism. Writing and Empire, 1780-1830*, Cambridge, Cambridge University Press, 1998.

39 William Hodges, *Travels in India during the Years 1780, 1781, 1782, & 1783*, London, Edwards, 1793, pp. iii–iv.

40 *Ibid.*, p. 2.

41 James Duncan, 'Dis-orientation: on the shock of the familiar in a far-away place', in Duncan and Gregory (eds), *Writes of Passage*.

42 George Forster, *A Journey from Bengal to England, through the Northern Part of India, Kashmire, Afghanistan, and Persia, and into Russia, by the Caspian Sea*, London, Faulder, 1798, p. x.

43 *Ibid.*, p. 96.

44 *Ibid.*, pp. 286, 291.

45 *Ibid.*, p. 295.

46 Dyson, *A Various Universe*, p. 32.

47 Ghose, *Women Travellers in Colonial India*, p. 158.

48 Jemima Kindersley, *Letters from the Island of Teneriffe, Brazil, the Cape of Good Hope, and the East Indies*, London, 1777, pp. 72–3.

49 *Ibid.*, p. 193.

50 *Ibid.*, p. 180.

51 *Ibid.*, p. 182.

52 Thomas Williamson, *The East India Vade-Mecum; or, Complete Guide to Gentlemen intended for the Civil, Military, or Naval Service of the Hon. East India Company*, London, Black, Parry and Kingsbury, 1810, p. v.

53 *Ibid.*, pp. 193–4.

54 *Ibid.*, pp. 200–1.

55 Kate Teltscher, *India Inscribed. European and British Writings on India, 1600-1800*,

Delhi, Oxford University Press, 1997, pp. 146–50.

56 Williamson, *The East India Vade-Mecum*, p. 398.

57 Teltscher, *India Inscribed*, p. 74.

58 See, for example, D.W. Bebbington, *Evangelicalism in Modern Britain. A History from the 1730s to the 1980s*, London, Unwin Hyman, 1989; Brian Stanley, *The Bible and the Flag. Protestant Missions and British Imperialism in the Nineteenth and Twentieth Centuries*, Leicester, Apollos, 1990; M.A. Noll, D.W. Bebbington and G.A. Rawlyk (eds), *Evangelicalism. Comparative Studies of Popular Protestantism in North America, the British Isles and Beyond, 1700–1990*, New York, Oxford University Press, 1994; John Woolfe (ed.), *Evangelical Faith and Public Zeal. Evangelicals and Society in Britain, 1780–1980*, London, SPCK, 1995; Susan Thorne, *Congregational Missions and the Making of an Imperial Culture in Nineteenth-Century England*, Stanford, Stanford University Press, 1999.

59 Thorne, *Congregational Missions*, Chapter 2.

60 Andrew Porter, 'Religion, missionary enthusiasm, and empire', in Andrew Porter (ed.), *The Oxford History of the British Empire. Vol. III. The Nineteenth Century*, Oxford, Oxford University Press, 1999.

61 Thorne, *Congregational Missions*, pp. 26–36.

62 See above, pp. 107–9.

63 Here Thorne's attempt to identify distinctions between the poor and the colonized is misplaced (*Congregational Missions*, p. 34). Her emphasis on the poor law and philanthropy leads to a neglect of other ways in which the poor were represented, most particularly their criminalization within a metropolitan context. And the emergence of more severe cultural – later, racial – coding was not the product of missionary endeavour. Rather missionaries had a particular take on, and were busy in promoting, conceptions of the colonized other that were being transformed by more general notions of progress.

64 Joseph White, *Sermons Preached before the University of Oxford, in the Year 1784*, London, Robinson, 1785.

65 The standard biographies are Henry Morris, *The Life of Charles Grant*, London, Murray, 1904, and Ainslie Embree, *Charles Grant and British Rule in India*, London, Allen and Unwin, 1962.

66 Embree, *Charles Grant*, p. 51. The idea of a conversion was originally put forward by Morris, but qualified by Embree on the grounds that it did not seem to exhibit the characteristic features of conversion described in evangelical narratives.

67 *Ibid.*, p. 65.

68 Letter from Charles Grant to Thomas Raikes, 23 October 1784, cited in Morris, *The Life of Charles Grant*, pp. 96–7.

69 No copy of this document has survived. The synopsis that follows is taken from a covering letter dated 17 September 1787, sent by Grant to Wilberforce with a copy of the Proposal (Morris, *The Life of Charles Grant*, pp. 108–14).

70 *Ibid.*, pp. 110–12.

71 Embree, *Charles Grant*, p. 119.

72 It was presented formally to the Board of Directors in 1797, and made generally available when published as a contribution to the debates on renewal of the charter in 1813 (*ibid.*, pp. 141–2).

73 Charles Grant, *Observations on the State of Society among the Asiatic Subjects of Great Britain, particularly with reference to Morals; and on the Means of improving it. Written chiefly in the Year 1792*, Parliamentary Papers, 1813, X, p. 5.

74 *Ibid.*, pp. 2, 5.

75 *Ibid.*, p. 13.

76 *Ibid.*, pp. 23–4.

77 Grant read selectively. Much of his evidence was based on quotations excavated from the archives of the Company, supplemented by Bernier's *Voyages*, Luke Scrafton's *Reflections on the Government of Indostan*, Holwell's *Historical Events*, Verelst's *View of the English Government in Bengal*, the parliamentary proceedings against Hastings, and John Shore's *Asiatic Researches*. Early travel accounts by the likes of

Roe, Hamilton, Baldaeus and Tavernier were omitted for the sake of brevity.

78 Grant, *Observations*, p. 26.

79 *Ibid.*, p. 39.

80 *Ibid.*, p. 75.

81 *Ibid.*, p. 79.

82 *Ibid.*, p. 80.

83 *Ibid.*, p. 112.

84 Penelope Carson, 'Soldiers of Christ: evangelicals and India, 1784–1833', unpublished PhD thesis, University of London, 1988.

85 Wilberforce was famously to declare to parliament in 1813: 'It was formerly my task to plead the cause of people whose woes affected every heart, who were finally rescued from the situation in which they groaned by the abolition of the slave trade. That cause was doubtless the cause of suffering humanity: but I declare that, even if we exclude the consideration of religion, humanity appears to me to be still more concerned in the cause I am now pleading, than in that of which I was formerly the advocate.'

86 William Carey, *An Enquiry into the Obligations of Christians to use Means for the Conversion of Heathens in which the Religious State of the different Nations of the World, the Success of former Undertakings, and the Practicability of further Undertakings, are considered*, Leicester, 1792, p. 5. Carey estimated that of the 731 million people in the world, 420 million were still in pagan darkness.

87 *Ibid.*, p. 12.

88 *Ibid.*, pp. 63–4.

89 *Ibid.*, p. 84.

90 For an interesting account of this early work, particularly with regard to street preaching, see Lata Mani, *Contentious Traditions. The Debate on Sati in Colonial India*, Berkeley, University of California Press, 1998.

91 The distinct theological positions evident in evangelicalism are usefully summarized in D.B. Hindmarsh, *John Newton and the English Evangelical Tradition Between the Conversions of Wesley and Wilberforce*, Oxford, Clarendon Press, 1996, pp. 124–5.

92 Heartened by early work in India, and to an extent using it as a model for further action, the BMS was to lead missionary endeavour in the Caribbean some twenty years later. It too was faced with fierce opposition from colonial interests, most notably the planters. On a wave of anti-slavery sentiment early in the 1820s, however, it was able to consolidate its activities in Jamaica. Caribbeans, like Indians, were seen to be lost in dark heathenism and savagery, but if anything even further down in the evolutionary chain. For reasons that have not been fully explored, striking contrasts existed in the outcomes of missionary endeavour. While in India evangelicals had little success in converting the indigenous population, in Jamaica thousands were converted in the period leading up to the 1840s. Proportionately this represented a far greater intervention (see the recent meticulous study by Catherine Hall, *Civilising Subjects. Metropole and Colony in the English Imagination, 1830–1867*, London, Polity, 2002).

93 I. Rivers, 'Strangers and pilgrims: sources and patterns of Methodist narrative', in J.C. Hilson, M.M.B. Jones and J.R. Watson (eds), *Augustan Worlds*, Leicester, Leicester University Press, 1978; P. Caldwell, *The Puritan Conversion Narrative*, Cambridge, Cambridge University Press, 1986; Hindmarsh, *John Newton and the English Evangelical Tradition*.

94 The text has been skilfully read by Hindmarsh, *John Newton and the Evangelical Tradition*.

95 *Ibid.*, p. 42.

96 Michael McKeon, *The Origins of the English Novel*, London, Radius, 1988, p. 104.

97 See, for example, Embree, *Charles Grant*; Eli Potts, *British Baptist Missionaries in India, 1793–1858*, Cambridge, Cambridge University Press, 1967; Carson, 'Soldiers of Christ'; Karen Chancey, 'The Star in the East: the controversy over Christian missions to India, 1805–1813', *Historian*, Spring, 1998.

98 See the retrospective account in Claudius Buchanan, *Christian Researches in Asia*

(1812), reproduced in *The Works of the Rev. Claudius Buchanan*, New York, Whiting and Watson, 1812. *Christian Researches* was based on Buchanan's travels around India during which he recorded detailed observations on the barbarities of Hindu customs. It was published in nine editions over two years, becoming the most widely read of his numerous publications.

99 Claudius Buchanan, *Memoir of the Expediency of an Ecclesiastical Establishment for British India* (1805), reproduced in *The Works of the Rev. Claudius Buchanan*, p. 188.

100 Buchanan was the first to point to the moral ambiguities of the pilgrim tax – a levy, as far as he was concerned, to raise revenue from such barbaric practices as Jagganath sacrifice.

101 *Ibid.*, p. 201.

102 *Ibid.*, p. 205.

103 *Ibid.*, pp. 209, 211.

104 Claudius Buchanan, *The Star in the East; a Sermon preached in the Parish Church of St. James, Bristol*, New York, Williams and Whiting, 1809.

105 George Bearce, *British Attitudes towards India, 1784–1858*, Oxford, Oxford University Press, 1961, p. 80.

106 See, for example, John Scott Waring, *Observations on the Present State of the East India Company*, London, 1808; *Remarks Preached before the University of Oxford*, London, 1808; *Remarks on Rev. Dr. Buchanan's Christian Researches in Asia*, London, Ridgway, 1812; Thomas Twining, *A Letter to the Chairman of the East India Company. On the Danger of Interfering in the Religious Opinions of the Natives of India*, London, 1807.

107 J.W. Cunningham, *Christianity in India. An essay on the Duty, Means, and Consequences, of introducing the Christian Religion among the Native Inhabitants of the British Dominions in the East*, London, Hatchard, 1808, p. xi.

108 *Ibid.*, p. 188.

109 Some 897 petitions were presented to parliament in the months leading up to the vote, 281 of which resulted from the efforts of 'friends and supporters' of the Baptist mission in India. To date, this was the largest number presented on any issue, and did much to bring India into the popular metropolitan imagination (Carson, 'Soldiers of Christ', p. 301; Mani, *Contentious Traditions*, p. 121).

110 East India Company Charter Act (1813), 53 Geo. III cap. 155, section 33.

111 Embree, *Charles Grant*, p. 155.

112 William Ward, *A View of the History, Literature and Mythology of the Hindoos*, 4 vols, London, British Missionary Society, 1817–20, Vol. I, p. xxiii.

113 *Ibid.*, Vol. III, pp. vii–viii.

114 Mani, *Contentious Traditions*, p. 128.

CHAPTER FOUR

A complete cyclopaedia

Unknown London

Despite Colquhoun's attempts to reveal the nature of the casual residuum, the sheer unknowability of the poor inhabiting the wider metropolitan landscape served only to intensify prevailing anxieties. In
response, a considerable body of literature emerged. Best remembered are
the writings of Charles Dickens and Henry Mayhew, but these were a
small part of the nineteenth-century endeavour by social reformers, novelists, evangelicals, illustrators and cartographers to organize new
knowledges of modern London and the poor who inhabited its inaccessible, seemingly primordial courts, rookeries and alleys. Neither were they
the first, for these writers drew inspiration from earlier work. It is thus to
Pierce Egan, George Smeeton, George Cruikshank, James Grant and others of the early nineteenth-century literary subculture that we have to look
for the defining moment.

Concern with the dissembling potentiality of the poor focused endeavour to know London as a modern city at that paradoxical moment when
the realization of this vision came to be recognized as problematic. Toward
the close of the eighteenth century a range of issues around aesthetics,
power and class featured in urban texts with unprecedented power and
complexity.[1] Previous writers, most notably Alexander Pope in *The
Dunciad* and John Gay in *Trivia* and *The Beggar's Opera*, had engaged
actively with the plurality of London life, assuming uncritically that it
could be described and represented. The profound change in sensibility
provoked by fears of disorder undermined this confidence, and from the
turn of the century writers approached the mapping and representation of
London with faltering appreciation of its immense, labyrinthine totality
now quite beyond the limits of comprehension found in earlier urban
rhetoric. Thus in Blake, Wordsworth, De Quincey and of course Dickens

emerged a more open-ended and circumspect exploration of London's dynamism:

> [W]e come to see the concatenation of discourses of the sublime and the outgrowth of terror in the face of urban immensity, the perplexing question of the formation of an urban bourgeois identity in the face of anonymity, the concern over proximity between East and West, rich and poor, and the fear of contamination in both a literal and metaphorical sense.... The city in the first part of the nineteenth century is written as a series of subjects (always plural) always in excess of expression and comprehension.[2]

These impulses, however, were not exclusively the concern of Romantic writers. The same sense of incomprehensibility pervaded popular literary appropriations of the metropolis that were beginning to appear. In the remarkable opening sections of the hugely popular *Life in London*, Pierce Egan struggles to define the epistemological and methodological underpinnings of his approach to the metropolis. 'An accurate knowledge of the manners, habits, and feelings of a brave and free people', he claims, 'is not to be acquired in the CLOSET, nor is it to be derived from the formal routine precepts of tutors.'

> It is only by means of a free and unrestrained intercourse with society ... that an intimate acquaintance is to be obtained with Englishmen: for this purpose it is necessary to view their pastimes, to hear their remarks, and, from such sources, to be enabled to study their *character*.[3]

Egan's desire was to represent the extraordinary material plurality of metropolitan life. For him London is a 'complete cyclopaedia' wherein the extremes and paradoxes of life happily coexist. To capture it, he provides a 'camera obscura view' for the reader in which the visual works alongside the textual, if not always in harmony. Here was an imagination that represented a fundamental shift in the status of the observing subject. It emerged from the novel ways of organizing vision in the early years of the nineteenth century as artists and writers broke with classical modes of representation, and set in motion the modernization of vision. Obvious manifestations were the changes in imagery promoted by new systems of representation, but more fundamental was the massive reorganization of knowledge that impacted on human capacities to produce, desire and perceive.[4] Such arguments have considerable implications for the ways in which the history of visual art in the nineteenth century have been thought. They suggest, for example, that modernist art of the 1870s and 1880s was a delayed symptom, made possible by the systemic shift in perception witnessed some fifty years earlier. And they help us to contextualize the problematic relationship between visual and textual materials evident in works like *Life in London*. Of equal significance, however, is the light shed on literary endeavour. For what emerged in the early decades of the nineteenth century was a new observer, operating in a range of social and artistic practices, and scientific and philosophical domains of knowledge, who attempted to appropriate the dislocating experiences of urban environments. This 'ambulatory observer shaped by a convergence of new urban spaces, technologies, and new economic and symbolic functions of images and products' abandoned the dominant, fixed and seemingly stable perceptions of the previous century, and sought a truth 'abstracted from any founding site or referent'.[5]

This new observer attempted to record his observations, creating a body of urban literature that constituted a formative moment in the cultural history of the metropolis.[6] Produced in the period from 1815 to 1845 by a relatively small number of writers, publishers and illustrators working on the fringes of a bohemian culture, this literature commanded unprecedented levels of attention from a reading public. In its innovative, diverse and self-conscious attempts to grasp the complex totality of London, the literature can be seen as an early popular modernism that laid the foundation for the writings of Dickens, Mayhew and their successors, and for popular Victorian theatre and graphic illustration.

This recognition of the important – but ultimately limited – practice of observation adopted by Egan and his contemporaries is critical to an understanding of their literary appropriation. The vision of the wider social drama of metropolitan life they offered was made possible by the liminality of the position they occupied within class relations. Thus, in contrast to the dominant visions held by planners and cartographers, and evident in elite town guides during the improvements to the built infrastructure of London, these writers attempted to capture high and low life through participation in and observation of their forms. Ultimately, however, they withdrew, and as *flâneurs* looked vicariously from a safe distance at the performance or the spectacle. In so doing, they represented, often in comic form, the troubling manifestations of poverty rather than revealing them through critique.[7]

Life in London is a work of transition. Although able to capture the instabilities of a totalizing vision and hence prepare the path for nineteenth-century literary appropriations of the metropolis, it simultaneously was indebted to eighteenth-century genres. Tricks-of-the-town travelogues in which unsophisticated gentlemen from the country are exposed to the various frauds and villainies of London during a tour conducted by a knowledgeable friend provide the narrative form for the adventures of the three heroes. And there are passing references to elite town guides in the descriptions of venues such as the Royal Academy and the curious detour around Carlton Palace. But from the outset Egan is determined to distance the work from hack writing:

That *intense* study formerly required to make up the *character* of an AUTHOR is at the present period (1820) greatly relieved, as it should seem that LITERATURE has kept pace with the new buildings in the Metropolis; and new street and new books have been produced, as it were, by magic. This rapid improvement made in the literary world, is owing to those extensive manufacturers of new works, Messrs. SCISSORS and PASTE.[8]

Instead, his invocation is to the legacy of eighteenth-century literature manifest in the '"*excellence*, NOVELTY, and *naivete*", which still hover about the heads of the MODERN WRITERS, who "*sit in the whirlpool of* LITERATURE, *and direct the* STORM" in the Metropolis'.[9] 'The Metropolis is now before me', he concludes, 'POUSSIN never had a more luxuriant, variegated, and interesting subject for a landscape; ... if I cannot command success, at least, it shall not be averred that I did not exert myself to deserve it.'[10]

It is in this attempt to portray – and express – the dislocating materiality of the city that Egan reveals the stirrings of modernist sensibility. For him, the metropolis is a

complete CYCLOPAEDIA.... Every SQUARE in the metropolis is a sort of *map* well worthy of exploring.... There is not a *street* also in London, but what may be compared to a large or small volume of intelligence ... a *court* or *alley* must be obscure indeed , if it does not afford some remarks; and even the *poorest* cellar contains some *trait* or other, in unison with the manners and feelings of this great city.[11]

London thus offers travellers the supreme opportunity to see life in all of its manifestations from the '*high-mettled* CORINTHIAN of St James's, *swaddled* in luxury, down to the *needy* FLUE-FAKER of Wapping, *born without a shirt*'. On this voyage of (self)-discovery they come to recognize the necessity of improvement by appreciating the 'advantages that experience holds forth'.[12]

Jon Bee in *A Living Picture of London, for 1828* is also alert to the profound changes in literary activity attendant on a sense of crisis in the imperial metropolis. The past quarter of a century, he argues, has witnessed the rise and progress of the 'present extended *taste for reading*', much of which was centred in London.[13] This 'march of intellect' has swept aside resistance from a corrupt state oligarchy which had precipitated a crisis in empire through the loss of the thirteen colonies, ferment in Europe and threat of yet further loss of India. From this struggle for power, the '*spirit of inquiry*' has gone forth promoting new approaches to the administration of the nation, improvements in manufacturing, and advances in the arts and sciences. Initially, this spirit was tempered by a literature which, although increasing rapidly in volume, remained 'of the most mawky nature'. But the swelling tide of demand for substantial authors among studious clerks, journeymen and mechanics was insatiable: 'all *read*, in some manner or other, *se defensio*, as 'twere, and the accumulation of little libraries on every floor and in every lodging' marked out a new reading public which soon abandoned 'flimsy novelists and hackneyed "histories"'.

For John Duncombe in *The Dens of London* (1835), 'Age of inquiry' best described this new spirit. Ancient romantic tales of love and heroism were no longer fashionable. The 'insipid stuff of the rhymer, and the equally sentimental trash of the getter-up of fiction' have been superseded by more rational publications such as *The Spectator* and *The Tatler* which are founded on truth and bear 'the stamp of newness'.[14] This change was fostered by a reading public which has turned away from the 'exaggerated imaginings of a diseased brain' and toward the writings of Scott in which could be found 'History beautifully blended with Fiction, or rather Truth, accurate descriptions of nature, and correct pictures of life, both high and low'. The present desire for change has engendered a new sensitivity to the condition of the people which even Egan's 'by-gone piece of notoriety' was unable to capture.

The sense of historicity is evident in other publications. George Smeeton's popular *Doings in London* uses detailed information to convey the historical lineages of London's modernity. Most striking are the statistics on the capital of companies that collapsed in the financial crisis of 1825.[15] Included 'as a curious and valuable record of the gullibility of the citizens of this overgrown metropolis', they simultaneously provide a modern perspective on the scale of loss that can be incurred through fraud in the financial capital of the world. A similar inventory appeared in *How to Live in London*, also published in 1828.[16] But it was the denial of fictional accounts that most defined their distinctive approaches to the representation of London. 'No fiction of the brain, no imaginary character, make any part of these pages', stated Jon Bee in the Preface to *A Living Picture of London*:

> I protest against, as I utterly eschew, all attempts at teaching this most perilous of worldly knowledge, by the machinery of 'pretty novel' or 'amusing narrative,' to which some excellent cerebral writers of the present day seem fondly addicted; those modern Bunyans, who couch whatever they write 'under the similitude of a dream'.[17]

Overall, this body of literature signalled a further shift in discursive appropriations of metropolitan life. Produced at a time of renewed anxiety about the poor, it represented a faltering attempt to resolve the problems attendant on the continued unknowability of London low life. John Badcock's *The London Guide* remained encased within the eighteenth-century genre of the gentleman's vade-mecum, revealing little beyond the activities of the criminalized poor and their use of canting slang.[18] He seeks, however, to confer empirical veracity on the urban travelogue by inclusion of material from seemingly authoritative surveys. Reference is constantly made to Colquhoun's *Treatise on the Police of the Metropolis*, and the evidence submitted to the Select Committee on the State of the Police.

The work of Egan, Smeeton and other members of the bohemian sub-culture was part of an important transitional phase in the literary representation of the metropolis. Out of this complex, plural literature struggling to capture the confused and contradictory totality of the metropolis emerged Charles Dickens and Henry Mayhew. Their links with Egan in particular were powerful. Egan's celebration of the exuberant diversity of metropolitan life through chance encounters with its characters provided inspiration for Dickens (best evidenced in the early novels *Sketches of Boz* and *Pickwick Papers*[19]), who creatively developed an urban vision by making these characters familiar and knowable. In Dickens, empathy displaced amused detachment; readers responded because the mimetic realism in the novels was one they recognized sympathetically. But this remained a middle-class or lower-middle-class sympathy, for Dickens rarely revealed the poor, even less the working class who are almost entirely absent. Occasionally, members of the criminal poor and metropolitan low life feature, but they are not offered as representative of a wider culture. In his novels the poor were sensed as Egan sensed them – as minor and shadowy characters who provided detail and contrast to the narrative rather than driving it forward.[20] Thus although a sense of London's poverty is always there, it is as a backdrop to the main characters. Ultimately, we know little about the lives of the various characters who are forced to suffer the quotidian oppression of poverty.

Mayhew took Egan in a different direction. The turmoil of street life encountered by the traveller is in Mayhew given voice by intimate observation and detailed recording of the experiences of the urban poor. His original project to map metropolitan poverty as a whole was never realized; what remains for the most part is explorations of the street sellers, performers and labourers who constituted a relatively small section of the London poor. But from these studies we can for the first time begin to know something of the histories, cultures and economies that structured the lived experiences of the street poor, and their emotional and cognitive responses.

The trinity of Egan, Dickens and Mayhew helped to define the course of urban exploration for the next thirty years. Their projects may have been distinct, but they shared a concern to reveal London's diversity at a time of anxiety over the threat posed by the poor, and simultaneously exerted an influence, the complex, individual strands of which can be untangled only with difficulty. This task was mediated, however, by the influence of evangelical narratives, which by mid century when the massive intervention into metropolitan poverty was under way were being read by increasing numbers of people. This intervention and the literature to which it gave rise also helped to shape perceptions to the extent that in some writings congruence with the genre established by urban explorers was almost complete.

Metropolitan evangelicalism

Toward the end of the eighteenth century London provided a distinct focus for evangelical activity. Here were to be found the Clapham Sect and the headquarters of leading societies. And we have seen that strong evangelical influence was felt in the activities and writings of the Society for Bettering the Condition of the Poor and the Mendicity Society, as well as local bodies such as the Association for the Relief of the Industrious Poor of Spitalfields. The most sustained intervention, however, began in the 1830s when evangelicals singled out the metropolis as a mission field of such importance that a national effort was required. From that time evangelicalism, with organization powerful enough to transcend denominational differences, embarked on an extraordinary campaign to bring the gospel to the metropolitan poor.

In *Lighten their Darkness* Donald Lewis has described well evangelical organizations and their armies of agents during the most intense period of activity from 1828 to 1860.[21] Inspired by the efforts and writings of Thomas Chalmers, who in his Glasgow parish twenty years earlier had claimed success for operations based on the locality, they directed their energies to aggressive proselytization through systematic house-to-house canvassing. The largest of the organizations was the London City Mission (LCM), founded in 1835 by the combined efforts of David Nasmith, Baptist Noel and Thomas Buxton. Although in their background and social philosophy there was little in common, they shared a vision that despite the misgivings of the church establishment the metropolitan poor could be reached through determined interdenominational effort. Nasmith provided the initial impulse, announcing on his arrival in the metropolis his intent to establish missions similar to those he had pioneered in Glasgow and Dublin under the influence of Chalmers. But the ground had been prepared by the publication a few months earlier of Baptist Noel's *The State of the Metropolis Considered*.[22] Drawing heavily on Colquhoun's statistics, the book reverberated with familiar concerns about the condition of the metropolitan poor. Mendicancy, alcohol, Sabbath breaking, gambling and robbery, he argued, were endemic witnesses to the moral destitution of the poor, in the face of which the church had proved ineffective.

The attendant demand for new initiatives was a clarion call to evangelicals. London's 'mass of heathenism ... more revolting than that of Benares or Calcutta' has failed to attract the same attention directed to foreign missions:

> England sends out her missionaries to the coasts of Guiana, to the tribes of Southern Africa, to the islands of the South Pacific, to North and South India, to Malacca and Canton: but 518,000 souls in the metropolis, within easy reach of hundreds of Christian ministers, and of thousands of intelligent Christian laymen with wealth and leisure, are almost entirely overlooked![23]

Extracts from the book were reproduced in the leading evangelical journal *The Record*, and quoted widely in sermons and lectures.[24] Nasmith recruited the active support also of Thomas Buxton, who not only agreed to become the LCM's treasurer, but also in the first precarious years guaranteed its financial survival by eliciting donations from his friends and family. Doctrinal stability, however, was rather more troublesome. Fearing that the interdenominational character of the LCM was being challenged by Nasmith's uncompromising independence, Anglican examiners resigned. But the critical blow was dealt by Noel, who in 1837 threatened resignation, forcing Nasmith to withdraw. Thereafter, effective control passed into the hands of Anglicans, although committee posts were shared equally with Nonconformists. On the basis of this new-found co-operation, the fortunes of the LCM were transformed. The number of agents employed increased from 50 in 1839 to 101 in 1844, eventually rising to 375 in 1860.[25] Since each agent was expected to visit the same 500 families every month, this constituted a massive intervention. In its 1855 Annual Report the LCM claimed to have made 1,484,563 visits in the previous year, during which over two million religious tracts had been distributed.[26] Agents were instructed to read and interpret portions of the scriptures, foregrounding the core tenets of evangelical belief. Those families without scriptures were provided with tracts approved by the committee in the hope that someone could read. Politics was studiously avoided. A daily journal was kept in which the agent was expected to record accurately facts relating to the circumstances of each family.[27]

Evangelical thinking of the poor during the period of intense activity in the metropolis was in many respects a faltering attempt to come to terms with the apocalyptic vision of Malthus.[28] Unfettered increase in population was perceived as the single most serious threat to the divinely ordered world, in response to which evangelicals sought methods to reassert its natural harmony. Optimists turned outward, stressing the capacity of humans in productive exertion to overcome the pathological consequences of overpopulation. The more pessimistically minded, on the other hand, interpreted the demographic calculus as a divine means of encouraging inner reform and sexual abstention among the lower orders, thereby erecting a 'system of moral theology, in which prudence and chastity were not merely rational responses to the crisis, but spiritual imperatives in their own right'.[29]

The practical consequences of this can be seen in the intellectual formation and activities of Chalmers. In evidence to the Select Committee on Mendicity, and in his *Christian and Civic Economy of Large Towns*,[30] Chalmers stated forcefully that intensive house-to-house visits were the only means of effecting moral regeneration of society. Evangelical missionaries, by promoting restraint, virtue and self-help among the poor, could provide a more lasting and humane solution to the problems of mendicity and vagrancy than any amount of reform to the system of poor relief. The poor may well be in need of material benefit, but without spiritual enlightenment it would provide at best temporary relief which in the long term would be self-defeating. 'I should count the salvation of a single soul of more value than the deliverance of a whole empire from pauperism'[31] may have overstated his case, but it suggested where his priorities lay.

Narrative forms of salvation were evident in evangelical writings throughout the long nineteenth century (pp. 90–1). Mass publication began in the troubled political climate of the 1790s when a group of church and lay workers led by the Clapham Sect sponsored anti-Jacobin and moral tracts. Hannah More was prominent in organizing a series of cheap repository tracts; by 1796 an estimated two million were in circulation.[32] Three years later the Religious Tract Society (RTS) was formed. From these activities emerged the vast tract literature published by the LCM, most notably tract tales for the young, millions of which were distributed by agents in their mission to evangelize the metropolitan poor. But the narratives shaped also the spiritual autobiographies of those working among the poor, and the lengthy commentaries on the state of moral and physical depravity they encountered.

The rapid increase in evangelical literature in this period was part of the massive effort conducted by various societies to evangelize London. This level of activity transformed knowledge of the poor. Lay agents became familiar figures on the urban landscape, as a result of which many developed a sympathetic concern for the material as well as spiritual welfare of the families they visited. Metropolitan sanitation, lodgings and ragged schools were of particular interest, and the information agents acquired on these and related issues through direct acquaintance with the poor was sought increasingly by members of parliament and other middle-class social reformers. And it was to city missionaries that Mayhew turned for guided tours around the slums.[33]

Racialization of the poor

I have attempted to demonstrate that approaches to an understanding of the metropolitan poor in the early nineteenth century have to be viewed with due recognition of the imperial context. As urban travellers and evangelicals came to confront the dogged persistence of the poor at a time of perceived progress, and the threat that the poor and colonial subjects posed to the future of the empire, imperial sentiment intensified. We need to be sensitive, however, to the contrasts that continued to exist between these two genres, particularly on the question of progress. In the writings of Egan, Smeeton and other members of their literary subculture, traces remain of eighteenth-century tricks-of-the-town narratives, but they are subordinated by a celebration of London's quotidian plurality in an age of enlightenment and intellect. 'LIFE IN LONDON', states Egan, 'is ... to admire the good and to avoid the vicious; but never to entertain an idea, that however bad and depraved some individuals may appear to be, that they are past any attempt to reclaim them from their evil ways.'[34] Thus recognition of the 'waste of wickedness' that is London is muted by comic displacement of low-life haunts, and joyous, cross-cultural encounters between their denizens and the three heroes representing 'some of the worthiest, most tender-hearted, liberal minds, and charitable dispositions, which ornament London, and render it the delight and happiness of society'.[35]

Smeeton, in his desire to 'show vice and deception in all their *real* deformity', displays a more leaden concern with the criminal propensities of London's poor,[36] but at no time is this linked to an apocalyptic vision of the future. Above all, his project was reliably to capture the same contradictoriness of the city's 'vast emporium of happiness and misery, splendour and wretchedness'.[37] And if Badcock has little of Smeeton's precocious eclecticism, there is a similar concern to avoid 'fiction of the brain [and] imaginary character' in revealing the darker side of London life.[38] In the end we are left with the thought that in spite of the litany of criminal activities described, the march of intellect and spirit of inquiry reigned: 'happiness, comfort, health, ease, and progressive improvement, are perceptible everywhere', he concluded.[39]

Contrast these writings with the stirrings of evangelical zeal in the metropolis. Noel's pioneering study of religious instruction in the metropolis employed detailed statistical information with much greater rigour and coherence than the early urban explorers. His purpose, however, was not to capture London's plurality, but to reveal the potentially grave consequences of religious neglect. Over half a million souls were living without religious instruction of any kind. This 'mass of heathenism ... more untaught in Divine truth than the New Zealanders, more unregarded than the Chinese',[40] has led to incalculable mischief. Labourers fail to attend church on the Sabbath, choosing instead to imbibe the poison on 'various blasphemous and revolutionary unstamped publications', saunter in suburban tea-gardens, or revel in drunken orgies. The consequence is mendicancy and crime on unprecedented scales, and an 'unspeakably painful contemplation of this mass of immortal beings ... without God and without hope'.[41]

This deep sense of foreboding does not pervade the more racy writings of James Grant. He admits to recent and general moral improvement, but simultaneously claims that among sections of the lower classes there is room for greater still. The chapter on Bartholomew and Greenwich fairs in *Sketches in London*, for example, concludes with a sustained condemnation of popular culture. Such fairs are the 'relics of a barbarous age, and were established for the sake of an ignorant and brutalized people. They are altogether unworthy of the nineteenth century: they are especially unworthy of a civilized and Christian land.'[42] Worrying also are penny theatres, the recent rapid increase of which has done great mischief in corrupting the youth. Abolition of fairs and popular theatres, therefore, is now an urgent matter since it would lead to an improvement in the morals of the lower classes, and amelioration of the conditions in which so many of them live.

Over the next decade, this sense of the corruption and demoralization intensified, and pessimism about the future was voiced with increasing shrillness. Out of this dystopian vision emerged the notion of race, used as a critical referent to help explain and express frustration over the continued failure to eradicate the pathological effects of poverty. To understand this process we need to go beyond stereotypical configurations of race. An awareness of the use of pejorative stereotypes, gleaned from the occasional isolated and decontextualized quotation, provides at best partial access to the problem because they were often merely manifestations of certain contemporary linguistic practices rather than the logical outcome of racial theory. Consequently, racist epithets do not reveal – because they have no necessary relationship to – metanarratives of racial formation. This is why an appreciation of the process of racialization, seen through the optic of broader theories and narratives that informed the construction of the poor as a race beneath or apart, assumes significance.[43] Furthermore, acknowledgement of the influence of racial and social theories has to be tempered by the recognition that they were adapted and implemented in ways that lacked rigour, coherence and consistency.[44]

In 1850 Thomas Beames, a preacher and assistant at St James, Westminster, wrote *The Rookeries of London*.[45] In its pages he surveyed the condition of the metropolis, contemplating how the terrible plight of the poor could be located within the unbroken ascent of the English nation.

When, he asked, did they appear?

> True, thoughts of Rookeries recall, if not old Saxon times, yet times when we
> Anglo-Saxons were one people, ere the First and Second Charles had driven
> out the stern Republicanism destined to bear such fruit in the next century;
> ere the traveller's gig broke down in a Cheshire village, and a night's lodging
> at the hospitable home of a stranger gave him a bride, and that bride gave the
> world George Washington, – ere, in a word, the Anglo-Saxon name, language
> and strong manly spirit had become common to vast nations in both hemi-
> spheres.[46]

And why?

> We like to know for what particular offences the justice and the wisdom of
> England thought proper to consign the dark and comfortless dwellings of the
> poor for whom religion bids us care, and in whose preservation is preserved
> a nation's well being; at what particular era the custom was introduced,
> whether refractory Barons inflicted confinements in such tenements as a
> punishment on the commons who supported the sovereign, or whether when
> cities and boroughs first achieved municipal privileges they thus tamed the
> spirits of rude retainers.[47]

Whenever they first appeared, or for what reasons, the poor remained,
constituting a greater threat to the future of the English nation than revolutionary upheaval:

> Strong as we are, secure as we have been, we may yet bear to listen to the
> teaching of history; its lessons are for us – for us, round whom the middle
> class reared an impregnable rampart, and who have lived through convul-
> sions which shook to the centre the great powers of Europe. That splendid
> monument of wisdom and courage, the English Constitution, may defy mi-
> nor attacks – afford to despise them; other nations are only now winning the
> privileges we enjoy – are opening their eyes slowly to the light which has long
> been our birthright. Yet with all this, if we forebear to renovate where time
> has ravaged, to remedy abuses which none can palliate, the day of retribu-
> tion must come, – our children may possess an heritage blasted by our neglect,
> and the swords their fathers have sharpened pierce them to the heart.[48]

Faced with such prospects, England must once again assume the mantle of
responsibility and embark on a mission to save not only herself but the
civilized world:

> England, our beloved country, the mother of freedom, the asylum of the
> persecuted, whose sons have gone forth from their island home to teach the
> British tongue, and hand down the British name to empires now just spring-
> ing into life; who, at the cost of twenty millions, willed that slavery should
> be no more. Look around at what she has done, and think not that her
> strength is spent, or her arm unnerved. If Rookeries be the canker-worms,

not of England but of Europe, may she, who is the first in arts and arms, be the first to sweep them from the land they disgrace – may she take the lead in the holy work, from whom the voice has oft gone forth which awoke Europe from her slumber.[49]

I have included the words of Beames at length because between the hyperbole they reveal much of significance about the political and historical specificity of the racialization of the poor. How was it, he inquired, that within a nation of an ancient Anglo-Saxon people whose wise and benign influence has shaped the modern world a poor population living in wretched conditions was formed? The question was an urgent one, for this population presented the nation with a moral obligation and a political dilemma that had not been resolved. Strong as England was through a liberal constitution that had survived revolutionary impulses convulsing the rest of Europe, the poor remained a malignant presence at the very heart. That presence threatened progress, for without social reform the poor, mindful of past neglect, would seek violent retribution. As in the past when the nation gave freedom to the civilized world, was a haven for the persecuted, bestowed civilization throughout its empire, and in complete disregard for self-interest abolished slavery, England had once again to meet the challenge and fulfil its historic destiny by sweeping away the slums.

Here is the discursive context within which racial theories of the poor came to prominence in nineteenth-century England.[50] The articulating principle was progress, for it was through the complex dialectic between the hope for a future built upon intellectual, imperial and industrial revolutions and the threat posed by their antinomies that the concept of race came to express the 'conundrum of inequality'.[51] The optimistic sense of inevitable progress promoted by eighteenth-century *philosophes* was re-cast by a sense of foreboding about the potential of regression and reversion. At this intersection, race embodied and helped construct the natural superiority of the progressive elites over their regressive class and imperial subjects.[52]

This was possible because race provided an historically secure and inviolable sense of community at a time of rapid change and fragmentation. In England this took the form of the imagined community of Anglo-Saxonism which gathered strength in the late eighteenth century, achieving its triumphant apogee in the mid nineteenth when the racial theorist Robert Knox could write, 'With me, race or hereditary descent is everything; it stamps the man'.[53] But such communities simultaneously consolidated divisions because they defined themselves by exclusion as much as by inclusion, thereby undermining the universalism of the Enlightenment project. And since exclusion operated against others beyond *and within* the territorial boundaries of the imagined community, internal class divisions came to be seen as racial.[54] Racialization in this sense, therefore, refers to the appropriation and subsequent reproduction of a particular conception of race within hegemonic structures. It can take two co-existent forms. In one, the racialized groups are incorporated within the social body in positions of subordination; in the other, they are excluded to the margins beyond the social body. Both serve to consolidate a racially based order.[55]

Wandering tribes

It seems well known that during a period of prolific writing over 1849–52 Henry Mayhew did more than any other to 'discover the poor'. The experiences of metropolitan street traders, thieves, prostitutes, beggars and other species of outcast London were recorded, much of the detail being provided from direct oral testimony of people he interviewed. Originally, the material appeared as regular articles in the *Morning Chronicle*, and later weekly pamphlets, but he is now remembered best for the four-volume compilation *London Labour and the London Poor* published over 1861–62. Its introductory chapter is replete with a social imagery representing the poor in cultural terms seemingly identical to those used by racial theorists and anthropologists to construct the colonial other. In the oft-quoted preface Mayhew described himself as a 'traveller in the undiscovered country of the poor ... of whom the public had less knowledge than of the most distant tribes of the earth'; indeed, there are references in the first section on costermongers to the travel accounts of writers such as Andrew Smith in South Africa, Captain Cochrane in Russia, and John Ross and Captain Parry in the polar regions. Mayhew then proceeded to define the object of inquiry by invoking a series of manichean dualisms:

> Of the thousand million of human beings that are said to constitute the population of this entire globe, there are – socially, morally, and perhaps even physically considered – but two distinct and broadly marked races, viz., the wanderers and the settlers – the vagabond and the citizen – the nomadic and the civilized tribes.[56]

These curious oppositions reveal the rather inchoate discursive formations about the poor that Mayhew inhabited at this early stage. The term 'wandering tribes' was widely used to describe the itinerant population of the countryside, and by ethnologists to describe nomadic peoples; only Mayhew applied it to metropolitan 'street-folk',[57] and here ambiguously since many of the life stories he recounted display patterns of settlement not migration. 'Vagabond', a term symptomatic of the criminalization of the poor, was contrasted with the politically laden concept of the citizen. But it was the opposition of nomadic and civilized tribes that had the greatest significance.

In a brief section entitled 'Of wandering tribes in general' Mayhew claimed that attitude and behaviour distinguish the nomad from the civilized man. The nomad had a 'repugnance to regular and continuous labour', a 'want of providence', a 'passion for stupefying herbs' and 'intoxicating fermented liquors', a 'delight in warfare', a 'vague sense of religion', and so on.[58] This moral and cultural construction, combined with an assertion that nomadic tribes are universal, clearly forged an identity between tribe and the prevalent notion of race; indeed, Mayhew used tribe and race interchangeably. Into this he inserted biology. Thus wandering races have 'broad, lozenge-shaped faces (owing to the great development of the cheek bones), and pyramidal skulls', while the most civilized races have 'oval or elliptical' skulls. He summed up:

> Here, then, we have a series of facts of utmost social importance. (1) There are two distinct races of men, viz.:- the wandering and the civilized tribes; (2) to each of these tribes a different form of head is peculiar, the wandering races being remarkable for the development of the bones of the face, as the jaws, cheek-bones, &c., and the civilized for the development of those of the head; (3) to each civilized tribe there is generally a wandering horde attached; (4) such wandering hordes have frequently a different language from the more civilized portion of the community, and that adopted with the intent of concealing their designs and exploits from them.[59]

The sources of such a racial typography were evident from references made to contemporary ethnographical work, most notably that of James Prichard,[60] whose influential *Natural History of Man*[61] had been republished the year before Mayhew began his survey, and from which Mayhew quotes ideas concerning distinctive physical characteristics. From a humanitarian perspective and in ways that anticipated Darwin, Prichard attempted to explain the development of racial types through monogenesis.[62] But many of the subtleties of his arguments were effaced by commentators. Thus Mayhew took the *physical* variations used by Prichard to demonstrate the essential unity of humankind as inherently *racial*, and assumed a physiognomic typology with which the lower races could readily be identified and the investigation of the metropolitan nomads could proceed.[63]

Unsurprisingly, Mayhew has been regarded by commentators as an unreconstructed racial theorist,[64] or ignored except as a source of information on the black metropolis.[65] A more reflexive assessment of Mayhew is required. Recent work has begun this, and while much of it has attempted to rethink Mayhew's location within the discursive domain of the political economy of the poor, it has opened up useful avenues of inquiry into his contribution to an understanding of their racial and cultural identity.[66] In a valuable analysis of Mayhew, Karel Williams has demonstrated that the non-unitary, unstable and unsystematic qualities of the material published in the *Morning Chronicle* and *London Labour and the London Poor* both defined its modernity and rendered impossible any essentialist reading.[67] Mayhew's approach was that of an inductive empiricist. He described himself as a mere collector of facts on the basis of which he would be able to formulate general laws governing the political economy of the poor. Classification was an essential component of this methodology, and became something of an obsession. Over time he struggled to structure the diversity of occupations into meaningful categories, but because of the absence of consistently applied empiricist techniques and an emphasis on descriptive categories this process became 'an active disorganizing principle' quite incapable of identifying causal connections between empirical variables.[68]

The diverse, promiscuous and chaotic empirical material amassed by Mayhew defied logical classification, and forced him occasionally to adopt an alternative methodology by conjuring up formal theory as a 'deductive *deus ex machina*'. This was the case when he attempted to formulate a theory of low wages, but more importantly to invoke contemporary ethnological theory. The putative distinctions between wanderers and settlers were made not on the basis of empirical material he collected, but introduced as a means of conferring status to the text and adding 'interpretative garnish to the facts'.[69] The result was that Mayhew did not attempt a radical vision of the poor, but 'simply endorsed the conventional wisdom of ethnology and identified the street folk as the wandering tribe in the midst of a civilised nation'.[70]

Here I part company with Williams, for Mayhew's use of ethnological theory cannot consistently be argued to be both an interpretative garnish and an endorsement of conventional wisdom. And it is simply not true that in *London Labour and the London Poor* Mayhew was complicit in his endorsement because he devalued the testimony of street folk and refused to represent them from their own point of view. Ethnological theory had little direct impact on Mayhew's material; indeed, for the most part the experiences recorded through personal testimony and the commentaries on them conflicted sharply with its logical suppositions.

Mayhew's treatment of costermongers provides a most appropriate test not least because it appears at the beginning of Volume I, immediately after the theoretical discussion on 'wandering tribes in general'; if ethnological theory is to be found, it is here. In a long and detailed section Mayhew described the numbers, earnings, dress, diet, language and homes of the costermongers, and more notably their culture and politics. Unsurprisingly, he introduced street sellers in terms that would have been familiar to racial theorists:

[I]t is always in those callings which are the most uncertain, that the greatest amount of improvidence and intemperance are found to exist.... Moreover, when the religious, moral, and intellectual degradation of the great majority of these fifty thousand people is impressed upon us, it becomes positively appalling to contemplate the vast amount of vice, ignorance and want, existing in these days in the very heart of our land. The public have but to read the following plain unvarnished account of the habits, amusements, dealings, education, politics, and religion of the London costermongers in the nineteenth century, and then to say whether they think it safe – even if it be thought fit – to allow men, women and children to continue in such a state.[71]

And there followed references to their 'continual warfare with force' and the 'treachery and cunning' found among 'savage nations'.[72] But this has to be seen against later arguments that stressed their qualities and the nature of the 'degradation' they are forced to suffer:

We have now had an inkling of the London costermonger's notions upon politics and religion. We have seen the brutified state in which he is allowed by society to remain though possessing the same faculties and susceptibilities as ourselves – the same power to perceive and admire the forms of truth, beauty, and goodness, as even the very highest in the state.[73]

He concluded:

My personal experience with this peculiar class [sic] justifies me in saying that they are far less dishonest than they are usually believed to be, and much more honest than their wandering habits, their want of education and 'principle' would lead even the most charitable to suppose.[74]

Most tellingly, and with a nice touch of irony, Mayhew quoted directly the words of a 'general dealer':

'You see, sir, the letters in the Morning Chronicle set people a talking, and some altered their way of business. Some were very angry at what was said in the articles on the street sellers, and swore that costers was gentlemen, and that they'd smash the men's noses that had told you, sir, if they knew who they were.'[75]

At no time was reference made to distinct physical characteristics.

Material on prostitutes, thieves and beggars was brought together in Volume IV of the series. This volume seems an anomaly. Some of the material on prostitution had appeared in the original two-volume edition of 1851, but when the volumes were expanded by the inclusion of new and recycled material on street folk, the publishers decided to place the prostitution material in a separate final volume along with sections on thieves, swindlers and beggars written by Mayhew's co-workers John Binny and

Andrew Halliday. Perhaps because of this, Volume IV has conventionally been seen as part of a distinct project.[76] In fact, it is difficult to see this as a project at all. Thieves, swindlers and beggars could legitimately be considered as street folk, even if they were numbered among Mayhew's 'those that cannot work, and those that will not work'. And although these sections were not written by Mayhew, the approach was his.

The material on prostitution, on the other hand, was quite distinct. Nearly three-quarters of it comprised a long historical survey of prostitution in various lands written by Mayhew and Bracebridge Hemyng. If there is evidence in Mayhew of a retreat from the critical edge of social inquiry to the refuge of racial ideology it is to be found here, for what is reproduced is little more than familiar perspectives gleaned from travel and evangelical writings. Those on India (included among the 'semi-civilized nations') are representative. Drawing on the notable works of people such as Buchanan, Hamilton, Grant, Ward, Mill, Heber and Dubois, the section on India surveyed in general terms the state of gender relations prior to the 1857 revolt. National characteristics, the authors claim, have much to do with 'climate and position' but more with 'government'. Under East India Company rule, it follows, we have witnessed a 'change in the manners and institutions of the people perfectly wonderful to contemplate'.[77] The abominations of child marriage, sati, and female infanticide perpetrated by the caste system have been mitigated through the efforts of the Company. The general state of women, however, has not improved, and as long as Hindus continue to revere the teachings of Manu nor is it likely to do so. The 'timid effeminate Bengalee appears of a sensual character, and regards his wife as little more than the instrument of his pleasure'. Women are therefore denied the advantages of education, and forbidden to mix with others. Among the 'more wild and barbarous tribes, as well as the more ignorant classes ... men frequently beat their wives'.[78]

Certain disjunctions exist, therefore, between the early and later Mayhew, and between commentary and oral testimony. Because of the peculiar relationship he had with the poor – much closer and more prolonged than other contemporary investigators – Mayhew came to recognize that the classificatory frameworks were inadequate if not irrelevant, and that ethnological theory was inappropriate. The sheer variety and profusion of experience he recorded increasingly challenged the crude cultural, racial and physiognomic topologies, until they collapsed under the weight. What Gagnier says of the socio-economic classification also applies to the racial:

> The road to his final, surprising analysis is one of distinctions multiplied indefinitely, until all that remains is not the abstract categories of political economists but the unique 'character' singularly embedded in its material

world, a world that Mayhew values above all other cultural configurations, classifications, and statistics. He differed from novelists of his class and time in never taking the individual 'character' as *representative* of the poor in general, but rather in multiplying their differences between one another ad infinitum.[79]

Questions on details of the socio-economic classifications employed by Mayhew – indeed on the very constituency of the poor he explored[80] – require further attention, but what is clear is that by celebrating the productivity of the poor, the *'fecund* materiality of the city',[81] he subverted contemporary perspectives. Examples abound of accounts that demonstrated the resourcefulness, physical presence, interdependence, cooperation, moral integrity and intelligence of the poor,[82] and simultaneously challenged pervasive racialized typologies of the same population as ignorant, isolated and primitive. Not until he considered 'less civilized' societies using evidence from evangelical and travel accounts did he lapse into more familiar racial categorizations (see pp. 153–5).

Mayhew's project was polymorphic.[83] Working in the troubled milieu following the 1848 revolution, the defeat of chartism, and a devastating outbreak of cholera, Mayhew – himself located contradictorily within the social formation – stood at an intersection between the radical potential of allowing the poor a voice and the regressive tendencies of racialized ethnographic theories. He went no further in realizing that potential; a variety of literary and journalistic endeavours of little note followed until his death in 1887 amidst poverty and obscurity.

His legacy is more difficult to assess. In the only study to date which attempts to present Mayhew's life and work, written at a time of renewed interest, Humpherys claims that Mayhew's innovatory contributions to social knowledge exerted no influence on his contemporaries.[84] Mayhew's investigative techniques were rapidly rendered obsolete by advances in the second half of the century. He may have been recognized and respected for the series published in the *Morning Chronicle*, but later work was largely ignored. Abrupt changes in the project and the considerable delay in publishing the collected work meant that the majority remained inaccessible to a reading public. By the time *London Labour and the London Poor* appeared, Mayhew's revelations were out of date. 'For this reason the four volume publication had practically no influence on either the sociology or the literature of the late Victorian period',[85] and by the 1860s he was at best remembered vaguely as the 'metropolitan correspondent' who revealed the plight of street sellers.

This is a harsh judgement, but justifiable if Mayhew's influence is thought as direct. His pioneering work on the London poor inspired no other sociological inquiries into metropolitan life. The next major project on poverty, Charles Booth's *London Life and London Labour*, was under-taken forty years later and bore little of the imprint of Mayhew. On the other hand, Mayhew's influence on literary genres was undeniable. The weekly editions of *London Labour and the London Poor* had sales of 13,000, the *Morning Chronicle* probably a third of that.[86] And they were widely reviewed in periodicals and the press. These responses provide insight into the real legacy. Reviewers for the most part commented on the 'strange', 'wonderful', 'piteous' and 'terrible' revelations of the unknown land, effectively appropriating Mayhew by inserting him within the traditions of travel writing and gothic fiction that were so deeply implicated in the literary imagination of the imperial formation.[87] Mayhew can be detected in Dickens, Thackeray and Kingsley, but his influence was not as the social investigator but as the source of bizarre and exotic characters. More important was the momentum given to the nascent tradition of semi-factual investigation into the metropolitan poor.

Mayhew's legacy

A variety of texts from the 1850s and 1860s reveal affinities with Mayhew. In 1853, John Garwood, secretary to the London City Mission, published *The Million Peopled City*.[88] Claiming the study to be a 'plain tale. The facts themselves are its only eloquence', Garwood included a detailed summary of an 1851 inquiry conducted by the mission into the London Irish, and long extracts from a lecture given in 1852 by the Rev. Samuel Garratt:

> A very little acquaintance with [the Irish] is sufficient to discover, in spite of all their social degradation, a peculiarity of character which would blend most usefully with their Saxon neighbours. The English labourer, with all his manliness and honesty, is often wanting in intellectual acuteness and in imaginative glow. In both these characteristics the Irish excel.... The worst parts in the character of the Irish of London are that they are idle and dirty; that they are without that honourable independence of mind which is so valuable a feature of the English character.[89]

Such sentiments may have displayed a degree of Christian sympathy with the urban poor, but of greater significance was the racialization of specific groups through identification of essential characteristics, and the fluidity of the boundaries of inclusion/exclusion operating between the groups. Here, faced with an Irish other, the English poor were readily incorporated into the Saxon race; but at times of profound anxiety for the imperial state other colonial subjects were introduced into the racial equation.

1857 was one such moment. Consider writings on the metropolitan poor around the time when the Indian revolt burst upon the psychic landscape of the English middle classes. A North American visitor, D.W.

Bartlett, some four years before 1857 described the prevalent disregard for India in a metropolis grown rich on the proceeds of wholesale plunder:

> A commercial company, called the East India Company, holds in trust for the crown this great India Empire, and has done so for many years. The iniquities which have been perpetrated upon the natives have often been exposed, but the English have never manifest national shame or repentance.... This influx of capital keeps the aristocratic classes rolling in splendour, and also renders them ... independent of the poverty-stricken condition of the English people. A panic at home does not touch them, for they lean upon India, and they can laugh when national calamity cometh.... [V]ery little is said in England about this great system of fraud and oppression save by a few men like George Thompson and John Bright. Exeter Hall resounds with eloquence directed against negro slavery – but India is passed over in silence.[90]

The revolt forced India onto the political agenda, not least by articulating – in the sense of both linking and expressing – more strikingly than heretofore anxieties around the metropolitan and colonial poor. Frederick Meyrick, a Fellow of Trinity College, Oxford, published in 1858 a series of sermons under the rubric of a compelling phrase from Psalm 82, 'Deliver the outcast and poor; save them from the hand of the ungodly'. He described vividly scenes at the London dock gates that were to become a powerful metaphor for the animalistic struggles of the metropolitan poor.[91] Such scenes, Meyrick claimed, promoted and were symptomatic of the 'two chief vices to which the Anglo-Saxon race is above other races prone', namely, 'drunkenness and mammonism – the intemperance which wallows senseless in the kennel, and the hard-heartedness which grinds the faces of the poor for the sake of adding gain to gain'.[92] We are left in no doubt, however, that despite these unfortunate propensities, the poor were included within this evangelical vision of the English race:

> My brethren, the persons ... I have cursorily described, are Englishmen – dwellers in this city – close to us – round about us.... As members of the human family, as countrymen, as men who ought to be, if they are not, Christians, they are our brethren; and it is a duty incumbent upon you to have regard for their spiritual and temporal welfare.[93]

In India, on the other hand, contemporary events had testified to the consequences of allowing a race outside the Anglo-Saxon to remain free from the healthy restraints of Christianity:

> God gave us the vast empire of India. Millions of souls He committed into the hand of England. They were sunk in debasing superstitions and immoralities, but we would not give them a better religion, or interfere with their wickedness.... And so we let them wallow on in their corruption and congratulate ourselves on our tolerance and freedom from bigotry. And then,

when we least expected it, the evil beast within them, which we had not chained by the wholesome restraints of Christian precept and example, rose up, and the demon passions which we had taken no pains to eradicate or repress awoke, and they turned the skill and craft and cleverness, which we had willingly fostered and cultivated, against ourselves, and deeds were done in the name of heaven, such as the devil and his worshippers alone can do.[94]

Later, as the reverberations from the revolt receded, Joseph Mullens, Foreign Secretary of the London Missionary Society, compared his extensive experiences of London and Calcutta. India, he claimed, had been the noblest site of missionary enterprise and Christian government. From early beginnings, the numbers of missionaries had increased rapidly, and wise and just government had provided the stability necessary for material and social prosperity. In Calcutta, however, as in London, there remained sites of degeneration almost beyond redemption:

There is a real heathenism, physically and socially degrading in the extreme; a heathenism widespread, involving myriads in its blackness, crushing all hope and purity and peace out of their life now, and leaving them hopeless in relation to a future world.... There are slums in London, known only to city missionaries and the men who work with them, in which violence and vice abound to a degree which cannot be told. But the slums of heathenism go a long way lower. They reach the very horrors of immorality.[95]

Parallels clearly existed in evangelical thought between perceptions of the conditions suffered by the metropolitan poor and colonial subjects, and of the political consequences threatened by their continued neglect. Where differences existed they were ascribed to the nature of the response of the constituencies to the Christian word. However, the fact that the metropolitan poor could be included as 'our brethren' even though not Christians, suggested that another mechanism of exclusion operated. Race was the most significant category of separation; as Mullens proceeded logically to argue, the most formidable opponent to Christianity in India was a caste system which could not be overthrown except through that 'large-hearted enlightenment which gives broad views of ... the connexion between man and man, race and race'.[96]

It was in the work of journalists, however, that the appropriation of Mayhew was most evident and a more strident racial coding occurred. Watts Phillips, an acquaintance of Mayhew, who had been in Paris at the time of the 1848 revolution, published in 1855 a popular book entitled, with ethnographic reference, The Wild Tribes of London.[97] Based on visits made to districts 'inhabited by those strange and neglected races', the sketches conveyed the full repertoire of new racial identities. Near Holborn, for example, he recalled courts which swarm with dirty unwashed men, who bear, Cain-like, on every brow a brand that warns you to avoid them – with rude, coarse women, whose wild language, fierce eyes, and strange lascivious gestures strike terror to the spectator's heart.... Children ... literally swarm about the road, half-naked, shaggy-headed little savages, who flock about you, and, with canting phrase and piteous whine, solicit charity for their dying father, – that broad shouldered, burly-looking Milesian, who has just reeled from the tavern-door.[98]

John Hollingshead, a staff member of Dickens's *Household Words* and the *Cornhill Magazine*, wrote in identical terms about a population whose history was marked by the 'five great divisions' of 'poverty, ignorance, dirt, immorality and crime':[99]

Fryingpan Alley ... is worse than anything in Whitechapel or Bethnal Green. The rooms are dustbins – everything but dwelling places. The women are masculine in appearance; they stand with coarse, folded arms and knotted hair, and are ready to fight for their castle of filth.... I should call Whitechapel by its more appropriate name of Blackchapel, and play with the East of London under the title St. Giles-in-the-Dirt.... Within a few yards of this refuge is New Court, a nest of thieves, filled with thick-lipped, broad-featured, rough-haired women, and hulking, leering men, who stand in knots, tossing for pennies, or lean against the walls at the entrances of the low courts ... The faces that peer out of the narrow windows are yellow and repulsive; some are the faces of Jews, some of Irishwomen, and some of sickly-looking infants.[100]

By 1861 these diverse racialized discourses on the metropolitan poor were being articulated into a complex whole. Within the metropolis an internal orient was perceived, prefiguring inevitable moral and physical decline not only in the metropolis itself but also in the empire:

Every year the manufactures and trade of the country will attract a greater proportion of the population into the larger towns. An actuary would predict the decade in which the deterioration and waste of the towns shall cease to be adequately sustained by healthy immigration from the country. From that moment the decadence of the British Empire will begin.[101]

The generation of social explorers in the immediate post-Mayhew period, however, is best exemplified by James Greenwood, whose career as a journalist and novelist spanned over forty years, in the course of which he published thirty-nine books and contributed numerous articles to the *Pall Mall Gazette* and the *Daily Telegraph*.[102] Greenwood began writing in the 1860s, largely in response to the devastating consequences of the severe social and economic dislocation in the metropolis attendant on financial collapse and a cholera epidemic. His investigations were based on close personal observation of the poor, made possible by the then unusual step of disguising himself as one of their number.

Writing under the pseudonyms 'The amateur casual', 'One of a crowd' and 'A London rambler', he first came to public attention in 1866 with a series of articles in the *Pall Mall Gazette* describing the horrors of a night in the casual ward of a workhouse, when he was forced to sleep on a blood-soaked mattress and converse with the other inmates.[103] There followed a steady stream of books, the titles to which suggest the impressionistic, semi-factual and racialized approach to the metropolitan poor Greenwood adopted: *Legends of Savage Life* (1866), *Seven Curses of London* (1869), *In Strange Company* (1873), *Wilds of London* (1874), *Low Life Deeps* (1875) and *The Wild Man at Home; or, Pictures of Life in Savage Lands* (1879). The description of women in the vicinities of the Costers Mission – 'A mission among city savages' – is representative of his portrayal of the metropolitan poor:

> The life that stirs in these black crooked lanes, not wider than the length of a walking stick, scarcely seems human. Creatures that you know to be female by the length and raggedness of hair that makes their heads hideous, and by their high-pitched voices, with bare red arms, and their bodies bundled in a complication of dirty rags, loll out of the patched and plastered holes in the wall that serve as windows, and exchange with their opposite neighbours compliments or blasphemous abuse.[104]

But Greenwood inhabited a broadly humanitarian perspective, and saw such cultural depravity not as an inherent immorality of the poor, but as a demoralization fostered by middle-class 'reform'. Of the 'seven curses of London', the worst was elision of boundaries between the deserving and undeserving poor by the indiscriminate distribution of charity. Even habitual violence was blamed on neglect:

> Did such accounts appear in the newspaper but rarely it might be assumed that the wanton brutality was done by some muscular blackguard who had drunk himself to the same condition of mind as the savage who, armed with a club and a hatchet, 'runs amuck' through his village, maiming and killing everyone he meets. But when such cases occur, sometimes three or four times a week, and the attendant circumstances are very much the same, one cannot help thinking that, at least in some instances, more responsible persons that men mad with drink are the evil doers.[105]

The body of semi-factual literature on the early nineteenth-century metropolitan poor constitutes a complex picture of contrast, contradiction and plurality but one in which distinct shifts are evident. In the course of the nineteenth century, and in the context of the imperial formation, the poor were constructed as a subordinate race. Around 1840 a preoccupation with the curious, bizarre and criminal propensities of the underworld was displaced by perspectives which although diverse were embedded in theorizations of the innate superiority of the bourgeois Anglo-Saxon subject over colonial and poor others.

Racial theories were rarely used by urban travellers in a consistent and rigorous way, not least because the theories themselves were riven by internal contradictions. Mayhew, for example, is generally regarded as seminal in the early construction of the poor as racially distinct, but the interpretative premises of the preface were effectively subverted by the logic of the empirical material that followed. Mayhew's legacy was to be found in a tradition of urban travel which appropriated selectively the ground he had prepared as evangelical and journalistic accounts revealed increasing evidence of racial coding. In this race was not an anterior category augmenting the inventory of elite concerns over order, citizenship and the empire, but from the outset was integral to ways in which these problems were defined and perceived, and to which solutions were sought.

In Greenwood we see the culmination of the tradition of urban exploration founded by Mayhew. Thereafter, as fears of social disorder and imperial decline took hold, the symbolic repertoires of dirt and degeneration imparted a sinister, intense and menacing turn to racialization of the poor. Faced with seemingly diverse, uncontrollable and unknowable low others, imperial theorists found in such repertoires a versatile means of transcoding physical difference into moral and cultural difference. Toward the end of the century when modernist impulses gained strength, the poor were displaced in the bourgeois imagination. The crowd and the abyss came to dominate the agenda of attempts to appropriate the metropolitan poor at a time of fragmentation and alienation. In this, however, race continued to act as a critical referent.

Notes

1 Julian Wolfreys, *Writing London. The Trace of the Urban Text from Blake to Dickens*, Basingstoke, Macmillan, 1998.
2 *Ibid.*, pp. 19, 24.
3 Pierce Egan, *Life in London*, London, Sherwood, Neely and Jones, 1821, p. vi.
4 Jonathan Crary, *Techniques of the Observer. On Vision and Modernity in the Nineteenth Century*, Cambridge, Massachusetts Institute of Technology Press, 1990.
5 *Ibid.*, p. 14.
6 I have recently gathered together the most influential texts and images in John Marriott (ed.), *Unknown London. Early Modernist Visions of the Metropolis, 1815–1845*, 6 vols, London, Pickering and Chatto, 2000.
7 Deborah Nord, *Walking the Victorian Streets. Women, Representation and the City*, Ithaca, Cornell University Press, 1995, pp. 30–3.
8 Egan, *Life in London*, p. 2.
9 *Ibid.*, p. 4.
10 *Ibid.*, p. 17.
11 *Ibid.*, p. 24.
12 *Ibid.*, p. 37.
13 Jon Bee [John Badcock], *A Living Picture of London, for 1828, and Stranger's Guide*,

London, Clarke, 1828, p. 120.

14 [John Duncombe], *The Dens of London Exposed*, London, Duncombe, 1835, p. 6.

15 George Smeeton, *Doings in London, or, Day and Night Scenes of Frauds, Frolics, Manners, and Depravities of the Metropolis*, London, Hodgson, 1828, pp. 376–8.

16 Anon., *How to Live in London; or, The Metropolitan Microscope*, London, Smith, 1828.

17 Bee, *A Living Picture of London*, p. v.

18 [John Badcock], *The London Guide, and Stranger's Safeguard*, London, Bumpus, 1818.

19 Raymond Williams, *The Country and the City*, London, The Hogarth Press, 1985, pp. 217–18; Nord, *Walking the Victorian Streets*, Chapter 2.

20 Peter J. Keating, *The Working Classes in Victorian Fiction*, London, Routledge and Kegan Paul, 1971, pp. 17–18. Significantly, however, Dickens was also a journalist, and it was in this role that he brought his considerable powers of observation to reveal the plight of the metropolitan poor. He started writing as a journalist, and although his imagination and supreme powers of observation were to find more fertile expression in the novel, they continued to be displayed in the numerous articles he continued to write on aspects of metropolitan low life. The best of these appeared in *Household Words* and *All The Year Round*, both of which were edited by Dickens. Among them were 'A walk in the workhouse', 'A December vision', and 'On duty with Inspector Field', which exposed the inhumanities of a system that condemned the poor (see Michael Slater (ed.), *The Dent Uniform Edition of Dickens' Journalism*, 3 vols, London, Dent, 1994–98, and my edited collection, *The Metropolitan Poor. Semi-Factual Accounts, 1795–1910*, 6 vols, London, Pickering and Chatto, 1999, Vol. I).

21 D.M. Lewis, *Lighten their Darkness. The Evangelical Mission to Working-Class London, 1828–1860*, New York, Greenwood Press, 1986.

22 Baptist Noel, *The State of the Metropolis Considered in a Letter to the Rt. Hon. and Right Reverend the Lord Bishop of London*, London, Nisbet, 1835.

23 *Ibid.*, p. 11. The passing reference to Benares and Calcutta masks Noel's deep and abiding interest in India. In the aftermath of emancipation and the declaration of independence by the Jamaica Baptist Union, the BMS turned with renewed attention to India. At its 1850 annual meeting he declared that although 'Hindoos were the slaves of the most complicated superstition the world has ever seen', and 'caste was a diabolical chain, holding them in servitude, inertness of mind, and foul superstition', they could not resist the superior intellect, morals and civilization of the British (cited in Catherine Hall, *Civilising Subjects. Metropole and Colony in the English Imagination, 1830–1867*, London, Polity, 2002, pp. 370–1).

24 Lewis, *Lighten their Darkness*, p. 50. Noel's findings predated the 1851 Religious Census by fifteen years. No one familiar with Noel could have been surprised by the revelations on church abstinence contained therein.

25 *Ibid.*, Appendix B, p. 279.

26 These visits were augmented by agents of the Scripture Readers' Association and the Ranyard Bible Mission, both of which were increasingly active during the 1850s. In 1860 it has been estimated that a total of 628 full-time agents were operating (*ibid.*).

27 See LCM, *Instructions to Missionaries*, reproduced in *ibid.*, Appendix E, pp. 283–4.

28 By far the most scholarly discussion on evangelical social thought is Boyd Hilton, *The Age of Atonement. The Influence of Evangelism on Social and Economic Thought, 1795–1865*, Oxford, Clarendon Press, 1988. Attitudes toward poverty are examined in Chapter 3, 'Poverty and passionate flesh'.

29 *Ibid.*, p. 79.

30 Thomas Chalmers, *Evidence before the Select Committee on Mendicity and Vagrancy in the Metropolis*, 1815; *Christian and Civic Economy of Large Towns*, Glasgow, Chalmers and Collins, 1821.

31 Chalmers to James Brown, 30 January 1819, cited in Hilton, *Age of Atonement*, p. 88.

32 M.N. Cutt, *Ministering Angels. A Study of Nineteenth Century Writings for Children*, London, Five Owls Press, 1979, p. 16. See also Edward Royle, 'Evangelicals and educa-

tion', in John Wolffe (ed.), *Evangelical Faith and Public Zeal. Evangelicals and Society in Britain, 1780–1980*, London, SPCK, 1995.

33 *Ibid.*, p. 122.

34 Egan, *Life in London*, p. 37.

35 *Ibid.*, p. 23.

36 Smeeton, *Doings in London*, p. iii.

37 *Ibid.*, p. 3.

38 Bee, *A Living Picture of London*, p. vi.

39 *Ibid.*, p. 264.

40 Noel, *The State of the Metropolis*, p. 11.

41 *Ibid.*, pp. 12–16, 24.

42 James Grant, *Sketches in London*, London, Orr, 1838, p. 320.

43 For a useful challenge to reductive representations of contemporary racism that takes due account of the complexities of theory and narrative, see P. Cohen, '"It's racism what dunnit": hidden narratives in theories of racism', in James Donald (ed.), *Race, Culture and Identity*, Milton Keynes, Open University/Harvester Press, 1992.

44 In writing this I have been mindful of Thomas's exhortation to avoid the 'Scylla of mindlessly particular conventional colonial history, which fails to move beyond the perceptions of whichever administrators or missionaries are being documented', and the 'Charybdis of colonial discourse theory which totalizes a hegemonic global ideology, neither much tainted by its conditions of production nor transformed by the pragmatics of colonial encounters and struggles' (Nicholas Thomas, *Colonialism's Culture. Anthropology, Travel and Government*, London, Polity Press, 1994, p. 60).

45 Thomas Beames, *The Rookeries of London. Past, Present and Prospective*, London, Bosworth, 1850.

46 *Ibid.*, pp. 3–4.

47 *Ibid.*, p. 45.

48 *Ibid.*, pp. 210–11.

49 *Ibid.*, p. 218.

50 A considerable body of literature now exists on the emergence of racial theories. I have found particularly useful Douglas A. Lorimer, *Colour, Class and the Victorians. English Attitudes to the Negro in the Mid-Nineteenth Century*, Leicester, Leicester University Press, 1978; idem, 'Race, science and culture: historical continuities and discontinuities, 1850–1914', in S. West (ed.), *The Victorians and Race*, London, Scolar Press, 1996; Kenan Malik, *The Meaning of Race. Race, History and Culture in Western Society*, Basingstoke, Macmillan, 1996; Robert Young, *Colonial Desire. Hybridity in Theory, Culture and Race*, London, Routledge, 1995.

51 Malik, *The Meaning of Race*, p. 72.

52 Paul Gilroy has argued persuasively for the necessity of rethinking modernity in the light of an experience of slavery actively legitimated by racial theory (*The Black Atlantic. Modernity and Double Consciousness*, London, Verso, 1993). The same argument obtains for the experience of imperial conquest.

53 R. Knox, *The Races of Men. A Fragment*, London, Renshaw, 1850, p. 6, cited in H.A. MacGougall, *Racial Myth in English History. Trojans, Teutons and Anglo-Saxons*, Montreal, Harvest House, 1982, p. 91, which explores intelligently the Anglo-Saxon myth of origin.

54 Malik, *The Meaning of Race*, p. 81.

55 For a useful elaboration of these idea see the endnotes to Barnor Hesse, 'White governmentality: urbanism, nationalism, racism', in Sally Westwood and John Williams (eds), *Imagining Cities. Scripts, Signs, Memory*, London, Routledge, 1997.

56 Henry Mayhew, *London Labour and the London Poor*, 4 vols, London, Cass, 1967 [1861–62], Vol. I, p. 1.

57 Gertrude Himmelfarb, *The Idea of Poverty. England in the Early Industrial Age*, London, Faber, 1984, p. 568.

58 Mayhew, *London Labour*, Vol. I, p. 2. See also the useful discussion in Himmelfarb, *The Idea of Poverty*, pp. 323–32.

59 *Ibid.*, p. 2.

60 T. Barringer, 'Images of otherness and the visual production of difference: race and labour in illustrated texts, 1850–1865', in West (ed.), *The Victorians and Race*.

61 J.C. Prichard, *The Natural History of Man; Comprising Inquiries into the Modifying Influence of Physical and Moral Agencies on the Different Tribes of the Human Families*, London, Bailliere, 1843.

62 Recent work on Prichard includes Lorimer, *Colour, Class and the Victorians*, pp. 134–7; Nancy Stepan, *The Idea of Race in Science. Great Britain 1800–1960*, London, Macmillan, 1982, pp. 29–39; Young, *Colonial Desire*, pp. 10–15.

63 Equally significantly, Mayhew displayed a cavalier use of the term race, and one inconsistent with that of Prichard. He claimed at the outset, for example, that humans are divided into two races, but then proceeded to argue that wanderers in England are part of the same community as 'the more industrious', later referring to them occasionally as a 'class', 'body', 'horde' or 'order'. Such lack of conceptual rigour was in part the product of Mayhew's casual use of ethnological theory, but is more appropriately seen as symptomatic of the estranged relationship between evidence and theory in his own writings.

64 See, for example, Himmelfarb, *The Idea of Poverty*, Chapter 14 (although she is aware of some of the difficulties), and Henrika Kuklick, *The Savage Within. The Social History of British Anthropology, 1885–1945*, Cambridge, Cambridge University Press, 1992, p. 100.

65 Lorimer, *Colour, Class and the Victorians*, pp. 41–3.

66 Barringer, 'Images of otherness'; Bernard O. Taithe, *The Essential Mayhew. Representing and Communicating the Poor*, London, Rivers Oram, 1996; Regina Gagnier, *Subjectivities. A History of Self-Representation in Britain, 1832–1920*, Oxford, Oxford University Press, 1991; Anne Humphreys, *Travels into the Poor Man's Country. The Work of Henry Mayhew*, Maryland, University of Georgia Press, 1977; Karel Williams, *From Pauperism to Poverty*, London, Routledge, 1981.

67 Williams, *From Pauperism to Poverty*.

68 *Ibid.*, p. 241.

69 *Ibid.*, p. 242.

70 *Ibid.*, p. 261.

71 *Ibid.*, p. 6.

72 *Ibid.*, p. 16.

73 *Ibid.*, p. 25.

74 *Ibid.*, p. 31.

75 *Ibid.*, p. 33. This quotation suggests that Mayhew's works were known to the costers. Evidence exists also from a meeting of ticket-of-leave men organized by Mayhew at Farringdon Hall in January 1857. One of an audience estimated at ninety stated that Mr Mayhew was 'making capital out of them all ... this ingenious gentleman merely gets them together in order to "suck their brains" and make up pretty stories for publication'. *The Times'* leader which reported the meeting suggested that it should have been held at Drury Lane (29 January 1857).

76 Williams deals with some of the arguments, but concludes that the fourth volume reinstated one of Mayhew's projects by providing an excuse for a piece of 'dirty journalism' – another example of Victorian soft porn (Williams, *From Pauperism to Poverty*, pp. 272–4).

77 Mayhew, *London Labour and the London Poor*, Vol. IV, p. 116.

78 *Ibid.*, p. 117.

79 Gagnier, *Subjectivities*, p. 84.

80 Mayhew's subjects were what he called the street folk – the relatively small 'wandering tribe' of musicians, beggars, sweepers, and so on – rather than the labouring poor or the pauper population as a whole.

81 The phrase is Gagnier's, *Subjectivities*, p. 86.

82 Exactly the same arguments apply to the visual imagery which was such an important part of Mayhew's project. Illustrations of the poor defy neat racial classification, and their sheer diversity defies any sense of an internal coherence necessary for construction of an other (Barringer, 'Images of otherness').

83 See Taithe, *The Essential Mayhew* – a curious title given the general thrust of the arguments, even though he claims that in the 'Answers to correspondents' printed on the covers to weekly instalments of *London Labour and the London Poor* over 1851–52 is to be found the key to Mayhew's project.

84 Humpherys, *Travels into the Poor Man's Country*, pp. 163–94.

85 *Ibid.*, pp. 165–6.

86 Himmelfarb, *The Idea of Poverty*, p. 355.

87 See, for example, P. Brantlinger, *Rule of Darkness. British Literature and Imperialism, 1830–1914*, Ithaca, Cornell University Press, 1988.

88 John Garwood, *The Million Peopled City, or One Half of the People of London Made Known to the Other Half*, London, Wertheim and Macintosh, 1853.

89 *Ibid.*, pp. 256, 263.

90 D.W. Bartlett, *What I Saw in London; or, Men and Things in the Great Metropolis*, Auburn, Derby and Miller, 1853, pp. 315–17.

91 Frederick Meyrick, *The Outcast and the Poor of London; or, Our Present Duties Toward the Poor: a Course of Sermons*, London, Rivingtons, 1858, p. 35.

92 *Ibid.*, p. 45.

93 *Ibid.*, p. 17.

94 *Ibid.*, p. 241.

95 Joseph Mullens, *London and Calcutta, Compared in their Heathenism, their Privileges and their Prospects*, London, Nisbet, 1869, pp. 16, 53.

96 *Ibid.*, p. 135.

97 Watts Phillips, *The Wild Tribes of London*, London, Ward and Lock, 1855.

98 *Ibid.*, pp. 10, 12.

99 John Hollingshead, *Ragged in London in 1861*, London, Smith, Elder and Co., 1861, p. 8. The book comprised a collection of articles previously published in the *Morning Post* under the title 'London horrors'. Interestingly, the pathology anticipated the five giants in postwar Britain that the Beveridge Report attempted to tackle, although Beveridge was a little more reticent about the morality.

100 *Ibid.*, pp. 30, 39, 44.

101 H.O. Davies, *'The Way Out'. A Letter Addressed (by permission) to The Earl of Derby in which the Evils of the Overcrowded Town Hovel and the Advantages of the Suburban Cottage are Constrained*, London, Longman Green, 1861, p. 6.

102 For a general assessment of Greenwood see Keating, *The Working Classes in Victorian Fiction*; the introduction by J. Richards in the reprint of Greenwood's *The Seven Curses of London*, London, Blackwell, 1981; and J.W. Robertson Scott, *The Story of the Pall Mall Gazette*, Oxford, Oxford University Press, 1950.

103 The articles were subsequently reprinted in full by *The Times* and as a book, *A Night in the Workhouse* (1866). They created a sensation. The editor of the *Morning Post*, Sir William Hardman, declared that he would rather 'brave a Crimean campaign or an Indian Mutiny than undertake such a deed of daring', and thought Greenwood was entitled to the Victoria Cross. *The Spectator*, on the other hand, remarked that 'the "Amateur casual" had spent only one night under conditions to which hundreds of his countrymen were condemned any day of their lives'. Stead, who himself was later to create the odd journalistic sensation or two in the pages of the *Pall Mall Gazette*, stated that from 'the storm of indignation' over 'that one night in a casual ward may be traced the beginning of the reform of our Poor Law' (Robertson Scott, *The Story of the Pall Mall Gazette*, pp. 168–9).

104 James Greenwood, *In Strange Company; being the Experiences of a Roving Correspondent*, London, King, 1874, pp. 14–15.

105 James Greenwood, *The Policeman's Lantern. Strange Stories of London Life*, London, Scott, 1888, p. 39.

CHAPTER FIVE

So immense an empire

A new mode of observation

As we have seen, many of the anxieties of imperial rule in India were played out in the debates leading up to 1813. The inclusion of the 'pious clause' in the East India Company's charter may have been hailed as a victory by the evangelical cause, but it signalled a limited acceptance that missionary endeavour could promote social and religious reform and hence consolidate British authority. Minimally, it suggested that fears of insurgency provoked by undue interference in Indian culture were temporarily suspended. The most significant consequence of the debates, however, was the emergence of a certain consensus on the nature of imperial rule, linked to particular conceptions of the colonized and to-be-colonized Indian peoples.

An emphasis in the literature on the high politics of these debates has led to the neglect of another critical intervention made by the Company at the time. On the orders of the Court of Directors in 1807 the Government of Bengal instigated a survey of the 'Eastern territories'. 'We are of the opinion', the Court declared, 'that a statistical survey of the country, under the immediate authority of your Presidency, would be attended with much utility.'[1] Dr Francis Buchanan, who had previously been involved in a survey of Mysore in the immediate aftermath of its fall to the British,[2] was appointed to take responsibility.

Buchanan recorded details of religion, condition of the people, agriculture, commerce, progress in arts and manufactures, and natural history found in the region.[3] The full survey, completed in 1816, was never published in its entirety, largely because relations between Buchanan and the Company had so deteriorated that work on editing and revision was no longer possible. Instead, Robert Montgomery Martin later published selections from the vast archives deposited in East India House. The 'intrinsic merit' of the survey has not diminished in the intervening twenty-two years, he suggested, since 'a few years makes no difference in the manners and habits of the people'.[4]

This survey – comprehensive, intricate, diligent – represents something of a departure in the production of knowledge on India. Until the late eighteenth century orientalist interests in ancient language and culture had prevailed. With the expansion of British control and the attendant demands for an efficient and informed administrative system, however, new types of knowledge were necessary. In its attempt to quantify peasant production, Henry Colebrooke's *Remarks on the Present State of Husbandry in Bengal* (1795) signalled a concern for information more directly related to the exigencies of managing land revenue. It provided the pattern for future surveys.[5] At one level, therefore, Buchanan's survey can be viewed as an imperial project. The accumulation of empirical material was the most determined attempt heretofore to know the Indian landscape and village life better to exercise economic and political authority.[6]

Equally, and to an extent autonomously of imperial exigencies, the survey represented a new mode of observation akin to that taking place in the metropolitan context. There were continuities with previous knowledge-producing processes, but in surveys the accumulation and commodification of observable materials as a scientific enterprise to know India was quite novel. A comparison with travel writings is instructive. As we have seen, this early genre did often valorize the act of first-hand observation in recording landscape and people. This was a process framed by the aesthetic, in particular the picturesque, which was designed to elicit emotional responses from the viewer through the delicate manipulation of natural imagery. The alien landscape of India was susceptible to the operation of this visual hegemony, and so picturesque representations gained a reputation for accuracy and objectivity. The scientific, geographical gaze, in contrast, was characterized by the 'empiricist rhetoric of observation'.[7] Here the focus was on the everyday rather than the novel, which was recorded mechanistically and faithfully – a statement of facts deriving from the visual, with little room for analysis. Images, maps, censuses and surveys, as well as the categories of knowledge from which they were constructed, all resulted from this desire to observe in a rational, ordered and coherent manner.[8] This vision, however, was neither secure nor comprehensive. Buchanan could not have undertaken the survey single-handedly; when circumstances demanded it he was forced to rely on the evidence of other surveyors employed on the project, or indigenous informants:

> In the town of Danapur the native officer of police, under the authority of the general, gave a statement of the number of houses. With regard to the other parts of the district I have followed the same plan that I did in Bhagalpur and Puraniya: from various statements and considerations I have conjectured the number of men required to cultivate each division, and then made

an allowance for the other classes of society according to estimates given by the most intelligent persons that I could procure. In doing this, however, I experienced much difficulty.[9]

Because none of the informants observed in the same way as Buchanan, no matter how well briefed, he dismissed some of their evidence on local history and culture as nonsensical, confused or exaggerated.[10] Where the data were incomplete or thought to be unreliable he resorted to averaging. Many of the estimates of population were devised in this way. Such evidence severely compromised the reliability of the survey, but these inadequacies could easily be masked within the framing narrative. Different types of evidence were brought together into a seamless, authoritative whole. Less reliable sources could thereby be incorporated into a single truth derived from personal observation that was often endowed with even greater authority by dating it according to a precise chronology. In those areas where Buchanan could not rely on first-hand evidence, the whole system seemed on the point of collapse. He did not visit Assam, for example, and was forced to rely on evidence over which he had no authority:

> The following account was collected partly from several natives of Bengal, who on different occasions had visited Asam [sic]; and partly from natives of that country, who were fugitives in Bengal. Some of the former had resided long in Asam, and had connections there, whose office gave the opportunity of being well informed.... The accounts on all points did not agree, nor can I be certain, that I have on all occasions been able to select the parts that approach nearest the truth.[11]

Buchanan's topographical surveys reached far into those inaccessible spaces beyond the military routes mapped by Rennell's project. He included detailed descriptions of such features as rivers, marshes, roads, hills and meteorology. The streets of Gaya in Bihar, for example, are described in terms that would have been familiar to many London residents:

> The streets are narrow, crooked, dirty, uneven, and often filled with large blocks of stone or projecting angles of rock, over which the people have for ages clambered, rather than take the trouble to remove such impediments. In some places an attempt has been made at paving, and in the rainy season it may be of use to keep people from being ingulphed; but in dry weather the inequalities of such rude work harbour all manner of filth.[12]

Likewise, his description of the poor in Patna:

> The necessitous poor are abundantly numerous, and their condition is nearly similar to that of the unfortunate of Bhagalpur, the doctrine of caste producing the same evils. The people here are however more straitened in the means of giving relief to the necessitous by an enormous number of religious men-

dicants, whose impudent importunity exceeds the usual measure of patience.... Many people, who are really necessitous, finding themselves deprived of assistance by these religious mendicants, have assumed the character, which must be considered a very venial offence.[13]

More important to contemporary knowledge of India was the publication in 1815 of Walter Hamilton's *East India Gazetteer*.[14] By this time the gazetteer was firmly established as a compendium of geographical and related information, and Hamilton simply adapted to India the example set by Brookes and Crutwell. His intention was to provide a 'summary and popular account of India', gleaned from the more important published materials, 'for the perusal of those who have never visited that quarter of the world, and whose leisure has not admitted of their examining the numerous volumes in which local descriptions are dispersed'.[15] For Hamilton it was a propitious moment. Until recently, he argued, the vicissitudes of Indian politics and ceaselessly changing boundaries had rendered any such venture impractical, but there was now a degree of stability, and although 'territorial divisions continue in many places perplexed ... these obstacles are not of such weight as to preclude an attempt to class the whole alphabetically'. It was an initiative that was to have significant long-term consequences for the production of knowledge of India.

For some, the hard empiricism of such surveys did little to further understanding of India. It was from a desire at this time to locate the accumulated knowledge on India within a wider theoretical framework that James Mill wrote his massive *The History of British India*.[16] At first glance there appears little rationale for the inclusion of the *History*. Mill remained hostile to accounts of India written by travellers and evangelicals, and set himself beyond the reach of the nascent visual epistemology. As far as he was concerned, a 'duly qualified' man could 'obtain more knowledge of India in one year in his closet in England than he could obtain during the course of longest life, by the use of his eyes and ears in India'.[17] Alien cultures could therefore be better understood at a distance; close contact only compromises objectivity. Furthermore, Mill's project to provide universal principles of progress was informed overwhelmingly by Benthamite utilitarianism. And yet the representations of Indian culture and society, in particular the damning indictment of Hinduism, drew upon diverse previous writings – including those of evangelicals – and were to exert a powerful influence over much subsequent thought.

It is tempting to view this influence as hegemonic. Ronald Inden, for example, has argued that indologists throughout the nineteenth century reiterated Mill's construct of India or debated with his ghost. Company servants at Haileybury College found the *History* required reading.[18] It was so because Mill's attempt to formulate the principles of progress on rational grounds confirmed India's subordination to European civilization, and legitimated British rule as the solution to the country's traditional backwardness.[19] Savagely critical though he was of orientalists in using myth and legend to reconstruct and celebrate India's past, and of the idiosyncratic excesses of Company rule, Mill employed their knowledge to reveal the irrationality of Indian society, and the necessity of combatting it with reformed imperial rule. In so doing, he defined the essential qualities of India as village life, the caste system, political tyranny and religious superstition.

A more recent revisionist account has questioned the confidence of Mill's putative project to use India as a laboratory for utilitarianism. Because of the ambivalent nature of philosophical radicalism, Javed Majeed contends, utilitarianism had only a limited impact on British rule in India.[20] Nowhere is this illustrated better than in the edition of the *History* edited by Horace Hyman Wilson, who defends orientalism against the 'harsh and illiberal spirit' of the book. And if India was the focus of Mill's attention, it was used as a vehicle with which to attack the history of English laws, and so to arrive at general principles governing all national forms. Little of this was recognized by nineteenth-century accounts. Remembered selectively were the fierce denunciations of Indian society and custom which, although hardly novel, were endowed by Mill with the status of philosophical rationality. Important too was his positioning of India in a particular scale of civilization. The scale may have been distinct in that it was calibrated by the pursuit of utility demonstrated by individual nations, but the outcome was the same – India was a paternal despotism, positioned in a hierarchy of progress between societies of savage independence and those of Europe. Indeed, Mill went as far as to deny the claims of orientalists that Indian culture had ancient roots of great sophistication. To the contrary, since ancient times India, because of lack of liberty and individuality, had not advanced. It was immature, weak and primitive – a *tabula rasa* upon which British rule could write advantageously to reform and progress India along the path of enlightened civilization. Such arguments, *mutatis mutandis*, were readily appropriated by evangelicals and Company servants.

The privilege of the traveller

It was within this shifting climate that evangelical and travel narratives strove toward a degree of maturity. In the period 1811–22 William Ward's studies of Hindu culture, for example, displayed a more determined effort to comprehend the seeming diversity of material he had accumulated (pp. 94–5). This was part of a more general trend that impacted also on travel writings. Something of their interrelationship is suggested by the fact that 1813 witnessed not only the passing of the pious clause in the Company's charter but also the publication of James Forbes's *Oriental Memoirs*, the substantial volumes of which mark a defining moment in travel literature of India.[21]

Forbes first arrived in India as a Company servant in 1765, leaving nearly twenty years later having made his fortune. As a keen traveller, diligent observer and amateur naturalist, he took an obsessive interest in the contemporary natural and human landscape of India. Observations were recorded in an extensive series of letters supplemented by a large number of drawings, which Forbes prepared for publication after his return to England. During this time he read voraciously on India, and became increasingly involved in debates on the future of missionary work, publishing in 1810 a treatise advocating the necessity of converting the Hindu population.[22] Forbes therefore drew promiscuously on a variety of influences to produce a heterogeneous knowledge of India:

> As to the method I have taken in this work, it is unconfined, such being the privilege of the traveller; not bounded within the narrow terms of an historian, nor loosely extravagant, like poetical fictions; but suited both to time and place, and agreeable to the nature of the relation; which, though it may make some unevenness of style, as where the ruggedness of the way interposes, or the subject matter is varied, it must happen; ... though I do declare my desire is, to shew my diligence in collecting, and sincerity in compiling, what may make the road more easy to the next adventurers, and satisfy the present inquirers.[23]

In sensuous and romantic descriptions of its flora and fauna, constant reference is made to orientalist writings. Similar impulses are evident in his observations on Indian society, where he freely uses extracts from previous writings 'to add value and authenticity to the work', but in the event produces an often awkward mix of statistics, first-hand observation, impressions, fragmented historical narrative, illustration and information from villagers. His description of Malabar women is a good example:

> Their black glossy hair, tied in a knot on the middle of the head, is copiously anointed with cocoa-nut oil, and perfumed with the essence of sandal, mogrees, and champahs; their ears, loaded with rings and heavy jewels, reach almost to their shoulders; this is esteemed a beauty.... Round their waist they wear a loose piece of muslin, while the bosom is entirely exposed; this is the only drapery of the Malabar women; but they are adorned with a profusion of gold and silver chains for necklaces, mixed with strings of Venetian and other gold coins.... Their skin is softened by aromatic oils.[24]

Overarching the *Memoirs*, however, was a nascent belief in the backwardness of Indian society and the concomitant necessity of conversion to Christianity. In ways emblematic of the shift from orientalist to hard-line evangelical perspectives, early attractions to the novelty and innocence of Indian character are gradually displaced by disdain. Forbes himself recognized this change. 'There was a time', he claimed, 'when I loved and venerated the character of a brahmin, leading a tranquil, innocent and studious life under the sacred groves.' But experience as a collector and district judge gave Forbes the opportunity of 'scrutinizing the Hindoo character', and his 'opinion materially changed':

> Their cruelty, avarice, craftiness, and duplicity, occasioned a thousand grievances, which I could neither counteract nor redress; and displayed such shocking traits, rooted and strengthened by religious opinions, prejudices of caste, and habits of oppression, as baffled all my endeavours to relieve the poor Ryots, suffering under their tyranny.[25]

Embittered, Forbes on his return to England embarked on extensive studies of Indian history and culture which merely confirmed his prejudices on India's location in the historical order. Relying for the most part on lengthy extracts from previous work, the arguments may have lacked originality or insight, but they gained weight from being based on the personal experience of a diligent observer who had undergone the experience of conversion:

> Civilization, as far as the Malabars are susceptible to it, has long attained its height: Egypt, Assyrian, Persian, Greece, and Rome, from the pinnacle of grandeur, perfection in the fine arts, and the luxury of opulence, have dwindled to a name: the Malabars seem to have been for some thousand years in the same state of mediocrity: on such a system, no new designs in building, no alteration in manners or dress, no improvements in art or science, are to be expected. This may be alleged of a great part of the world besides; but I do not compare the Negroes and Hottentots of Africa, nor the savages of America, with the natives of India, or the generalities of the Asiatics: these are certainly placed on a higher scale.[26]

Consistent with mainstream evangelism, Forbes concluded that Christianity would guarantee the stability of the Raj, promote commerce, and bring India into modern civilization. Hinduism was seen increasingly as a barrier to this project, as a result of which what prevails is a sombre and apocalyptic vision of a heathen India redeemable only through the destruction of its entire way of life.

As the British consolidated control over Indian territories so the opportunities for travel increased. Among the new generation of travel writers that appeared in the early decades of the nineteenth century there was the same struggle to comprehend the diversity of Indian society. Conspicuous was the presence of women, most of whom had experience of extensive travel abroad.[27] Conscious of their strategy to assert themselves as intrepid and self-confident travellers in their own right, these women sought to provide knowledge that was framed broadly by orientalist perspectives but derived from privileged access to areas seemingly beyond the preserve of men. In her *Journal of a Residence in India* (1813) Maria Graham contrasted her role as a 'mere idle or philosophical observer' of India to that of imperial agents:

> [T]he greater part are too constantly occupied with the cares and duties of their respective vocations as statesmen, soldiers, or traders, to pay much attention to what is merely curious or interesting to a contemplative spectator.... Almost all our modern publications on the subject of India, are entirely occupied with its political and military history, – details and suggestions upon its trade and commercial resources, – and occasionally with discussions upon the more recondite parts of its literary or mythological antiquities.[28]

In the ensuing pages, however, Graham soon disavows any notion that she is an idle recorder of the curious and anecdotal. She brings to bear an extensive knowledge of orientalist research, which she uses to compare her own observations, or to identify gaps which are then filled by detailed observation and information from native informants. In contrast to Forbes, she decried the prejudice displayed by many Britons, and continued to hold in high esteem the achievements of Indian culture. Progress for her depended less on the civilizing mission of the British, than on a reawakening of ancient morality:

> Our missionaries are very apt to split upon this rock, and in order to place our religion in the brightest light ... they lay claim exclusively to all the sublime maxims of morality, and tell those who they wish to convert, that their own books contain nothing but abominations, the belief that they must abandon in order to receive the purer doctrine of Christianity. Mistaken men! Could they desire a better opening to their hopes than to find already established that morality which says, it is enjoined to man even at the moment of destruction to wish to benefit his foes, '*as the sandal tree in the instant of its overthrow sheds perfume on the axe that fells it*'. In short I consider morality like the science and arts, to be only slumbering not forgotten in India; and that to awaken the Hindus to a knowledge of the treasures in their own hands is the only thing wanting to set them fairly in the course of improvement with other nations. Everywhere in the ancient Hindu books we find the maxims of that pure and sound morality which is found on the nature of man as a rational and social being.[29]

Few could match Graham's erudition. More common were impressionistic accounts of Indian life and character that drew upon and consolidated pejorative rhetoric. First sights, so often from the vantage point of the boat approaching Calcutta, were recorded with a particular sense of wonder and bewilderment. Lady Maria Nugent reached India early in 1812, and recorded her observations in terms virtually identical to those of Jemima Kindersley nearly thirty years earlier:

> We can see a long line of low coast, and this is Saugur Island. Many ships are lying in the road. Several fishing boats came, with fresh fish, which was a great treat. The fishermen were a very dark olive, almost black, with very slight figures, but very good countenances. They were dressed in turbans, and had large muslin shawls round them, but they throw this off, when at work, and have only a bit round their waists.... They look like a mild innocent race of people, but I should imagine, from their listless manner, that they are without any energy of character.... In the morning, they seemed to be very sensitive of the cold, for they wrapped the coarse muslin, or cotton shawls round them, and squatted down like so many monkies, smoking a sort of odd shaped pipe called a hookah; but they sung occasionally, and seemed very merry.... In the middle of the day, they all jumped up, as if by word of command, and began to sing; then they set to work to mend their nets.... They make as much use of their feet as their hands, and both are as small and delicate as a woman's – indeed, the only thing that makes them look like men, is their whiskers, and they are immense.[30]

A similar rhetoric is later employed to describe the good Lady's 'poor outcast' chambermaid with telling effect:

> She never makes her appearance, unless called for by the ayah, but sits squatting like a cat on the back stairs, with a long veil, which covers not only her head, face and shoulders, but her whole person – her dress is a coarse petticoat, very full, and plaited around her, like a Dutch woman's, and so long that it covers her feet – then the veil I have just mentioned covers the rest of the dress, concealing almost every thing but her eyes; – her arms are covered with silver bracelets, and are really remarkably pretty, and well shaped, otherwise she would be hideously ugly, and her caste is held in the greatest contempt by all the natives.[31]

This complex discourse singling out low-caste Indian women as particular objects of disgust stood in sharp contrast to comments on fair-skinned Indian women who were invariably described as possessing such exquisite features and soft expressions that differences from European complexions were soon forgotten. This was so because within this discourse race was articulated to class, gender and sexuality. William Huggins, for example, was so taken with the beauty of some Indian women at fairs that he overcame objections to their dark complexions. In noting that upper-caste Brahmin women were the most attractive, lowest-caste women the least, he commented that

> this is easily accounted for: the one live retired, feed daintily, and have abundant time to devote to the care of their persons and improvement of their charms; the other, exposed to the sun and weather, become dark and coarse,

assuming a figure that corresponds with their harassing duties and lowly condition.[32]

Occasionally, this coding acquired even greater complexity through an articulation to evangelical concerns about the effects of heathenism on the Indian people. Here is Mary Sherwood describing her reaction to the sight of women on the streets of Madras:

> The character of the countenances which are seen is such as I have never beheld in an English woman. The old women especially are fearful to look upon; their skin is shrivelled and hanging loose, the lips thin and black, and the whole expression that of persons hardened by misery and without hope, having in youth exhausted all that life can give ... all this evident misery, without counting the many secret cruelties which abound in every heathen land, in every dark corner of the earth, being the effect, either direct or indirect, of those abominable creeds which we think it an act of charity not merely to tolerate but to patronise.[33]

While acknowledging the particular horror she felt on first seeing Madras women, Sherwood felt unable to account for it

> unless it may be from this circumstance that even in Europe degradation of character is always more evident (as it is more irrecoverable) in a female than in a man. As religion, whether true or otherwise, has more influence on the female mind than on that of men, so the abominable administrators of a corrupt worship have a much stronger and more detestable influence over the minds of the weaker than the stronger sex.[34]

It is misleading to suggest, however, that all travel accounts of this period demonstrated such explicit racial coding. The hugely popular narrative of Bishop Heber, published in 1828, was written in a spirit of genuine sympathy for Indian people.[35] Compare, for example, the description of boatmen encountered on his arrival in Calcutta with those above:

> [T]he crew were chiefly naked, except for a cloth around their loins; the colour of all was the darkest shade of antique bronze, and together with the elegant forms and well turned limbs of many among them, gave the spectator a perfect impression of Grecian statues of that metal.... Two observations struck me forcibly; first, that the deep bronze tint is more naturally agreeable to the human eye than the fair skins of Europe ... The second observation was, how entirely the idea of indelicacy, which would naturally belong to such figures as those now around us if they were white, is prevented by their being of a different colour from ourselves. So much are we children of association and habit, and so instinctively and immediately do our feelings adapt themselves to a total change of circumstances; it is the partial and inconsistent change only which affects us.[36]

By the time Reginald Heber was appointed as Bishop of Calcutta in 1823 he was an experienced European traveller, and almost immediately embarked on extensive travels over India. His death in an accident three years later silenced one of the more humane commentators on Indian society. Although Heber's private letters tend to reveal harsh judgements on Hinduism in keeping with his evangelical leanings, the travel diaries convey a sense of a sympathetic project to understand difference and diversity. In this he was quite prepared to challenge received wisdom:

> I have ... understood from many quarters that the Bengalees are regarded as the greatest cowards in India; and that partly owing to this reputation, and partly to their inferior size, the Sepoy regiments are always recruited from Bahar and the Upper Provinces. Yet that little army with which Lord Clive did such wonders, was chiefly raised in Bengal. So much are all men creatures of circumstance and training.[37]

Indeed, many pejorative characterizations of Indians are either dismissed by Heber or understood as rational responses to the economic, religious and political conditions they were forced to endure. There is little sense of the innate or hereditary. Unlike the response of Forbes to prolonged contact with Indians, Heber's impression of Indian society seems to grow more favourable. Overall, the impression he conveys is of a people active, charitable, loyal and affectionate; divested of heathen propensities, they would prove superior to Europeans.

From the sheer diversity of published accounts emerged what was arguably the first attempt to provide a comprehensive guide to India for the general reader. As we have seen, previous surveys had been undertaken, but they were regional and specialist in nature; the archives of Buchanan still lay hidden in the vaults of East India House. In 1820 Walter Hamilton used the material gathered for his *East India Gazetteer* to 'reduce the Geography of Hindostan to a more systematic form'. Thirty years had passed since the appearance of Rennell, during which time the revolution in 'our knowledge' had rendered many of his observations obsolete. Furthermore, the supremacy of British rule was now so complete that India must be viewed not as a 'mere assemblage of Nabobs, Sultans and Rajas, but as a component portion of the British empire'.[38] The result was *A Geographical, Statistical and Historical Description of Hindostan*. This epistemological appropriation, however, was not without problems. Much extant knowledge was suppressed or was selected in pursuit of political objectives which have little contemporary relevance, as a result of which it is unreliable and incomplete. 'It is impossible', Hamilton is forced to conclude, thereby revealing the limits of any such endeavour, 'to describe so vast and populous a country in a small compass, or by a few phrases, some of which apply universally.' His objective was rather more modest and contingent:

It is obvious ... that a satisfactory delineation of so immense an empire must be the result of a progressive accumulation of facts, and that acquiescence on the prior details of accidental travellers tends to perpetuate errors. Many of the statements here collected will probably require future correction, many remote tracts and sources in information remain to be explored, and new discoveries hereafter will disturb and confound all previous systems and arrangements.[39]

In the event, even this overstated Hamilton's ambitions. The book ultimately was a work of synthesis intended for 'persons who have never visited India'. As in the *Gazetteer*, information was gleaned and presented from orientalist researches, regional surveys, evangelical tracts and East India Company archives, inevitably transmitting much of their ideological baggage. Hamilton found Bengalese, for example, a

lively, handsome race of men; there is also a softness in their features, corresponding to the general mildness, or perhaps, pusillanimity of their character; and were it not for the uncharitable operation of caste, they would ... be a friendly and inoffensive race.... As subjects they are quiet, patient, industrious, and governed with a facility almost incredible; and that one European may sleep secure, amidst a million of Bengalese, without a lock on his door, or a weapon of offence in his vicinity. We mention this as a notorious matter of fact, experienced by every European of character, who has ever resided among the genuine Bengalese, remote from the contamination of Calcutta, and of European society.[40]

Indian society, however, remains resistant to modernization. Its sense of the past derives from traditions 'preserved among ignorant people' or from 'monstrous fables'. Hindus, in sum, have 'nothing deserving with the name of history'. Their ideas 'run equally counter to all European notions of civil liberty'; indeed, the very idea 'never seems to have been contemplated, and is to this day without a name in the languages of India'.[41] Hamilton concludes:

On the British Government will devolve the task of inculcating the principles of mild and equitable rule, distinct notions of social observances, and just sense of moral obligations, the progressive result of which must inevitably be the adoption of a purer and more sublime system of religion.[42]

The demand for general guides to India was partially sated also by the publication in 1825 of a revised edition of Williamson's *The General East India Guide and Vade Mecum*. Edited by J. Borthwich Gilchrist, the former Professor of Hindoostanee at Fort William College, it aimed to simplify the original by omitting now familiar details on Indian sects, languages and literature.[43] The most significant revision, however, was its attempt to standardize Hindi orthography. Gilchrist included – rather incongruously

– a discussion of the 'vulgar mode of spelling Hindustanee' and long extracts from his *Collection of Dialogues English and Hindoostane* which had originaly been published in 1804 as part of a project to establish Hindi as a preferred language of command.[44]

Formal recognition was finally bestowed on the world traveller with the publication in 1828 of Josiah Conder's multi-volume *The Modern Traveller*.[45] In contrast to older travel accounts which are 'amusing and often valuable, but abound with obsolete errors and are barren of scientific information', Conder asserted, information in this collection was given in a succinct and popular form with accurate references.[46] India, which occupied the first four volumes, presented a particular problem for the editors, for in spite of the work of Rennell, military writings and trigonometrical surveys, our geographical and statistical knowledge remained in an 'extremely crude and imperfect state'. In addition, although numerous valuable studies of India's history and religion had appeared in transactions and journals, 'little or nothing has been effected in the competent and scientific arrangement of these stores of information'.

Demonstrating none of Hamilton's reticence, Conder plunders previous works shamelessly. Material on history and natural history is little more than a reworking of Rennell, Robertson, Mill, Ward, Hamilton, Prinsep and Elphinstone, while that on topography relies almost exclusively on Buchanan, Forbes and the travel writings of Heber and Graham. Underpinning these narratives is the same valorization of British rule, which has 'performed a splendid act of justice, policy and humanity, which fairly entitles it to be regarded as a conservative and beneficent power, whose supremacy has been the deliverance of the people'.[47]

With the publication in 1838 of Montgomery Martin's three-volume digest of Buchanan's archives this genre reached its apogee. The first volume was widely reviewed in the periodical, national and regional press, reviewers for the most part expressing gratitude to Martin for his industry in recovering such a valuable source of information on India. The *Literary Gazette*, for example, was 'glad to see the commencement of an undertaking which bids fair to redeem a large portion of British India from the dark state, in which it has heretofore remained'.[48] Faced with the mass of evidence accumulated by Buchanan, however, Martin seemed overwhelmed by this act of redemption:

> To offer an analysis of the facts contained in these three volumes would be a difficult task, and it would fail to convey an accurate impression as to the reality of the case; the whole work should be read and pondered on; the very minutiae of detail conveys to a thinking mind a clearer view of what the condition of people so situated must be, than any other mode of description; while those who are in the habit of contemplating the progress of society, and whose mental faculties are sufficiently comprehensive to examine all

the elements of social wealth and happiness will philosophically scrutinize the materials on which alone sound and just opinions can be based.[49]

His object in rescuing the manuscripts was rather to 'arouse in some measure, the people of England to some sense of feeling for the condition of the myriads of their fellow subjects now pining and perishing of famine, disease and all the slow but sure concomitants attendant on long continued want and slavery'.[50] He concludes with a remarkably prescient warning:

> England treats India with a despotism which has no parallel in ancient or modern history. But injustice acts like the scorpion's sting on its possessor, and the temporary and trifling advantage which England gains by her cruel and ungenerous treatment of India, will, if persevered in, recoil with tenfold effect on the persecutor.[51]

Thus in the period leading up to 1840 we can detect distinct shifts in the India created for domestic consumption. Travel and evangelical narratives continued to appear, but in spite of their popularity India remained shrouded in ignorance and mystery. In response, certain convergences took place that signalled commitment to a more total vision. Travellers such as Graham subordinated the vicarious and anecdotal to scholarly observations on Indian history and culture, while evangelicals such as Heber relegated theological invective against Hinduism to the sympathetic observations on Indians encountered on his extensive travels around the country. Personal accounts, however, no matter how well informed, could provide only partial truths; more systematic, empirical, standardized and comprehensive perspectives were needed. Hamilton, Conder and Montgomery Martin in their various ways represented attempts to meet this need.

Christopher Bayly has talked of the emergence of a new information order in these years, and although his emphasis is on intelligence gathering administered by the imperial state in India, I find much of relevance to an understanding of related changes in knowledge production for a popular domestic readership.[52] The demand for 'useful knowledge' was prompted and fuelled by the need to improve communication within the state, to provide social and economic statistics at a time of commercial crisis, and to establish cultural hegemony through the subordination of indigenous knowledge, particularly in the sphere of education. This new knowledge took the form increasingly of quantitative, routinized, abstract surveys which may have borrowed from indigenous knowledge and been rich in empirical detail but rarely penetrated beneath surface reality to reveal the inner workings of Indian society. Indeed, despite the exponential growth of empirical projects based on more sophisticated methodologies, the 'deeper social knowledge' of India receded. Colonial knowledge of India remained partial and contradictory.

As we have seen, these totalizing endeavours were increasingly evident in the production of knowledge for popular consumption. Most shared a belief in the providential nature of British rule and a concomitant desire to understand the complexities of Indian culture, but the more critical among them acknowledged that India defied totalization. Against this backdrop of self-doubt and insecurity those aspects of India most remote from the inquiring gaze of imperial administrators, travellers and evangelicals attracted undue concern. Enough had been done to provide a reasonably secure knowledge of India's languages, history and, increasingly, topography, and militarily the position seemed strong, but there remained worrying silences about Indian culture which, if unaddressed, would come to threaten the entire fabric of British authority. From such concern emerged increasingly virulent forms of racial coding.

Racialization of India

The notion of race derived authority from its versatility both in providing putative answers to a range of questions around Indian society and progress, and in legitimating the continuance of imperial rule.[53] The precise 'moment' of this racism is difficult to establish. It seems likely that racist sentiment existed in 'traditional' Indian society, and that this was readily articulated by imperial authorities into an orthodoxy.[54] The impact of this elective affinity was profound, for whereas racist sentiment in Indian society had been limited in scope and effect, colonial modernity consolidated and generalized racism into an ideology that shaped attitudes and policies toward virtually every facet of Indian society. It even penetrated into the heart of Hindu intellectual thought, not by engaging Indian elites in the modernizing project but by provoking as a form of resistance a retreat into myths of a rigidly hierarchical Indian past.

We have already encountered diverse elements of racial thought in the early writings of travellers and evangelicals. One of the most influential emerged from the geographical imagination of the Enlightenment. Here the concern was to explore putative relationships between the physical environment and its human occupants as a means of understanding regional characteristics. Some topographical studies emphasized the significance of landscape, agriculture and climate, while ethnologists tended to stress cultural formation, pattern of inhabitation and economy, but the boundaries between the approaches were crudely drawn. Attempts were made reductively to refer indigenous temperament to environment in ways that engendered racial thinking. In his *Essay on the Origin of Language*, Rousseau attributed the softness of the languages spoken in the southern hemisphere to its warmth and natural abundance. In Asia, people are close to nature; they have little to do but express love and tenderness. Europeans, on the other hand, are forced to work, and therefore re-press natural instincts. This utopian vision, however, was readily inverted by those seeking a naturalization of European supremacy.[55] Civilization, it came to be argued, had attained its heights in Europe because its temperate climate produced a vigorous and virile race, while tropical countries were inhabited by carnal and indolent peoples, incapable of improvement.

Toward the end of the eighteenth century writings on India displayed aspects of this geographical imagination. William Robertson's *An Histori-cal Disquisition* (1791) noted that India had over a long period of time been able to form extensive states even under its 'genial climate' and in its 'rich soil'.[56] More significantly, the stereotype of the Hindu as enervated, incurious, apathetic and listless, commonly found in the contemporary writings of Orme, Scrafton, Tennant and Claudius Buchanan, was given pseudo-scientific credence by being linked to the Indian climate. Charles Grant in his *Observations on the State of Society among the Asiatic Sub-jects of Great Britain* (1792) identified climate as one of the principal causes of the Hindu character, although qualified this by adding that any improvement had to come from moral reform. But it was James Forbes who identified the relationship with greater rigour:

> That the heat of the torrid zone debilitates the body, and enervates the mind, is very obvious: to this cause may be attributed the want of curiosity, enterprize, and vigour, among the Malabars: their inclinations are chiefly passive; indolence constitutes their happiness, and you cannot impose a severer task than mental employment ... from this habitual indolence they become incapable of exertion; and thus the laws, manners, and customs, are at this day as they were some thousand years ago.[57]

Forbes was too assiduous an observer to claim that the whole of India languished in such torpor, but his recognition of environmental diversity served only to consolidate the orthodoxy. Employing a typology that was to become familiar, he contrasted lowland peoples such as indolent Malabars and effeminate Bengalis with caste-free, energetic and rugged Sikhs and Rajputs found in mountainous regions, and wild, predatory, tribal Bheels. Over time, and with the application of a nascent interest in ethnology, more elaborate racial taxonomies emerged. In the writings of Francis Buchanan, for example, a sophisticated sense of topography pro-vided a platform for deliberations on racial physiognomy:

> The mountain tribes are, I believe, the descendants of the original inhabit-ants of the country, very little, if at all, mixed with foreign colonies. Their features and complexion resemble those of all rude tribes, that I have seen on the hills from the Ganges to Malabar.... [T]heir noses are seldom arched, and are rather thick at the points, owing to their nostrils being generally circular; but they are not so diminutive as the noses of the tartar nations, not

flattened like those of the African Negro. Their faces are oval, and not shaped like a lozenge, as those of the Chinese are. Their lips are full, but not at all like those of the Negro; on the contrary, their mouths are generally well formed. Their eyes, instead of being hidden in fat, and placed obliquely, like those of the Chinese, are exactly like those of the Europeans.[58]

In some contrast to the denunciations of a pan-Indian heathenism apparent in evangelical writings, travel writings displayed a heightened concern with particular populations perceived to be beyond both the interpretative skills of European observers and the civilizing influence of Hinduism. Bengalis, tribals and criminal sects were singled out. Complex codings were used by early travellers to describe the seemingly uncertain gender and racial identity of Bengali fishermen and ayahs (p. 138), but it was the tribals who continued to attract the most virulent forms of racist representation:

> The great mass of the Hindoo and Mahommedan population throughout Hindoostan has nearly reached the same stage of civilization, but intermixed with them are certain races of mountaineers, probably the true aborigines, whose languages have little affinity with the Sanscrit, and whose customs retain all their primitive barbarity. The most remarkable of these tribes are the Gonds, Bheels and Coolies; but there are many others of less note, such as the hill people of Boglepoor, and the Kookies of Chittagong.[59]

Henry Spry, of the Bengal Medical Staff, sensitive to the fact that 'men of profound learning ... have chosen subjects which ... are not generally interesting', sought to prove that there were 'no subjects more attractive that those relating to a country upon which so much apathy and ignorance have hitherto prevailed'.[60] He cited as influences the works of Heber and Emma Roberts; indeed, something of their humane sentiment prevails, but it is allied to an environmental determinism. 'The sensibility of men's natural or inborn character', he argues, 'must depend principally on the climate and products of the soil.'[61] The people of Hindustan, it follows, are 'frugal and primitive; their pastoral habits being nearly the same as they were in the time of the patriarchs of old'. Their national character does not deserve 'that unqualified censure which has been so lavishly heaped on it'. Indeed, even while respecting the 'authority of so great a name as Mill', Spry contends that Indian culture is 'not so much attributable ... to the inherent bad qualities of the mind of the people themselves, as to the selfish and unhealthy form of government under which they have been nurtured'.[62] In descriptions of Bengalees, however, Spry had recourse to a harsher racial typology:

> The Bengalees are a race distinct in many respects from the people who inhabit the provinces of Benares, Rohilcund, Bundlekund, Rajpootana, Malda, or the Nerbuddah. Their style of living is different, and their manners and

their climate are different, the latter particularly so; the climate of Bengal being damp, and the heat and the cold more tempered than in the provinces of Upper Hindustan. They have, moreover, a dialect peculiar to themselves, which is intelligible to persons only conversant with the Hindustanee language. In their social relations they are characterized as a degenerate class of people, being notorious for low cunning and deceit, and for the readiness with which they will enter into schemes of fraud and treachery.[63]

But it was in his characterization of tribals that Spry revealed the most strident racist sentiment:

The Kookees ... only differ from more civilized natives, forced by necessity upon expedients of the kind, by living constantly in trees, in other respects there is fortunately no similarity, even to the most degraded beings of the human race. They openly boast of their feats of cannibalism, showing, with the strongest expressions of satisfaction, the bones and residue of their fellow creatures who have fallen prey to their horrible appetites.[64]

Similarly, he felt compelled to mention

a race of native mountaineers, called Goands, who live in the hill jungles of Central India, particularly the southern parts. The Goands observe manners and customs which are peculiar to themselves, – their physiognomy partakes neither of the intelligence of the Mahomedan nor the effeminacy of the Hindu. They have hard set features. The lips, particularly the upper, thick; a receding forehead, and a general unintellectual expression of countenance. The skin is very black. The hair in the head thick, with an approach to woolliness, offering, in short, in their external physical characteristics, a striking resemblance to the well-known features of the African.... In the wild unreclaimed jungles in the eastern part of the Jubbulpore division, ... these people are no other than savages, and wander about when and where inclination prompts.[65]

In the uncertain political climate of the 1830s British colonial authorities sought to secure the frontiers of their expanding empire and facilitate movement of personnel over military and commercial routes. They met with resistance from indigenous populations whose customary rights of control and access were thereby threatened. Riots erupted that were conveniently blamed on tribals occupying adjacent areas of waste land. In February 1832, reported Lieutenant Thomas Bacon,

A popular disturbance took place among the Koles, a wild uncultivated race of men, inhabiting a tract of country ... forging the northern boundary of the province of Orissa.... There is little cultivation of the soil, and where it does exist, the operations of agriculture are performed in the most primitive and uncivilized fashion, the natives being far too stupid to benefit by example, and too superstitious to venture upon any innovation of their established usages or to desire improvement of any kind. They are well made and athletic in person, of very dark complexion, and coarse savage features; in temper they are sullen; dissipated in their habits, being slaves to excitement produced by fermented liquors; and tyrannical and revengeful in disposition. Without restrictions of any distinct religion ... the most revolting part of their savage degeneracy exists in the almost indiscriminate connexions or marriages which take place between members of the same family, and the neglect of other decencies, which form the most distinctive line between humanity and the brute creation.[66]

It was at this moment that the Thuggee Act of 1836 was introduced. It had novel and distinctive features; it could be applied retrospectively, and to territories beyond the Company's control, effectively extending its jurisdiction.[67] In this, the Act represented the most significant authoritarian intervention into the sphere of criminality, and we need briefly to consider its genesis.

Castes of robbers and thieves

Various forms of collective activity had long been recognized as a source of concern and therefore criminalized. From the inauguration of the Company's judicial framework in 1772, and in the belief that dacoits were robbers by profession, even birth, Warren Hastings included an article extending punishment from the individual criminal to his family and village.[68] Toward the close of the eighteenth century the British periodical press featured regular accounts of robberies and murders committed by dacoity gangs.[69] Seemingly undeterred by the threat of imprisonment or execution introduced by British authority, armed gangs were described as stalking the fashionable streets of Calcutta, occasionally abetted by European sailors in disguise. Riverside dacoits, operating in as many as twenty-four boats, attacked travellers, robbing them of everything of value. And in the surrounding countryside, gangs successfully plundered military camps without raising the alarm. How such daring could be displayed by a population known to be effeminate and cowardly puzzled Charles Grant; the answer was to be found in identification of hereditary criminality:

Though the Bengaleze in general have not sufficient resolution to rent their resentment against each other in open combat, yet robberies, thefts, burglaries, river piracies, and all sort of depredations where darkness, secrecy, or surprize can give advantage are exceedingly common.... There are castes of robbers and thieves, who consider themselves acting in their proper profession, and having united their families, train their children in it. Nowhere in the world are ruffians more adroit or more hardened. Troops of these banditti ... are generally employed and harboured by the zemindars of the districts, who are sharers in their booty.[70]

Grant, however, anticipated rather than instigated thinking on criminal activity. The notion of hereditary criminality was not to emerge as a system of thought in India for some forty years; instead, it surfaced at particular moments to explain threats to the social order, and to justify punitive measures that reached beyond procedural boundaries. It was during the war against the Marathas, for example, that a prolonged campaign was organized by colonial authorities to put down the Pindaris. One of its commanders, Lt. Col. Fitzclarence, described them:

> The horrid predatory system which has so long desolated India with the ravages of an active banditti, formed of the refuse of all countries and religions, and presenting the uncommon spectacle of a community of robbers (exceeding in numbers any of which history furnishes an example), yet permitted to exist in the states which made no attempt to eradicate them, was an anomaly in the political world.... The Pindarries had in 1812, 1816, and 1817, 'rushed like a torrent' upon the provinces of Mirzapoor, Gintoor, and Gangam, all in our possession, and with the barbarity so common, ... had committed the most cruel and wanton excesses on our subjects.[71]

Fitzclarence proceeded – and perhaps going to heart of the matter – to record that peasants used the plunder to excuse themselves from payment of rent arrears to government, resulting in a loss of revenue greater than that taken by the Pindaris. The Marquis of Hastings refused to negotiate with them; the Pindaris, as far as he was concerned, were public robbers who had to be eradicated by military means. Even the rights of war were denied. On capture, Pindaris were tried and, if found guilty, summarily executed. By 1818 Hastings could report that the campaign had been successfully completed. Rumours subsequently flourished, however, that rural labourers continued to join the Pindaris.[72]

The campaign against mercenary bands did little to solve the problem of robber gangs; indeed, it may have exacerbated the situation, for smaller groups of itinerant predators were less likely to attract the attention of military contingents.[73] From the insecure territories of Sagar and Narbada, annexed from the Marathas in 1817–18, emerged the new threat of thuggee that in the colonial imagination acted as a potent articulating principle of hereditary criminality. Within ten years, thuggee came to dominate fears about the limits of colonial knowledge and authority, and prompt wholesale changes in surveillance and the operation of law.

Thugs were, like dacoits and Pindaris, organized into groups numbering in their hundreds, led an itinerant existence, and preyed upon innocent victims. In other respects, however, Thugs were seen as distinct. They were secretive, hereditary murderers who inhabited cults with their own cant and superstitions, and followed their calling as an act of devotion to the popular Hindu goddess of destruction Kali. For some, this confirmed the inherent evil of Hinduism. 'The genius of Paganism', stated Edward Thornton, 'which has deified every vice, and thus provided a justification of the indulgence of every evil propensity, has furnished the Thugs with a patron goddess, worthy of those whom she is believed to protect.'[74]

Early encounters with Thugs had excited little interest. After the conquest of Seringapatam in 1799 approximately one hundred such robbers were apprehended, but there was no suspicion that they formed a band of hereditary murderers.[75] The idea of thuggee was taken more seriously by Thomas Perry, a magistrate in the frontier region of Etawah. Faced with a local population hostile to colonial authority, and regular looting from temples and rich inhabitants, Perry was persuaded that criminal bands were responsible. He used the term Thug to describe the miscreants – although for indigenous informants it meant little more than a cheat – and in the ensuing years recorded increasing numbers of Thug activities as a means of extending his police powers and resources.[76] By 1815 thuggee was recognized as a particular form of organized crime, and in the ensuing years entered into popular imagination. Writing of his exploits in the early 1830s, Lieutenant Bacon, who had previously singled out tribals for attention, had difficulty in locating Thugs on any known scale of humanity:

> [T]hugs ... are subjects affording ample scope for the investigations of the metaphysician and the philosopher; there is more filth from the sink of superstition than we can find in any other record of savage depravity; even cannibalism falls short of the diabolical influence which in *thugs* has spread over thousands of square miles, and among all ranks and sects.[77]

It was not, however, until the establishment of the Thuggee and Dacoity Department, and, more particularly, the appointment of Captain W.H. Sleeman as Assistant to the Agent to the Governor-General in the Sagar and Narbada territories, that a grand narrative of thuggee emerged.[78] Thornton found it remarkable that after a period of nearly two hundred years the British should have been ignorant of the 'existence and habits of a body so dangerous to the public peace',[79] but it was Sleeman who took on the task of revealing the underworld of thuggee as a prelude to its extirpation. He traced its origins to the time of the Arab, Afghan and Mughal conquests of India when similar practices were in evidence. Thereafter, he claimed, thuggee was allowed to flourish by the rulers of independent states and local zemindars, many of whom entertained a dread of Thugs but benefited handsomely from Thug revenue.

More significantly, through minute scrutiny of official records, including cross-examinations of suspected Thugs, Sleeman attempted to decode its hidden rituals, practices and language.[80] Thuggee, however, resisted rationalization. No explanation of the phenomenon was offered, nor was the phenomenon defined with any precision. The early identification with ritual strangulation was abandoned after the 1830s, and the notion of thuggee came to apply to a wide range of organized criminal activity including kidnapping and poisoning. And although tropes of the hereditary and itinerant were maintained, these seemed only to confound any understanding colonial authorities had of the location occupied by Thugs within Indian society. At times seen as a community apart, preying upon the indigenous population, at others as a natural expression of certain essential Hindu values, thuggee could not readily be incorporated epistemologically into caste or religion. It was discovered that Muslims frequently joined Thug gangs; in Oude, for example, they comprised 90 per cent of those apprehended.[81] And many of the Thugs arrested turned out to be among the most respected members of the community – merchants, tradesmen and loyal soldiers in the service of the Company. It was this unknowability, combined with the public invisibility of Thug misdeeds, that helps to explain why a criminal activity that never threatened British persons came to demand so much attention from colonial authorities, and entered so vividly into popular mythologies of Indian culture. As Parama Roy puts it:

> There is an ongoing and strenuous endeavour in the discourse of *thuggee* to interpellate the thug as an essence, a move which attests to the anxiety of rupture that subtends the totalizing epistemologies of colonialism. Yet the thug as discursive object is strikingly resistant to such fixity; he is all things to all people. If native identity can be staged, can be plural, then what are the implications for colonial authority and colonialism's project of information retrieval? *Thuggee*, I would suggest, introduces a disturbance on the paradigm of information retrieval ... as well as [in] the notion of native authenticity and ontological purity that is a governing trope of colonial discourse.[82]

Sleeman displayed rare zeal in cracking the code of thuggee. He mapped the activities of Thugs, constructed genealogies, and completed a dictionary of their secret cant, Ramasee.[83] This project, however, was never solely one of reading Indian criminality; it laid the foundation for a transformation in the rhetoric and practice of colonial authoritarianism. Drawing upon experience of anti-Thug campaigns in the Sagar and Narbada territories, and given legal sanction by the 1836 Thuggee Act, the colonial state instituted a draconian regime of arrest, trial, conviction and punishment that came to be applied to virtually all acts of collective crime – and indirectly to itinerant activity – across the whole of India. At the height of the campaign in 1840, 3,689 Thugs were committed; of these, 466 were hanged, 1,504 transported and 933 sentenced to life imprisonment.[84] Radical new techniques of ethnographic classification were also introduced. Here, Henry Spry, medical officer of Sagar, appeared on the scene. In the interests of science, he forwarded to the phrenological society at

Edinburgh seven skulls of Thug leaders executed at Sagar.[85] The findings were to inform his later deliberations on tribal societies (p. 147).

The reactions provoked among colonial authorities by the discovery of tribal and criminal societies in the first decades of the nineteenth century had a material basis. Frontier regions in west and central India, wherein most of the societies were located, were politically insecure. Troublesome tribal societies such as the Kolis and Bhils, which earlier had been granted rights by the Marathas to control access to mountain and forest routes, found themselves in conflict with a newly won British authority intent on securing its commercial and military operations.[86] Simultaneously, land revenue, so necessary to finance Britain's precarious expansionist policies, was under threat from armed banditti who successfully plundered ill-protected villages. The solution was to be found in the break-up of those forest and waste land areas adjacent to arable land which had provided sanctuary for unruly elements, and the promotion of settlement, or at least the orderly migration of labour instead of untrammelled movement of criminal fraternities. Despite the completion by 1820 of the conquest of most of the Indian states, continued financial insecurity prevented the Raj from stabilizing its frontiers.[87] It was against the disturbed conditions of the 1820s and 1830s when revolts broke out in border areas, and the severe fall in government revenue during the 1830s and 1840s, that the Thug panic has to be seen. It represented an exaggerated response to fears of all nomadic peoples.

This period therefore witnessed a distinct shift in representations of both the metropolitan poor and sections of the indigenous Indian population. On the surface this was evident in the emergence of a certain linguistic repertoire. Epithets such as 'wild tribes', 'wandering tribes', 'savage races' and 'nomad races' were invoked by Henry Mayhew, Watts Phillips and James Greenwood to describe the metropolitan street poor, and by William Sleeman, Edward Thornton other social investigators to describe predatory bands and tribal peoples in India. Underpinning this vocabulary, however, was a radical new attempt to comprehend constituencies previously beyond observation. As was so often the case when faced with such epistemological insecurity, writers turned to older discursive strategies. I wish to argue that the field of understanding created by these explorers was one structured largely by an awkward reworking of the idea of wildness.

Wildness had an ancient lineage.[88] In the founding traditions of both Judeo-Christian and Hellenic-Roman thought the notion of the wild man was associated with areas of wilderness such as the desert, forest, jungle and mountains that had yet to be domesticated and thus brought within knowledge. As these areas became known, so the wild man was 'progressively despatialized', and in the modern era wildness was no longer thought as a physical entity beyond geographical knowledge, but internalized as the 'repressed content of *both* civilized *and* primitive humanity'. In the course of this long transformation, wildness was used variously to denote a stage in human development, a moral condition and a category in cultural anthropology, each of which bore traces of its complex origins. Hebrew thought tended to stress wildness as an evil condition. Wild men were hunters and nomads who lived in a state of ignorance below animality, sowed the seeds of destruction, and violated the laws of God, most notably by transgressing the natural order through species corruption.[89] Descended from Ham, they were also seen as black. As the early modern era began to liberate emotions from the stifling influence of medieval Christian thought, so the more benign influence of classical conceptions of the wildness came into play, and primitivism briefly celebrated a state of natural desire unconstrained by civilization.

This cosmography framed much contemporary thought on the nature of populations seen to be beyond civilization. Thus in the eighteenth century Henry Fielding could compare London's criminal haunts to the 'desarts of Africa'. With the discovery of the threatening presence of an endemic poor on the streets of London and predatory populations in India nearly a century later, the discourse of wildness provided an amenable trope of representation, not necessarily to reveal the real conditions of existence of these populations, but rather to locate them in the human order:

> The notion of 'wildness' (or, in its Latinate form, 'savagery') belongs to a set of culturally self-authenticating devices which includes, among many others, the ideas of 'madness' and 'heresy' as well. These terms are used not merely to designate a specific condition or state of being but also to confirm the value of their dialectical antitheses 'civilization,' 'sanity,' and 'orthodoxy,' respectively. Thus, they do not so much refer to a specific thing, place, or condition as dictate a particular attitude governing a relationship between a lived reality and some area of problematical existence that cannot be accommodated easily to conventional conceptions of the normal or familiar.[90]

This, I believe, was the political and intellectual context of Prichard, Mayhew and Sleeman. That they were familiar with India is not in doubt. In his survey of the ethnography of human societies Prichard included a detailed description of 'Hindus' based for the most part on the accounts of travellers including Orme, Heber, Tod, Abbe Dubois and Elphinstone. Hindus, he concluded, belong to Indo-European stock, and provided 'striking and conclusive proof' that their complexion is due to climate.[91] Aboriginal 'races' were not of the same stock. Mountaineers and 'wild tribes', including Bhils, Gonds and Coolies, spoke languages distinct from Sanskrit, and demonstrated diverse physical characteristics. Ethnology, however, is in 'far too imperfect a state to render it possible at present to determine what relation these tribes bear to each other, and to the civilized nations who are nearest to them'.[92] Mayhew made few direct references to India in his work on street folk, but the section on India in the long chapter on prostitution relied heavily on travel and evangelical accounts. Bernier, Forster, Hamilton, Wilson, Malcolm, Ward, Grant and Thornton were among many cited.[93]

It is in this context that we can better appreciate Mayhew's contribution to the understanding of metropolitan poverty. Despite his problematic use of Prichard and absence of detailed references to India, the rhetoric and tropes employed by Mayhew emerge from earlier concerns of colonial authorities and travellers in India to locate the troublesome presence of nomadic populations. 'The notions of morality among these people', Mayhew states in his discussion of coster girls, 'agree strangely ... with those of many savage tribes – indeed, it would be curious if it were otherwise. They are part of the Nomades [sic] of England, neither knowing nor caring for the enjoyments of home.'[94] And he proceeds to describe habits where 'passion is the sole rule of action', and where 'every appetite of our animal nature is indulged in without the least restraint'. Indeed, such imagery can be found in descriptions of many of the varieties of street poor that came under Mayhew's gaze. But he rarely lapsed into crude racial typologies. Thus the tentative suggestions of distinct physiognomies appearing in the preface were never applied to the poor. Mayhew was too much of a humanitarian and too good a sociologist to allow this. Thus the immorality of coster girls was not due to some hereditary traits, but to the conditions which they were forced to endure. Coster girls grow up, he argues, without the beneficial guidance of parents, without education, and under the cruel rigours of street life. Their fathers are in the tap room, mothers away tending the stall or hawking goods from morning to night. Under such circumstances, girls pick their morals 'from the gutter', the only notion of wrong formed by 'what the policeman will permit them to do'. 'I say this much', he concludes,

> Because I am anxious to make others feel, as I do myself, that *we* are the culpable parties in these matters. That the poor things should do as they do is but human nature – but that *we* should allow them to remain thus destitute of every blessing vouchsafed for ourselves – that we should willingly shape what we enjoy with our brethren at the Antipodes, and yet leave those who are nearer and who, therefore, should be dearer to us, to want even the commonest moral necessaries is a paradox that gives to the zeal of our Christianity a strong savour of the chicanery of Cant.[95]

And yet these fears expressed also a profound sense of unease about the state of colonial knowledge. Those populations that were seen to bar the progress of colonial modernity were precisely those about which so little was known. New narratives of knowledge – based largely on racialized categories – were constructed as a means of addressing the silence. Events in 1857 were to explode this project, and set in motion the consolidation of more systematic, centralized, totalizing and abstract bodies of knowledge based on fundamental discourses of race, caste and criminality.

Notes

1 R. Montgomery Martin, *The History, Antiquities, Topography, and Statistics of Eastern India*, 3 vols, London, Allen and Lane, 1838, Vol. I, p. vii. This is a digest of Buchanan's unpublished survey completed over twenty years earlier.

2 Francis Buchanan, *A Journey from Madras through the countries of Mysore, Canara, and Malabar ... for the Express Purpose of Investigating the State of Agriculture, Arts and Commerce; the Religion, Manners, and Customs; the History Natural and Civil and Antiquities, in the Dominions of the Rajah of Mysore, and the Countries Acquired by the Honourable East India Company, in the Late and Former Wars, from Tippoo Sultaun*, London, Cadell and Davies, 1807.

3 Marika Vicziany claims that Buchanan's real interests lay in botany. Certainly, he devotes a disproportionate amount of space to it, and the subordination of other aspects in the survey created tensions with the Company (see 'Imperialism, botany and statistics in early nineteenth-century India: the surveys of Francis Buchanan (1762–1829)', *Modern Asian Studies*, 20, 1986, pp. 625–60). Some light is shed on this by a comparison between Buchanan's interests and the topics of interest identified by the Company for the Mysore and Bengal surveys. For the Mysore survey 'Agriculture' is singled out as the 'first great and essential object', and given prominence also in the Bengal survey. Here the priority is with cultivation and its improvement. The Bengal survey includes a requirement to forward to the Company's botanical garden 'useful or rare and curious plants and seeds', but it is almost as a postscript (see the tables in Matthew Edney, *Mapping an Empire. The Geographical Construction of British India, 1765–1843*, Chicago, University of Chicago Press, 1997, pp. 46–7).

4 Montgomery Martin, *The History*, Vol. I, p. x.

5 C.A. Bayly, *Indian Society and the Making of the British Empire*, The New Cambridge History of India Vol. II.1, Cambridge, Cambridge University Press, 1988, p. 87.

6 But if it was part of such a project its location was somewhat ambiguous. Buchanan's priorities were botanical, and although this did not automatically disqualify him as an active agent of imperial endeavour, it did lead to seemingly irreconcilable differences of opinion between him and the Company on the nature of the project and the final product. Furthermore, Buchanan can equally well be located in the Scottish Enlightenment. Influential though Colebrooke was to the development of the survey of India, Buchanan's more immediate inspiration was John Sinclair's *Statistical Account of Scotland*, published in twenty-one volumes between 1791 and 1798 (Vicziany, 'Imperialism, botany and statistics', p. 649).

7 Edney, *Mapping an Empire*, p. 66.

8 See the exemplary discussion in *ibid*.

9 Montgomery Martin, *The History*, Vol. I, p. 110.

10 Vicziany, 'Imperialism, botany and statistics', p. 646.

11 Montgomery Martin, *The History*, Vol. III, p. 600.

12 *Ibid.*, Vol. I, p. 49.

13 *Ibid.*, p. 126.

14 Walter Hamilton, *The East India Gazetteer; containing particular Descriptions ... of Hindostan, and the Adjacent Countries; ... together with Sketches of the Manners, Customs, Institutions, Agriculture, Commerce, Manufactures, Revenues, Population, Castes, Religion, History, &c., of their Various Inhabitants*, London, Murray, 1815.

15 *Ibid.*, p. vii.
16 James Mill, *The History of British India*, ed. H.H. Wilson, 10 vols, London, Madden, Piper, Stephenson and Spence, 1858 [1817].
17 *Ibid.*, Vol. I, p. xxiii.
18 Ronald Inden, *Imagining India*, Bloomington, Indiana University Press, 2000 [1990], p. 45.
19 David Ludden, 'Oriental empiricism: transformations of colonial knowledge', in Carol A. Breckenridge and Peter van der Veer (eds), *Orientalism and the Postcolonial Predicament*, Philadelphia, University of Philadelphia Press, 1993, p. 263.
20 Javed Majeed, *Ungoverned Imaginings. James Mill's* The History of British India *and Orientalism*, Oxford, Clarendon Press, 1992, p. 129.
21 James Forbes, *Oriental Memoirs: Selected and Abridged from a Series of Familiar Letters Written during Seventeen Years Residence in India: including Observations on Parts of Africa and South America, and a Narrative of Occurences in Four Indian Voyages*, 4 vols, London, White, Cochrane and Co., 1813.
22 James Forbes, *Reflections on the character of the Hindoos; and on the importance of converting them to Christianity. Being a Preface to, and Conclusion of, a Series of Oriental Letters, which will be shortly published*, London, 1810. For background detail on Forbes, see Ketaki Kushari Dyson, *A Various Universe. A Study of the Journals and Memoirs of British Men and Women in the Indian Subcontinent, 1765–1856*, Delhi, Oxford University Press, 1978.
23 Forbes, *Oriental Memoirs*, Vol. I, pp. xii–xiii.
24 *Ibid.*, p. 390.
25 *Ibid.*, Vol. IV, p. 306.
26 *Ibid.*, Vol. I, p. 381.
27 Among the accounts recorded by female travellers in this period are: Lady Maria Nugent, *A Journal from the Year 1811 till the Year 1815, including a Voyage to and Residence in India, with a Tour to the North-Western Parts of the British Possessions in that Country, under the Bengal Government*, 2 vols, London, 1839; Maria Graham, *Journal of a Residence in India*, Edinburgh, Constable, 1813; Mary Sherwood, *The Life and Times of Mrs. Sherwood (1775–1851) from the Diaries of Captain and Mrs. Sherwood*, London, Wells Gardner and Co., 1910; Anne Elwood, *Narrative of a Journey Overland from England, by the Continent of Europe, Egypt, and the Red Sea, to India; including a Residence there, and Voyage Home, in the years 1825, 26, 27, and 28*, London, Colburn and Bentley, 1830; Emma Roberts, *Scenes and Characteristics of Hindostan, with Sketches of Anglo-Indian Society*, London, Allen, 1835; Fanny Parks, *Wanderings of a Pilgrim in Search of the Picturesque, during four-and-twenty years in the East; with Revelations of Life in the Zenana*, London, 1850; Marianne Postans, *Western India in 1838*, London, Saunders and Otley, 1839. Most of these are mentioned in Dyson, *A Various Universe* and in Indira Ghose, *Women Travellers in Colonial India. The Power of the Female Gaze*, Delhi, Oxford University Press, 1998.
28 Graham, *Journal of a Residence in India*, pp. v–vi.
29 *Ibid.*, pp. 85–8.
30 Nugent, *A Journal from the Year 1811 till the Year 1815*, Vol. I, pp. 68–70.
31 *Ibid.*, pp. 88–9.
32 William Huggins, *Sketches in India, treating on Subjects connected with the Government; Civil and Military Establishments; Characters of the European, and Customs of the Native Inhabitants*, London, 1824, p. 207, cited in Dyson, *A Various Universe*, p. 95.
33 Sherwood, *The Life and Times of Mrs. Sherwood*, pp. 252–3, cited in Dyson, *A Various Universe*, p. 96.
34 *Ibid.*, p. 253.
35 Reginald Heber, *Narrative of a Journey through the Upper Provinces of India, from Calcutta to Bombay, 1824–1825, with Notes upon Ceylon, and Account of a Journey to Madras and the Southern Provinces, 1826, and Letters written in India*, 2 vols, London, Murray, 1828.
36 *Ibid.*, Vol. I, pp. 3–4.

37 *Ibid.*, pp. 85–6.
38 Walter Hamilton, *A Geographical, Statistical and Historical Description of Hindostan, and the Adjacent Countries*, 2 vols, London, Murray, 1820, p. v.
39 *Ibid.*, Vol. I, pp. xii–xiii.
40 *Ibid.*, pp. 102, 113.
41 *Ibid.*, pp. xxx–xxxi.
42 *Ibid.*, p. xli.
43 John Borthwick Gilchrist, *The General East India Guide and Vade Mecum, for the Public Functionary, Government Officer, Private Agent, Trader or Foreign Sojourner, in British India, and the Adjacent Parts of Asia immediately connected with the Hon. East India Company, being a Digest of the Work of the Late Capt. Williamson*, London, Kingsbury, Parbury and Allen, 1825.
44 See the useful discussion in C.A. Bayly, *Empire and Information. Intelligence Gathering and Social Communication in India, 1780–1870*, Cambridge, Cambridge University Press, 1996, pp. 287–93. 'Unlike Persian', Bayly argues, 'Hindustani was a language with which to marshal the lowly servant and sepoy.'
45 [Josiah Conder], *The Modern Traveller. A Popular Description. Geographical, Historical, and Topographical, of the Various Countries of the Globe*, 10 vols, London, Duncan, 1828. The first four volumes of the series are devoted to India. Two years later Conder published a revision edition in thirty volumes; those on India were numbered VII–X.
46 *Ibid.*, Vol. III, p. 11.
47 *Ibid.*, p. 29.
48 *Literary Gazette*, 24 March 1838, cited in Martin, *The History*, Vol. III, endpaper.
49 Montgomery Martin, *The History*, Vol. III, p. iv.
50 *Ibid.*, p. v.
51 *Ibid.*, p. xxii.
52 Bayly, *Empire and Information*.
53 Although the literature is copious, there remains no consensus on the theorization of race. For the purposes of this study, I take the position that racial theory is predicated on the identification of essential characteristics in particular populations. This identification is fluid. Historically, it has involved cultural, religious and physical attributes, and, with the emergence of 'scientific' racism in the nineteenth century, hereditary biological traits. It always results in the hierarchical ordering of populations.
54 For impressive discussions of this complex issue see David Washbrook, 'Ethnicity and racialism in colonial Indian society', in R. Ross (ed.), *Racism and Colonialism. Essays on Ideology and Social Structure*, The Hague, Martinus Nijhoff, 1982; Inden, *Imagining India*; Peter Robb, 'Introduction: South Asia and the concept of race', in Robb (ed.), *The Concept of Race in South Asia*, Delhi, Oxford University Press, 1997.
55 David Spurr, *The Rhetoric of Empire. Colonial Discourse in Journalism, Travel Writing and Imperial Administration*, Durham, Duke University Press, 1993, p. 157.
56 William Robertson, *An Historical Disquisition concerning the Knowledge which the Ancients had of India*, London, Cadell and Davies, 1817 [1791], p. 205.
57 Forbes, *Oriental Memoirs*, Vol. I, p. 382.
58 Montgomery Martin, *The History*, Vol. II, p. 123.
59 Hamilton, *A Geographical, Statistical and Historical Description of Hindostan*, p. xxiv.
60 Henry Spry, *Modern India; with Illustrations of the Resources and Capabilities of Hindustan*, 2 vols, London, Whittaker, 1837, Vol. I, pp. vi–vii.
61 *Ibid.*, Vol. II, p. 152.
62 *Ibid.*, p. 4.
63 *Ibid.*, Vol. I, p. 3.
64 *Ibid.*, p. 17.
65 *Ibid.*, Vol. II, pp. 139–40.
66 Thomas Bacon, *First Impressions and Studies from Nature in Hindostan, embracing an Outline of the Voyage to Calcutta, and Five Years Residence in Bengal and the Doab from 1831 to 1836*, 2 vols, London, Allen, 1837, Vol. I, pp. 199–200.
67 Radhika Singha, *A Despotism of Law. Crime and Justice in Early Colonial India,*

Delhi, Oxford University Press, 1998, Chapter 5.

68 *Ibid.*, p. 169.

69 W.H. Carey (ed.), *The Good Old Days of Honorable John Company, 1600–1858*, Calcutta, Cambray, 1906, pp. 358–61.

70 Charles Grant, *Observations on the State of Society among the Asiatic Subjects of Great Britain, ... Written chiefly in the year 1792*, Parliamentary Papers, 1813, p. 28.

71 Lt. Col. Fitzclarence, *Journal of a Route across India, through Egypt to England in the latter end of the Year 1817, and the beginning of 1818*, London, Murray, 1819, pp. 1–2.

72 Singha, *A Despotism of Law*, p. 177.

73 As early as 1822, officials such as Ochterlony and Bentinck suggested that Thugs had formed out of the 'remnants of the Maratha Pindari evil' (*ibid.*, pp. 178–9). In fact, mercenary bands in search of service with Indian rulers were in evidence throughout the eighteenth century. The extension of British authority probably added to their numbers.

74 [Edward Thornton], *Illustrations of the History and Practices of the Thugs, and Notices of some of the Proceedings of the Government of India for the Suppression of the Crimes of Thuggee*, London, Allen, 1837, p. 44.

75 *Ibid.*, p. 2.

76 Bayly, *Empire and Information*, pp. 174–5.

77 Bacon, *First Impressions and Studies from Nature in Hindostan*, Vol. II, p. 410.

78 I have relied here on the useful account to be found in Parama Roy, *Indian Traffic. Identities in Question in Colonial and Postcolonial India*, Berkeley, University of California Press, 1999, especially Chapter 2, 'Discovering India, imagining *Thuggee*'.

79 [Thornton], *Illustrations of the History and Practices of Thugs*, p. 2.

80 The findings were widely reported in popular publications, most notably W.H. Sleeman, *Ramaseeana, or a Vocabulary of the Peculiar Language used by the Thugs*, Calcutta, Huttman, 1836; *The Thugs or Phansigars of India, comprising a History of the Rise and Progress of that extraordinary fraternity of Assassins*, Philadelphia, Carey and Hart, 1839; *Report on the Depredations Committed by the Thug Gangs of Upper and Central India*, Calcutta, Huttman, 1840; *Report on Budhuk Alias Bagree Dacoits and Other Gang Robbers by Hereditary Profession*, Calcutta, Sherriff, 1849. The Thug mythology created for the domestic reading public of the nineteenth century, however, was probably facilitated more by publications such as Edward Thornton, *Illustrations of the History and Practices of Thugs*, London, Allen, 1837, and James Hutton, *A Popular Account of the Thugs and Dacoits, the Hereditary Garroters and Gang-Robbers of India*, London, Allen, 1857. Although published over a twenty-year period, this body of literature displayed little variation in style, content or rhetoric.

81 Hutton, *A Popular Account of Thugs and Dacoits*, p. 25.

82 Roy, *Indian Traffic*, p. 55.

83 The parallels with earlier canting dictionaries of metropolitan low life are clear.

84 Hutton, *A Popular Account of the Thugs and Dacoits*, pp. 93–4.

85 Henry Spry, 'Some accounts of the gangmurders of central India, commonly called Thugs', *Phrenological Journal*, 8, December 1832 – June 1834, pp. 511–30, cited in Singha, *A Despotism of Law*, p. 208.

86 Bayly, *Indian Society and the Making of the British Empire*, p. 107.

87 *Ibid.*, p. 120.

88 Hayden White, 'The forms of wildness: archaeology of and idea', in *Tropics of Discourse. Essays in Cultural Criticism*, Baltimore, The Johns Hopkins University Press, 1978.

89 *Ibid.*, p. 160.

90 White, 'The forms of wildness', p. 151.

91 James Prichard, *The Natural History of Man; comprising Inquiries into the Modifying Influence of Physical and Moral Agencies on the Different Tribes of the Human Family*, London, Bailliere, 1843, p. 169.

92 *Ibid.*, p. 248.

93 Henry Mayhew, *London Labour and the London Poor*, 4 vols, London, Cass, 1967

[1861–62], Vol. IV, pp. 116–25. This chapter was co-written by Bracebridge Hemyng, Mayhew's long-time collaborator. The section on India was actually devoted almost exclusively to denouncing the lot of Indian women in general, and said little about prostitution.

94 *Ibid.*, Vol. I, p. 43.
95 *Ibid.*, p. 43.

CHAPTER SIX

In darkest England

As we have seen, in the first half of the nineteenth century social reformist and evangelical journalists, laying distinct claim to have access to the metropolitan poor, abandoned iconographies of the criminal, bizarre and grotesque, to develop perspectives deeply embedded in theorizations of the innate superiority of the Anglo-Saxon subject over both poor and colonial others. These urban travellers, however, rarely used racial theory with rigour and coherence. The pioneering Henry Mayhew borrowed freely from contemporary racial theory in writing the interpretative preface to his *London Labour and the London Poor*, but any putative logic was undermined by the plurality of empirical material on the experience of the poor recorded in the corpus of the work. Nonetheless, the tradition of urban exploration that followed displayed an increasingly intensified concern with race. Around 1860, as fears of social disorder and imperial decline gripped the bourgeois imagination, writings of journalists such as James Greenwood took a sinister turn, manifest particularly in their use of symbolic repertoires of dirt and degeneration.

The trope of racialization locates shifts in the construction of the poor within the *imperial* formation, and provides a more satisfactory explanation of their chronology and nature than those focusing exclusively on domestic politics and social policy. In the following I wish to explore the workings of this symbolic process. To understand the active construction of racial identities in this period, we need to go beyond the convention of identifying characteristics of racial stereotyping, to an investigation of the subtle and powerful mechanisms through which they were created. From there I proceed to consider how modernist impulses transformed the discursive realm of the poor. Toward the end of the century anonymous crowds from an unknown abyss surfaced upon the urban landscape; race, however, remained the principal referent.

The meaning of dirt

Dirt featured prominently in the imaginative universe constructed around the nineteenth-century metropolitan and colonial poor. Consider, for example, the Rev. Garratt, who in 1852 lectured to the London City Mission on the problem of the London Irish. While displaying admirable qualities of 'intellectual acuteness and imaginative glow', he claimed, the London Irish were 'idle and dirty', and 'without that honourable independence of mind which is so valuable a feature of the English character'.[1] John Hollingshead, a staff member of Dickens's *Household Words*, in a sociological flourish anticipating William Beveridge by nearly a hundred years, talked of the poor as a population marked by the 'five great divisions ... of poverty, ignorance, dirt, immorality and crime'.[2] And James Greenwood referred to 'creatures that you know to be female by the length and raggedness of hair that makes their heads hideous, and by their high pitched voices, with bare red arms and their bodies bundled in a complication of dirty rags'.[3] This physicality was linked increasingly to urban topography. Watts Phillips's 'Wild tribes of London' crouched in 'darkness, dirt, and disease';[4] Hollingshead's 'Ragged London' were 'half buried in black kitchens and sewer-like courts and alleys'.[5] In 1863, W. Cosens, Secretary of the Additional Curates Society, spelt out the necessary lessons:

> The purity of the moral atmosphere in which we live exercises over us an influence as real as the purity of the physical atmosphere.... The parallel between the infection of disease and the infection of crime holds strictly; if we suffer pollution to remain unabashed in the hovel it will take its revenge on the palace.[6]

Most influential, however, was George Godwin, editor of *The Builder* – the most important architectural and building periodical of the time – who wrote prolifically on the relationship between living conditions and the social pathology of the poor. Although investigation was 'a task of no small danger and difficulty; it is necessary to brave the risks of fever and other injuries to health, and the contact of men and women often as lawless as the Arab or the Kaffir',[7] he persevered, and in the 1850s published a series of articles, collected later in *Town Swamps and Social Bridges*.[8] Guided by the maxim 'As the homes, so the people', he described vividly the housing environments suffered by the poor in ways that were to become very familiar. By a Thames tributary, for example:

> Dwelling-houses are built on the sewer wall, and around it. The people living about here have, in most instances, sickly children, who in a measure resemble the poor plants observable in some of the windows about. Everything around is bad. The bank, when the tide goes out, is covered with filth; and when the number of the similar tributaries which flow to Father Thames, both night and day, is recollected, his state is not to be wondered at.[9]

The 'hybrid suburb' of Canning Town, then in the initial stages of a tumultuous growth, was similarly depicted:

> In 1857 an outbreak of cholera proved the truth of the prediction [of evils resulting from poisoned cesspools], and great efforts were made to obtain improvements in the drainage of the place.... The President of the Board, the Right Hon. Mr. Cowper, went down immediately, and found houses without drainage, without ventilation, without water-supply, except of the worst description, ditches presenting an evaporating surface of the foulest kind, and the roads a mass of mud and filth; the whole being a marsh seven feet below high-water mark.[10]

In their notable *The Politics and Poetics of Transgression*, Peter Stallybrass and Allon White have elaborated the cultural significance of a coding that separated the slum, the sewer, the poor and the prostitute from the suburb.[11] This separation enabled the social reformer, as part of a process of validation of the bourgeois imaginary, to survey and classify its *own antithesis*.[12] Dirt was crucial because while it moved readily across the symbolic domains, it was always matter in the wrong place. Furthermore, the physical filth of the poor and the colonized became a metonym for moral defilement and impurity. Thus 'contagion' and 'contamination' were the tropes through which the imperial formation appropriated the metropolis and the colonies, and expressed fears that dismantling of boundaries between suburb and slum, public and private would threaten class distinctions.[13]

These symbolic hierarchies, however, contained inherent contradictions. Filthy bodies and geographical spaces were held ambivalently between disgust and fascination, repugnance and desire in a way that suggested that the low was not a marginalized other but laid as an 'eroticized constituent' at the centre of the bourgeois imaginary. Prostitutes, rookeries, the body of the poor, the lascar and other sources of contagion in the Victorian metropolis attracted a degree of attention incommensurate with their 'real' presence, thereby revealing the symbolic centrality of the socially and economically peripheral. The preoccupation with social reform, slumming, visits from members of the Charity Organization Society, urban exploration and prostitution were therefore in part an encoding of fascination with the transgressive qualities of the dirty, low other.

Important though this analysis is to an understanding of how dirt moves freely around symbolic domains, in focusing on the consolidation of *class*-based hierarchies certain limitations are exposed. In the imperial formation the category of class was articulated with gender and race in ways that denied any essential privileging; class, gender and race existed only as relational categories in a state of 'dynamic, shifting and intimate interdependence'.[14] This imparts a new range of meanings to dirt, some of which have been explored by Anne McClintock in her *Imperial Leather*. Dirt, she argues, was used symbolically in Victorian culture to define and transgress social boundaries. The middle class, for example, had an obsession with dirt – evidenced nicely in the deification of soap – which was used imaginatively to define identity. Since dirt was visible evidence of manual labour it had to be eliminated from the body and clothes; if not then the symbolic encoding of class boundaries would have been under threat.[15] Similar arguments obtained in the sphere of sexuality. In the course of the nineteenth century, therefore, the 'iconography of dirt became a poetics of surveillance' in policing the boundaries not only between 'normal' and 'dirty' work, but also between 'normal' and 'dirty' sexuality.

These arguments, however, do not capture fully the nuanced repertoire of dirt. The dirt of manual labour was not the dirt of the metropolitan poor. Despite their enforced remoteness from the bourgeois imaginary, a cultural void existed between the 'honest', 'manufactured' dirt of the artisan (grease, sweat, oil, dust and grime) and the 'grotesque', 'faecal' dirt of the poor (filth, sewage, swamp, slime and putrefaction). This distinction was of considerable significance in a number of interrelated ways:

1 The vocabulary was used in a highly selective way; the coding of manual dirt was rarely deployed in descriptions of the poor.
2 As the dirt of the poor became subject to surveillance, so it was mapped in distinctive ways. 'Honest' dirt was to be found on the hands and the brow; 'grotesque' dirt was located on the whole body of the poor, and within the body of the metropolis that they inhabited.
3 It is specifically the dirt of the poor that enters the bourgeois psyche as a repugnant low other.

These processes never operated independently. In the construction of symbolic hierarchies of the body, for example, they are all in evidence:

> But whilst the 'low' of the bourgeois body becomes unmentionable, we hear an ever increasing garrulity about the *city's* 'low' – the slum, the rag-picker, the prostitute, the sewer – the 'dirt' which is 'down there'. In other words, the axis of the body is transcoded through the axis of the city, and whilst the bodily low is 'forgotten', the city low becomes a site of obsessive preoccupation, a preoccupation which is itself intimately conceptualized in terms of discourses of the body.[16]

A more significant omission in McClintock – given her focus on the invention of race in the imperial metropolis – is any recognition of the ways in which the iconography of dirt contributed to the racialization of the poor. Dirt was colour-coded; it was neither brown nor grey, but unambiguously black. This was no semantic or poetic device. This synonymic association was part of a structuring process through which a complex chain of signification was established in a series of binary oppositions: dirt/filth – cleanliness; unwashed – washed; darkness/shadow – light; impure – pure; black – white; low – high.[17] Until the 1850s much of this coding was muted; for most Victorians heretofore race described social rather than colour distinctions.[18] Thus the poor lived in 'miserable hovels, many of them underneath the ground, without glass windows, or indeed without windows of any kind – the only light and air being admitted through the horizontal door'.[19] Phillips guided the reader through the courts of St Giles: 'Let us cross the road, and pausing before that dark archway, that seems to have retreated from the ill-paved street, and slink, as it were, into the shadow of the wall, glance into the pandemonium which lies beyond.... Such courts are the headquarters of filth and fever.'[20]

During the 1880s, however, the associations with 'black' became more direct. In the East End 'the angular meanness of the buildings is veiled by the dusk, and there stretches on either hand a hummocked wilderness of mysterious murk.... In the by-streets the lamps are so few and dim the feeble flickering light they cast upon the house fronts is only less dark than the pitchy blackness that broods above the lonely-looking roofs.'[21] The Rev. Rice-Jones visited the vicinity of St Giles Mission House: 'The walls are stained black with dirt; the passage and the stairs are thickly carpeted with dirt; and wherever you go, dirt reigns supreme', while its inhabitants had 'bare black feet, as black as the hands and face; shapeless boots, ungartered hose falling over the instep; brimless hats, low-looking eared caps drawn athwart the wickedest little faces possible to imagine'.[22]

This black/white coding constituted a manichean allegory which became a critical trope in the imperial formation of the late nineteenth century.[23] Stereotypical images based on physical characteristics, most notably skin colour, had existed ever since a black presence was known. But at determinate historical moments the coding took on particular forms. The wretched history of slavery provides abundant evidence of how virulent racial forms emerged as a means of validating the practice of enslavement, and were mobilized by pro-slave interests when they felt threatened by the impulses of abolition and slave revolt. And in India, the caste system – the internal boundaries of which were defined by precisely the same allegory articulated to notions of purity and cleanliness – was reconstructed and rigidified by imperial intervention after 1850 (see Chapter 7).[24] It was at this time that racial discourse, cultivated by scientific theory, shifted from the bestowal of arbitrary features to the systematic ascription of natural and essential signs.[25] Faced with seemingly diverse, uncontrollable and unknowable low others, the imperial formation found in the allegory a versatile means of transforming physical difference into moral and cultural difference. The superiority of white over black (with all their respective chains of signification) was naturalized and thereby consolidated. Eventually, through improvised extensions, such allegorical forms dominated most spheres of the imperial formation, implicating sympathizers and critics alike.

Peculiar problems were created within the metropolis. Here the poor were for the most part white, that is, without the visual sign of otherness. The poor presented a radical disruption to order by forcing the conjunction of a culturally constituted whiteness with its own metaphors of difference;[26] they could be embraced within a symbolic dualism and hence resolved only by being constructed as black. The Irish, as both colonial subjects and urban poor, were doubly problematic, and it comes as no surprise to find that the most strident racial coding was deployed on them. The examples previously cited testify to this. Better known are Carlyle's epithet in *Sartor Resartus* of the Irish as 'white negroes', and Kingsley's impressions on his tour of Ireland in 1860:

> But I am haunted by the human chimpanzees I saw along that hundred miles of horrible country. I don't believe they are our fault. I believe there are not only many more of them than of old, but that they are happier, better, more comfortably fed and lodged under our rule than they ever were. But to see white chimpanzees is dreadful; if they were black, one would not feel it so much, but their skins, except where tanned by exposure, are as white as ours.[27]

Such sentiments were examples of a more general process through which the Irish were increasingly 'simianized'. Between 1840 and 1890 visual representations of Irish physiognomy gradually changed; the early 1860s was a critical period, for it was then that the early emphasis on big-mouthed and prognathous faces was displaced by stereotypes with ape-like features.[28] In the aftermath of the explosions at Clerkenwell and Manchester when Fenians had attempted to liberate some of their leaders from police custody, cartoonists in popular periodicals such as *Punch*, *Judy* and *Puck* drew upon the early Francophobic anthropomorphisms of Gillray and Cruikshank to invent the Irish ape. A second wave of simianization occurred during the 1880s following the Phoenix Park assassination, renewed land wars and the rise of Parnellite nationalism. Similarities between Tenniel's famous 1882 cartoon of the Irish Frankenstein and his 1888 portrayal of the spectral Ripper were striking. Thus although simianization was evident in depictions of other subjects, the most virulent forms were retained for the Irish. Occasionally members of the English poor were endowed with ape-like features, but they were very much the exception. Even the brutal stereotypes of Africans at the time did not 'come close in terms of monstrousness to the Irish and Irish American gorillas of the Fenian era'.[29]

Dirt therefore was a versatile metaphor that helped give meaning to shifting and complex fields of racial hierarchies. It assumed a distinct significance in the 1860s when a peculiar conjunction of metropolitan and imperial crises forced a reconstitution of the racial order. The Indian revolt of 1857 and the Morant Bay rebellion of 1865 shook seismically the foundations of the imperial formation by demonstrating unequivocally that colonial subjects were no longer prepared to tolerate imperial authority or, in the aftermath of the abolition of slavery, the state of free wage labour, and that in mounting such challenges they revealed the dangers of an endemic savagery out of the control.[30] Across the Atlantic the course of the American Civil War – closely watched in this country – placed in sharp relief a kaleidoscopic range of racial tensions. Meanwhile, the 1860s represented something of a watershed in metropolitan history. The collapse of traditional industry in East London cast tens of thousands of workers into the residuum, precipitating a series of bread riots, undermining the actuarial basis of poor relief, and threatening the moral virtue and economic rationality upon which liberal utopian visions of the future were based.[31]

Degeneration and desire

It was at this moment that notions of degeneration assailed the discursive realm of the metropolitan poor. Expressing certain anxieties about the stability of the social order in the face of revolutionary upheaval, such ideas had surfaced occasionally to influence post-Enlightenment thought, but they remained relatively minor components within large theories of social and political evolution.[32] Now, at a time when an unprecedented crisis in the imperial formation catalysed a loss of confidence in progress, and in the context of a measured scientific valorization promoted by social Darwinism, degeneration took on dramatic new significance. The attractions were obvious. Degeneration was a fluid category; it shifted readily and was thereby reconstituted between the human sciences, fiction and social commentary, rendering it irreducible to any fixed theory and unidentifiable with any single political cause.[33] But in the second half of the nineteenth century, degeneration was increasingly articulated with race. Thus, for example, it was used to explain the pathological condition of the urban poor as symptomatic of a degenerative process within the imperial race, and the natural savagery of colonial subjects as a characteristic degeneration from the ideal white race,[34] and provided an ominous portent which could be mobilized to legitimate an extensive repertoire of repressive measures.

Theories of degeneration imparted a sinister and menacing twist to the racialization of the poor. Social pathologies, it was argued, were due to characteristic hereditary factors not to the social conditions which the poor inhabited. This effectively rendered their presence invisible, and even more of a threat. For while heredity encouraged the racial separation of the poor, their persistence – indeed, their increased presence within the bourgeois imaginary – suggested simultaneously that the poor constituted a degenerative and threatening strain within the Anglo-Saxon race. For many, this invisible enemy within posed a 'far greater problem than the racial inferiority of non-European peoples';[35] it also helped to explain why the racialization of the metropolitan poor assumed its most pernicious forms after the 1860s when the immediate crises in imperial rule precipitated by colonial insurrection had been superseded by fears that dissembling processes were operating at the heart of empire.

Robert Young has argued skilfully that in the troubled climate manifest by theories of degeneration, hybridity emerged as a key cultural signifier.[36] Drawing upon examples from animal and plant kingdoms, racial theorists of the nineteenth century surmised that because hybrid offspring had diminishing fertility sexual unions between people from two different races threatened the propagation of the human race. In the worst case scenario, the intermixing of races gave rise to a raceless mass, a chaos of indiscrimination that threatened to contaminate and hence subvert the vigour of the pure race with which it came into contact. At the core of emergent racial theory, therefore, 'hybridity also maps out its most anxious, vulnerable site: a fulcrum at its edge and centre where its dialectics of injustice, hatred and oppression can find themselves effaced and expunged'.[37] But this preoccupation with hybridity betrayed an ambivalence between desire and repulsion, thereby revealing the centrality of sexuality in race and culture, and suggested that racial theories were deeply implicated in theories of desire. A dialectic existed between a structure of covert colonial desire promoting racial intermixing and a structure of repulsion in which racial antagonisms were perpetuated.

Racial theorists can most conveniently be located within a colonial context. Gobineau, for example, who in his *Essay on the Inequality of Races*, published in 1853–55, laid the foundation for European racial theory, was explicit about colonial desire, indeed erected hybridity rather than racial purity as the defining feature of modern civilization.[38] He elaborated the principle that internal poison resulting from continual adulteration of the race would eventually prove fatal. Thus while the attraction felt by the white (male) race for yellow and brown (female) races was critical to the development of civilization, the same imperative would bring about its downfall. The idea here that generation contains the seeds of its own destruction was clearly linked to fears about the fall of empire. And the most recent work on the mediation of race and culture with sexuality has been within the broad ambit of postcolonial theory.[39]

But the parallels with contemporary discourses about the metropolitan

poor are unmistakable. As we have seen, the same dialectic between fascination and disgust informed the imaginary relationship with the low
other. Equally significantly, the trope of degeneration assumed a new salience from the 1860s as the presence of the poor and colonial others – seen
as part of an internal orient – became subject to urgent concern and surveillance. Indian herbalists and tract sellers had been noted by Mayhew
among the street poor, but later in the 1850s, as records of their plight
came to the attention of magistrates and poor law authorities, evangelicals
sought to understand their condition and provide relief. Joseph Salter embarked on missionary work among Asians in the metropolis, leading to
the establishment in 1856 of the Asiatic Strangers' Home. His account of
this work echoed the earlier sentiments of Joseph Mullens (p. 122). The
progressive influence of civilization on Indian peoples, he declared, had
done much to encourage a questioning of their heathen beliefs and prepare
the grounds for their salvation. Citing a missionary in India, he argued
that British modernization had undermined the caste system. Railways
have 'ploughed up the soil consecrated to Gunga and Kalee', and lightning
is 'dispatched along its wire path ... more quickly than Ram escaped from
Ceylon to the continent'.[40] Indians who had migrated to London were discussed in sympathetic terms. Many risked defilement but on their return
had been praised for their courage. The majority proved themselves hard-
working and open to Christian influence. The more educated – apothecar-
ies and interpreters – rarely thought their ancient religion worth struggling
to save. But in London they are exposed to various frauds and cheats, lose
any money they have, and rapidly sink into begging and crime. Noticed by
few until seen shivering in rags, cared for by none, many perish on the cold
streets. One body found at Shadwell had 'horny hands' that bore evidence
of 'honest labour and hard toil'.[41] Quite apart from the human suffering
exacted, Salter concluded, 'the treatment they had received had evidently
produced upon their minds the very reverse of a favourable impression of
the Christian religion'.[42] More importantly, profound neglect had forced
them to associate with the depraved poor, serving only to build a dangerous moral isolation:

> The heathens of the heathen land associate here with the heathens of Chris-
> tian London; and, truly, they both dwell in the valley of the shadow of death.
> Between these waifs from the banks of the Indus and Ganges, and the repu-
> table white man brought up on the banks of the Thames, there is a great gulf
> fixed, and this gulf is crossed by very few. The difficulty of colloquial com-
> munication is one barrier that stands in the way; but far more formidable, as
> a division, is the foul atmosphere of human depravity in which these Orientals
> live and suffer.... The heathen mind is dark, and the vices of the various
> heathen systems in which the Asiatic is so brought up, as to form part of his
> nature, are bad enough when unmingled with European sin in his own land

of superstition; but here is an interchange of sin and an unholy compound of both.[43]

This sense of impenetrable isolation combined with cultural fantasies redolent of De Quincey constructed the opium den as *the* site of orientalist disgust and desire, hybridity and degradation. Accounts of the metropolitan poor came routinely to include descriptions of dens and their inhabitants. In 'Tiger Bay' (Brunswick St, Wapping) was discovered a cellar in which

> four lascars roll their yellow and black eyes upon us as they glare silently at each other, and smoke from one bamboo pipe.... The two wretched women who are cooking some rice at a scanty fire are English, but so degraded, even below the degradation of such a neighbourhood, that they answer only with ghastly grins and a cringing paucity of words.... Rooms where dark-skinned, snake-like Hindoos (beggars and tract-sellers by day) live with English and Irish women as their wives, and live, as it would seem, not always so miserably as might be imagined.[44]

Popular as Tiger Bay was as a haunt of social investigators, it was eclipsed by the den at Bluegate Fields off the Ratcliff Highway, which entered into popular iconography. J.C. Parkinson described it in familiar terms:

> There is a little colony of Orientals in the centre of Bluegate-fields, and in the centre of this colony is the opium den.... The livid, cadaverous, corpse-like visage of Yahee, the wild excited glare of the young Lascar who opens the door, the stolid sheep-like ruminations of Lazarus and the other Chinamen coiled together on the floor, the incoherent anecdotes of the Bengalee squatted on the bed, the fiery gesticulations of the mulatoo and the Manilla-man who are in conversation by the fire, the semi-idiotic jabber of the negroes huddled up behind Yahee, are all due to the same fumes.[45]

Ewing Ritchie inquired further into the effects of opium, expressing little surprise that the oriental experienced none of the mystical pleasures induced in the English mind:

> With the somewhat doubtful confessions of De Quincey and Coleridge in my memory, I tried to get them to acknowledge sudden impulses, poetic inspirations, splendid dreams; but of such things these little fellows had never conceived; the highest eulogism I heard was: 'You have pains – pain in de liver, pain in de head – you smoke – all de pains go'.[46]

Tiger Bay was demolished and the Ratcliff Highway cleared as part of a slum clearance programme in the mid 1870s, but the area continued to hold the same grim fascination for scribbling visitors because like all such waterside spaces it provided refuge for a transient seafaring population and the readiest opportunities for racial intermixing. But with the obliteration of the dens peculiar interest was focused on one of the previously identified and most visible participants – the site of the most profound moral danger and desire – the active, orientalized, predatory female. *Wonderful London*, published in 1878, welcomed the abolition of Tiger Bay, where 'swarms of Lascars and Malays herded together to indulge in mad opium orgies', but noted that 'the tigresses remain'.[47] Here a reversal was effected. A savage was not the male who 'tracks and brings down the game to share it with the she', but was the female who 'hunts, while the he creature lurks in ambush to give assistance if need be, or remains home at the den'. And while the Highway was a 'spectacle which no visitor from the country should miss; the whole human family ... is here perambulating the streets, with every shade of colour', tigresses were not always alert to this 'great variety of game', because like 'other carnivora, they are not partial to hunting by daylight'.[48]

Such images were by this time becoming part of a popular currency. Taine recorded in 1873 his impressions of numerous visits to London. In Shadwell, another waterside area, he found conditions with which the bad quarters of Marseilles, Antwerp and Paris could not compare. In the low houses, he noted

> unmade beds, women dancing. Thrice in ten minutes ... crowds collected at the doors; fights were going on, chiefly fights between women; one of them, her face bleeding, tears in her eyes, drunk, shouted with a sharp and harsh voice, and wished to fling herself upon a man. The bystanders laughed; the noise caused the adjacent lanes to be emptied of their occupants; ragged, poor children, harlots – it was like a human sewer suddenly discharging its contents.[49]

Home missionaries discovered similar scenes while working in East London. In one article entitled 'Degradation', we are confronted with the terrible prospect of missionary work amongst a poor population in which overcrowding subverted the normal boundaries of Christian and racial morality:

> [T]here are hideous cases of the most revolting incest occasionally coming to the surface, which tell how near the level of the brutes some of the masses of our people are fallen.... Enter one of these houses, and from cellar to garret it is packed with people, each floor let and sublet again with different families, herding together in a way from which even the beasts that perish would instinctively shrink. In such a part the work of a clergyman is as truly missionary as if his labours were being carried on in Central Africa.[50]

Some of the scenes reached such low depths of depravation that even heathens found them shocking. In 'Measured by a Mahometan's standard' (and no doubt that also of the home missionary), we learn that:

They beheld the streets swarming with prostitutes, and they were horrified at the sensuality and the sin which such scenes suggested.... And so they fled, terrified and amazed at the spectacle. Instead of being attracted by the outer manifestation of England's religion, they thanked the God they worshipped, and the false prophet by whom they had been misled, that this religion was not their religion.[51]

This nexus of hybridity, orientalization, degradation and covert desire marked both an apotheosis of the racialization of the poor and the onset of a transformation, for from this point the poor assumed a more threatening aspect which could not be theorized so readily using contemporary racial discourse. The predatory prostitute was emblematic of a new and distinctly modern sense that the poor were transgressing the imaginative and spatial boundaries of the metropolis. The prostitute's attraction for urban travellers since the time of Mayhew can only in part be explained by her position within male voyeuristic fantasies; the prostitute also transgressed the gendered boundaries of the metropolis.[52] By asserting an active presence within the public spaces of the city, the prostitute challenged defiantly prevalent norms of female virtue centred on a passive domesticity, and around the body of the prostitute was articulated moral, sexual and medical concern.

Crowds bred in the abyss

In the course of the 1870s anxieties about the transgressive threat of the prostitute were generalized to include the metropolitan poor as a whole:

> The savage class in question comprises the 'roughs' who infest every one of the hundreds of shady slums and blind alleys that, despite metropolitan improvements, still disgrace the great city. We held up our hands in speechless horror and indignation at the time when the scum and dregs of humanity which cling to the bedraggled skirts of Communism committed such frightful ravages in Paris; but it is as certain as that night succeeds day, that we have lurking in our undercurrents a horde of ruffianism fully equal to similar feats of carnage, plunder, and incendiarism, should occasion serve.[53]

Here was signalled something of the transformation in constructions of the poor. Detectable elements of earlier racialized discourses around savagery, dirt and degradation were to be expected, but qualitatively new was the politicization and spatial reordering of the poor. The modern metropolis, in spite of improvements undertaken as part of a civic mission to rid its streets of the residuum, was found still to be infested by their numbers. Indeed, the suggestion was that their presence had increased. No longer savage tribes confined to the racialized spaces of East and South London, the poor were a mob which, guided by the example of the 1871 Paris

Commune, threatened in an act of supreme transgression to seize the metropolis as a whole.

This transformation was underpinned by structural change within the metropolis.[54] The social and economic crisis of the 1880s was deeper and more widespread than that of the 1860s. The cyclical depression impacted on a far broader range of occupations, slum clearance schemes and housing reform had done little to solve the chronic problem of working-class housing let alone the slums, evangelical missions had for the most part been met with indifference even hostility by the poor, and the spectre appeared of socialist currents in working-class organization and thought. Incidences of the poor rampaging through the streets of the respectable West End bore witness that the worst fears of mob rule were being realized. All this fostered in the bourgeois consciousness a sense of fragmentation, self-doubt and loss of confidence in inexorable progress at a time of imperial expansion. The attendant 'epistemological crisis ... precipitated changes in the visual image of the city that produced new representations of the self and the Other'.[55]

In the course of the 1880s the metropolitan poor were rediscovered and reconstituted in ways that defy neat generalizations. The sensational revelations of a new breed of social investigators articulated older discursive formations with contemporary political and moral concerns. Of these, Andrew Mearns's *The Bitter Cry of Outcast London* had the greatest impact.[56] Originally published as a pamphlet of approximately 8,000 words in 1883, it appeared to have little sociological or literary merit. It had neither the originality of Mayhew nor the flair of Greenwood; it was poorly structured, misquoted sources and was based fragilely on an extremely limited survey of housing in Bermondsey, Ratcliff and Shadwell. But its unprecedented reception suggests that the pamphlet resonated powerfully with the growing sense of unease and guilt about the state of the metropolitan poor.

Mearns highlighted the gulf that was daily widening between the 'lower classes of the community' and 'all decency and civilization', as a result of which a 'TERRIBLE FLOOD OF SIN AND MISERY IS GAINING UPON US'.[57] This population, however, was not racially distinct, but belonged 'as much as you, to the race for whom Christ died', and given the appalling conditions in which they were condemned to exist they were 'entitled to credit for not being twenty times more depraved than they are'.[58] If urgent measures were not taken, then the political consequences would be dire:

> The only check upon communism in this regard is jealousy and not virtue. The vilest practices are looked upon with the most matter-of-fact indifference. The low parts of London are the sink into which the filthy and abominable from all parts of the country seem to flow.[59]

And the measures? These from the outset had to be based on a comprehensive collectivism:

> [W]ithout State interference nothing effectual can be accomplished upon any large scale.... The State must make short work of this iniquitous traffic [rack renting], and secure for the poorest the rights of citizenship; the right to live in something better than fever dens; the right to live as something better than the uncleanest of brute beasts.[60]

This confused and contradictory text best represented the stumbling attempts to recognize the nature of a problem that had beset the Victorian metropolis but which at a time of a crisis of confidence in the imperial formation assumed an unprecedented political urgency. The flood of moral depravity evident amongst the lowest sections of the population had to be stemmed, Mearns contended, by social and political reform lest the nation as a whole be engulfed by communism.

The contemporaneous writings of George Sims reveal the source of inspiration for much of Mearns's pamphlet. Working in the tradition of urban travel, Sims published an influential series of articles throughout the 1880s, which were collected in *How the Poor Live*.[61] The prose was less restrained than Mearns's, but the message was the same:

> This mighty mob of famished, diseased, and filthy helots is getting dangerous, physically, morally, politically dangerous. The barriers that have kept it back are rotten and giving way, and it may do the State a mischief if it be not looked to in time. Its fevers and its filth may have spread to the homes of the wealthy; its lawless armies may sally forth and give us a taste of the lesson the mob has tried to teach now and again in Paris, when long years of neglect have done their worst.[62]

And while Sims's arguments were replete with racist characterizations of 'savage tribes' which commanded the attention of much missionary activity, and references to the 'quaint sayings and peculiar wit of the nigger breed', the metropolitan poor are not thought as a race apart; indeed, the poor are entitled along with the rest of British society to participate in the benefits of empire:

> There are people who will contend that in these islands the great blessing of the natives of all degrees is that they are Great Britons. Our patriotic songs bid us all rejoice greatly in this fact, and patriotism is not a class privilege. The starved outcast, crouching for shelter on a wild March night on one of the stone recesses of London Bridge has a right to exclaim with the same pride as the Marquis of Westminster –
> 'Far as the breeze can bear the billow's foam
> Survey our empire and behold our home.'[63]

As the poor demonstrated an increased propensity to transgress spatial barriers and bring closer the lessons of Paris, so anxiety escalated. H.J. Goldsmid, travelling among lodging houses, recorded his impressions of discontented dossers:

> We have not been without warnings. When last winter a brutal mob rushed through the streets and looted the shops of the West-end, most people said it was the work of roughs and larrikins whose only object was plunder. They grievously misunderstood the facts. Many – nay most – of the men who took part in the riots of that day came from the low lodging houses, and though the majority were actuated solely by cupidity and greed, there were many a stern, determined man there who believed that in plundering and destroying he was merely executing the righteous wrath of starved, oppressed, and discontented labour against harsh, bloated, and unsympathetic capital.... [B]efore very many years have flown we shall be compelled to read in haggard, wolfish faces, robbed of every tender or human expression, to hear in coarse cries of menace, ay, even of lawless triumph, that lesson that has been taught so sharply in other lands than ours – that what might once, not long since, have been reformed, has grown and swelled and gathered force and volume until the torrent can no longer be stemmed, and we are confronted by REVOLUTION.[64]

Events around the 1889 dock strike and the early struggles of new unionism dissipated heightened political anxiety. Fears that an impoverished residuum organized by a socialist-inspired leadership would provoke mob rule were not realized; instead bands of dockers marched in orderly and good-humoured fashion in furtherance of modest demands. The more militant and threatening struggles of gasworkers were defeated by military-style police tactics which enabled employers to bring in large numbers of unskilled, strike-breaking labourers.[65] But if immediate political fears had receded, the problem remained of incorporating the poor within an interpretative framework for the metropolis as a distinctly modern totality.

The seventeen volumes of Charles Booth's *Life and Labour of the People in London* published over 1889–1902 constituted the single most comprehensive and systematic attempt to capture this totality.[66] Fired by a vision of social and moral progress removed from the orthodoxies of contemporary political economy, Booth set out to classify and quantify the metropolitan poor as the first step in formulating ameliorative measures. The focus was on production and distribution, and the multiplicity of social – and to a lesser extent cultural – relations built upon them. As the investigation progressed in a climate of relative political ease, so the diversity and dynamism of the metropolitan experience emerged. Although this challenged convenient polarizations of the poor and respectable so characteristic of previous social inquiry, Booth was unable to break completely with the genre. He and his army of co-workers remained urban travellers inhabiting psychological oppositions between the bourgeois and the low other, carrying with them all the familiar baggage of degeneration, depravity and gender disorder.[67]

The Booth survey was situated uneasily – and in some respects defined the moment – between past racializations of the poor and modernist impulses to see them as part of the metropolitan totality. The theory of hereditary urban degeneration may have been endowed with a certain authority by the survey,[68] but the theory implied no essential racial separateness; on the contrary, it both generalized and encompassed the poor within the metropolitan – and hence national – whole. And while slum dwellers were perceived as degenerate populations whose pathological features were transmitted from one generation to another and who carried contamination with them when forced as a body to migrate, there was little sense in Booth that degeneracy was the product of irreversible hereditary processes.[69] Recommendations for eliminating poverty were moral and socio-economic, not social Darwinist. At other times the poor were perceived in terms of a modern experience. Mile End fair was described as a vortex attracting the young, and the East End as a 'rush of human life as fascinating to watch as the current of a river to which human life is so often likened'.[70]

It was only with respect to the wave of Jewish immigration in the 1880s that more familiar racial constructions obtained. Even then there were contradictions. Jews may have possessed characteristic features of a racial other – high cheekbones, thickened lips, darker complexion and unmistakable noses – but they were sober and industrious, private and respectable. 'The Jews', Walkowitz concludes, 'were a peculiar people who eluded and challenged Booth's categories of class and gender Otherness.'[71]

The same ambiguities were evident in much of the considerable literature that addressed the problems posed by this immigration. Thus while the East End was seen to contain an internal orient larger and more visible than before, there is little of same sense of moral degradation or political threat. Thus H. Walker, writing in 1896, argued:

> But we soon begin to make the great and startling discovery which awaits every newcomer into Whitechapel. Here, in spite of English-looking surroundings, he is practically in a foreign land, so far as language and race are concerned. The people are neither French nor English, Germans nor Americans, but Jews. In this Whitechapel ghetto the English visitor almost feels himself one of a subject race in the presence of dominant and overwhelming invaders.[72]

Such a 'disaffected population might have been a standing menace to London', but Whitechapel was not the home of 'malcontent refugees or political anarchists': 'Nothing, in fact, is more remarkable on Sunday than the quiet and orderliness of a great population of aliens in faith and speech who ... are less aggressive in the streets than many of their better circumstanced co-residents'.[73]

The popular works of Walter Besant went further, actually identifying the *re*generational potential of English culture. Thus in *East London* he observed the 'narrow-chested and pasty-faced Polish Jew', asking one of their scholars if this was the 'race which defied the legions of Titus', or a descendant of 'Joshua's valiant captains'? The scholar answered that 'these are the children of the Ghetto.... Come again in ten years' time. In the free air of Anglo-Saxon rule they will grow; you will not know them again.'[74]

By actively constructing a threat, however, these racial ambiguities could be resolved. In a discussion of the furniture trade in East London, for example, F. Hird pointed to the capacity of Jews to force British workers out by undercutting the price of labour. Racial barriers were firmly erected around a diverse but unified population:

> [T]hese districts are a little world of Israels, where the Poles, Armenians, Russians, and Germans of the faith live and have their being amidst the babel of foreign tongues, and in an environment of dirt indescribable. But however interesting from the point of view of the picturesque the presence of these strangers within our gates may be, their effect upon the East End is truly lamentable.[75]

In a similar vein, George Haw claimed that Jewish landlords were 'coming down on the clamouring poor like a wolf on the fold ... and were now driving out the Christian poor in a more merciless way than they themselves were ever persecuted and driven out of Russia or Poland'.[76]

Problems of the race

Other writers saw the racialization of the poor less ambivalently. Arnold White began his publishing career in 1886 with *The Problems of a Great City*.[77] Here the problems of the great city were the 'problems of the race', which had to be resolved through a 'moral revolution' rather than delegation 'to governments or to a clerical caste' lest the 'dark seeds of poisonous and eternal evil' were sown to threaten the empire:

> Distress in London is not the distress of a great city – it is the distress of a great empire.... The social question in England is shrouded in greater darkness than the social questions of Imperial Germany or Republican France.... Great as the sum of poverty and degradation inherited by this generation from that which preceded it, we are making no sensible reductions of this debt to humanity, and in fair way to hand down to the next generation greater

embarrassment, with more efficient machinery for the manufacture of larger masses of human degradation.[78]

Mayhew was then rallied to the social Darwinist cause:

> Compared with the nomadic tribes of tropic countries, where the curse of civilization is unknown, the nomads of London are but miserable savages.... Criminal and pauperised classes with low cerebral development renew their race more rapidly than those of higher nervous natures.... The fecundity of starving people is notorious, and has again and again been exemplified in famine districts in India. A policy based on relief from funds collected in a hurry, and administered by a machinery raised in a night, can be but a temporary policy. The evil grows by what it feeds on.[79]

Instead White proposed legislation to sterilize the unfit, ban early marriages and force emigration, which with eugenicist logic he claimed would harmonize with 'the inexorable tendencies of our natural law'. By linking the social crisis caused by the threat of the metropolitan poor to fears in the imperial formation via theories of degeneration, White intensified the racialization of the poor. He may have been an erratic figure, working in isolation, but he represented an important response to the crisis.

William Booth emerged as part of the same strand of social imperialism; his writings were enormously popular, however, providing a secure financial and ideological basis for the expansion of the Salvation Army. *In Darkest England and the Way Out*, published in 1890, sold 200,000 copies in the first year.[80] The referent was Henry M. Stanley's *In Darkest Africa*, in which the explorer described an immense area 'where the rays of sunshine never penetrate, where in the dark, dank air, filled with the steam of the heated morass, human beings dwarfed into pygmies and brutalised into cannibals lurk and live and die'.[81] The parallels between degenerated Africans living in foetid darkness and the metropolitan poor were only too obvious:

> It is a terrible picture, and one that has engraved itself deep on the heart of civilisation. But while brooding over the awful presentation of life as it exists in the vast African forest, it seemed to me only too vivid a picture of many parts of our own land. As there is a darkest Africa is there not also a darkest England? Civilisation, which can breed its own barbarians, does it not also breed its own pygmies?[82]

Within this barbarian population, the racialized female reappeared to occupy a privileged site:

> The lot of a negress in the Equatorial Forest is not, perhaps, a very happy one, but is it so very much worse than that of many a pretty orphan girl in our Christian capital? We talk about the brutalities of the dark ages, and we

profess to shudder as we read in books of the shameful exaction of the rights of feudal superior. And yet here, beneath our very eyes, in our theatres, in our restaurants, and in many other places, unspeakable though it be to name it, the same hideous abuse flourishes unchecked.[83]

The impact of social imperialism was to be felt in the formation of the Edwardian welfare state.[84] But as the century turned, more pressing concerns around continued immigration and the standard of recruits for the Boer War intensified fears that degeneration was consuming the heart of empire.[85] With this more extreme current of racial theory surfaced views that seemed to traverse political boundaries. George Haw cited with approval Lord Rosebery when he asked, 'What is an Empire unless it is pillared on an Imperial race, and what are you doing to allow this Imperial race to be vitiated and poisoned in the dens of crime and horror in which too many of them are reared at this moment?'[86]

And Major W. Evans-Gordon, a leading voice in the Royal Commission on Alien Immigration, claimed that there was

> almost a spell which brings the Jewish immigrants into the already crammed and congested areas of the East End, where their brethren are aggregated and segregated.... The Hebrew colony, then, unlike any other alien colony in the land, forms a solid and permanently distinct block – a race apart, as it were, in an enduring island of extraneous thought and custom.... Many English people living in the neighbourhood have summed up the situation in a phrase 'We are living in a foreign country'.[87]

A rather different current simultaneously began to take shape and gain momentum, particularly among the liberal intelligentsia. Evident in embryonic form among Charles Booth's descriptions of East End crowds, and as part of the totalizing project, racialized conceptions of the metropolitan poor were displaced by modernist fears of the crowd. The French psychologist Gustave LeBon theorized contemporary perceptions in *The Psychology of Peoples*, first published in 1894. The crowd, according to LeBon, took different forms; the common denominator was faceless anonymity, but in the bourgeois mind of late Victorian Britain it was the irrational, aggressive, savage, instinctual and *feminine* crowd that prevailed.[88]

In the troubled context of an extended franchise and the failure of social reform to eradicate poverty, this crowd represented the hidden presence in modern society of destructive atavistic features – a regressive trend in civilization which by signalling the onset of mass irrationality marked the end of human development. The crowd thus became the dominant site of degeneration, effectively displacing the individual, the family and the 'tribe'; linked to the threat of social chaos and the fall of empire, the crowd was 'a commentary upon modernity itself'.[89] Paradoxically, as Young has noted, these raceless masses, by threatening to erase difference, both asserted and subverted the trope of degeneracy, leading to a more intense and sinister racialization of the crowd.[90]

Modernist accounts of the metropolis began with *The Heart of the Empire*, an important collection of articles written by the vanguard of the new liberal intelligentsia.[91] 'The Victorian era has definitely closed', announced the editor Charles Masterman at the outset:

> For many years it was manifest that the forces characteristic of that period had become expended, and that new problems were arising with a new age. But during the latter years of the nineteenth century men were content to confront the evils of national life with the old remedies.[92]

But the expressed intent of the authors to distance themselves from nineteenth-century approaches to the poor and the imperialist sentiment of Gladstonian Liberalism evident in Rosebery was not fully realized. Thus while the increase in the poor was described in sympathetically modernist terms as 'the continual impetuous multiplication of the dwellers of the abyss', they were still perceived through the lens of social imperialism:

> The second generation of the immigrants has been reared in the courts and crowded ways of the great metropolis, with cramped physical accessories, hot, fretful life, and long hours of sedentary or unhealthy toil. The problem of the coming years is just the problem of this New Town type; upon their development and action depend the future progress of the Anglo-Saxon Race, and for the next half-century at least the policy of the British Empire in the world.[93]

A year later Masterman's modern consciousness was given free rein. In *From the Abyss* he described in a striking manner the 'dense black masses from the eastern railways [that] have streamed across the bridges from the marshes and desolate places beyond the river':

> We have seen a ghost; we are striving to readjust our stable ideas. The newspapers stir uneasily, talk in a shamefaced manner about natural ebullitions of patriotism, police inefficiency, and other irrelevant topics, deprecate the too frequent repetition of the ceremony, and praise the humour of a modern crowd. But within there is a cloud in men's minds, and a half-stifled recognition of the presence of a new force hitherto unreckoned; the creeping into conscious existence of the quaint and innumerable populations bred in the abyss.[94]

The plural is significant, for the populations Masterman refers to extend well beyond the metropolitan poor of nineteenth-century observers. In the immediate aftermath of the Boer War when the fitness of recruits to the British army became a matter of intense concern, fears surfaced of a 'weird and uncanny people' who comprise the 'dense black masses from the eastern railways' streaming 'across the bridges from the marshes and desolate places beyond the river'. These are the new city types, 'aged men in beards and bowlers shambling hastily forward; work girls, mechanics, active boys, neat little clerks' who blinked in the sunshine, surged through London streets with a power that even they seemed afraid of, and who as night fell relapsed into carnivalesque revelry. Then in a remarkable passage calling upon the full repertoire of race, degeneration and social Darwinism, the abyss from which these denizens emerged and to which they retreated is likened to a forest where the unremitting yet hopeless struggle for life of the imperial nation takes place:

> Everywhere exuberant, many-featured life, struggling under the tropical sun; a struggle continued ardently year after year, through innumerable succeeding generations. Only always at length the end. Some inexplicable change; slowly, imperceptibly, the torrent of life has overreached itself; the struggle has become too terrific; the vitality is gradually dying. And then, as the whole mass festers in all the gorgeous, wonderful beauty of decay, comes the mangrove – dark-leafed, dank, slippery, unlovely, sign and symbol of the inevitable end. And with the mangrove the black-marsh and the reeking, pestilential mud.[95]

'Crowd' and 'abyss' lay at the centre of imaginative attempts to appropriate metropolitan masses at a time of alienation and fragmentation. The abyss was a swamp in which the crowd dwelled, but as a site of existential despair it offered the modern subject an opportunity for renewal.[96] Jack London, for example, in the tradition of the urban traveller explored the abyss, recording his observations in The People of the Abyss.[97] And Ford Madox Ford, in the same journey of self-discovery, produced one of the first modernist texts – The Soul of London – which rendered impressionistically the urban landscape.[98] For Madox Ford modern urban society provided the most urgent challenge to imaginative writers who were better placed than 'gatherers of facts' to become 'intimately acquainted with the lives of those around us' and hence avoid the 'great danger of losing human knowledge and human sympathy'.[99] Within the metropolis, the eastern parts attracted his particular concern:

> They are grim, they are overhung with perpetual miasma, they lie low in damp marshes. Square and stumpy chimneys rise everywhere in clusters like the columns of ruined temples overhung with smirchings of vapour. Great fields are covered with scraps of rusty iron and heaps of fluttering rags; dismal pools of water reflect back on black waste grounds the dim skies. But all these things, if one is in the mood, one may find stimulating, because they tell of human toil, of human endeavour towards some end with some ideal at that end. But the other thing is sinister, since the other influences are working invisible, like malign and conscious fates, below the horizon.[100]

In evangelical and journalistic accounts located within the tradition of urban exploration founded by Mayhew, racial coding assumed stridently novel forms, at the heart of which lay the symbolic repertoires of dirt and degeneration. By linking physical appearance to moral and cultural difference, the metaphor of dirt gave meaning to and legitimized racial hierarchies; by ascribing innateness, the trope of degeneration gave racialization a sinister and menacing twist. Degeneration assumed increasing significance as fears of social disorder and imperial decline took hold, and attention turned to internal dangers. Perceived threats in the late 1880s from the poor and from Jewish immigration redefined racial boundaries. Social imperialists took up extreme eugenicist stances on the degenerative strains identified within the imperial race, and on the threats posed by the increased presence of the Jewish race. More influential were modernist impulses, the key imaginative sites of which were occupied by the crowd from the abyss. A new liberal intelligentsia infused with evangelism and critical of older imperialist sentiment also redefined racial boundaries.

The shifting and unstable boundaries of racialization of the poor resulted from attempts to understand the anachronistic presence in the modern metropolis of a population that defied modernity.[101] It was historically coterminous with the emergence of a distinctly modern colonialism characterized by a 'coherently "anthropological" mode of typifying natives'.[102] In this endeavour race was originally an analytical category with which human culture could be thought; over time it became '*the* crucial determinant, not only of culture but of human character and of all history'.[103] Race facilitated the imagined interconnectedness of colonial and metropolitan others in the imperial formation as it strove to survey and position them within an objective totality, and hence to assimilate threats to its future. The task to 'find a single, comprehensive principle of explanation which would underpin a rational theodicy of racial privilege and anchor structural inequality within an organic image of the body politic' found urgent application in both domestic and colonial spaces.[104] This process was strategically partial and complex, as a result of which within broad shifts there were continuities, and within continuities there were shifts. Nonetheless, overall the dialectic of capitalist modernization in asserting the superiority of colonizers over the colonized necessarily constructed inferiority at home; this suggests why the poor were racialized in the first instance and why toward the end of the century as the forces of modernization accelerated racialized boundaries expanded to encompass not only the poor but the masses as a whole.

Notes

1   John Garwood, *The Million Peopled City, or One Half of the People of London Made Known to the Other Half*, London, Werthleim and Macintosh, 1853, p. 263.

2   John Hollingshead, *Ragged in London in 1861*, London, Smith, Elder and Co., 1861, p. 8.

3   James Greenwood, *In Strange Company; Being the Experiences of a Roving Correspondent*, London, King, 1874, p. 14.

4   Watts Phillips, *The Wild Tribes of London*, London, Ward and Lock, 1855, p. 12.

5   Hollingshead, *Ragged London*, p. 44.

6   William Cosens, *London Dens and Mission Work Among Them; a Lecture*, London, Rivingtons, 1863, p. 7. Note that Prince Albert had died of typhus two years earlier.

7   George Godwin, *London Shadows; a Glance at the Homes of the Thousands*, London, Routledge and Kegan Paul, 1854, p. 1.

8   George Godwin, *Town Swamps and Social Bridges*, London, Routledge and Kegan Paul, 1859, reprinted with an introduction by A.D. King in 1972 by Leicester University Press. Although swamps referred most immediately to the housing conditions of the poor, they were a metaphor for a whole range of related social pathologies including crime, poverty, disease, ignorance and superstition. Bridges were the institutional infrastructures required in an urban society to combat them, particularly adequate schooling and public health. Godwin's manifesto was 'Drain the swamps and increase the bridges' (*ibid.*, p. 102).

9   *Ibid.*, p. 56.

10   *Ibid.*, p. 58.

11   Peter Stallybrass and Allon White, *The Politics and Poetics of Transgression*, London, Methuen, 1986.

12   *Ibid.*, p. 128.

13   *Ibid.*, p. 135. Stallybrass and White actually refer only to the city, but as I will attempt to demonstrate, the arguments apply equally validly to the colonies. See also the useful discussion on the materiality of dirt in the bourgeois imagination, in Phil Cohen, 'The perversions of inheritance', in Phil Cohen and H.S. Bains (eds), *Multiracist Britain*, Basingstoke, Macmillan, 1988, pp. 72–3.

14   Anne McClintock, *Imperial Leather. Race, Gender and Sexuality in the Colonial Context*, London, Routledge, 1995, p. 61.

15   *Ibid.*, pp. 152–5.

16   Stallybrass and White, *The Politics and Poetics of Transgression*, p. 145.

17   Note that in a curious inversion collectors of dog shit described in Mayhew were known as pure finders.

18   Douglas A. Lorimer, *Colour, Class and the Victorians. English Attitudes to the Negro in the Mid-Nineteenth Century*, Leicester, Leicester University Press, 1978, pp. 67–8; Kenan Malik, *The Meaning of Race. Race, History and Culture in Western Society*, Basingstoke, Macmillan, 1996, p. 91.

19   James Grant, *Lights and Shadows of London Life*, London, Saunders and Otley, 1841, p. 164.

20   Phillips, *The Wild Tribes of London*, p. 10.

21   R. Rowe, *Picked Up in the Streets, or Struggles for Life Amongst the London Poor*, London, Allen and Co., 1880, p. 4.

22   D. Rice-Jones, *In the Slums. Pages from the Notebook of a London Diocesan Home Missionary*, London, Nisbet, 1884, pp. 69, 149.

23   See the useful A.R. JanMohamed, 'The economy of the manichean allegory: the function of racial difference in colonialist literature', *Critical Inquiry*, 12, 1985, pp. 59–87.

24   Ronald Inden, *Imagining India*, Bloomington, Indiana University Press, 2000 [1990], p. 45.

25   This is a reworking of David Lloyd's formulation in 'Race under representation', *Oxford Literary Review*, 13, 1991, pp. 62–94.

26   *Ibid.*, p. 77.

27   Cited in *ibid.*, pp. 76–7, and in Mary Hickman, *Religion, Class and Identity. The State,*

the Catholic Church and the Education of the Irish in Britain, London, Avebury, 1995, p. 49. These are two of very few examples of where the term 'white' was used. 'White' was more generally noted by its absence in racial discourses – an indication of any felt need to subject it to scrutiny. This is a silence that has recently been broken, albeit in a different context, by Theodor Allen, The Invention of the White Race. Racial Oppression and Social Control, London, Verso, 1994, and David Roediger, Towards the Abolition of Whiteness. Essays on Race, Politics and Working-Class History, London, Verso, 1994.

28   The most impressive work on this is L.P. Curtis, Apes and Angels. The Irishman in Victorian Caricature, Washington, Smithsonian Institution Press, 1997, particularly Chapter 4, 'Simianizing the Irish Celt'. This is a revised version of the 1971 edition, with a new chapter – 'Historical revisionism and constructions of Paddy and Pat' – in which Curtis, drawing upon recent writings from postcolonial theory, effectively challenges critiques of the earlier work.

29   Ibid., p. 121.

30   It was at this time that the term 'nigger' was widely used to describe not only blacks and the Irish, but also Indians (James Walvin, 'Recurring themes: white images of black life during and after slavery', Slavery and Abolition, 5, 1984, pp. 118–40).

31   Gareth Stedman Jones, Outcast London. A Study in the Relationship Between Classes in Victorian Society, Oxford, Clarendon Press, 1971, p. 15.

32   Daniel Pick, Faces of Degeneration. A European Disorder, c.1848–1914, Cambridge, Cambridge University Press, 1989, pp. 38–9; see also Malik, The Meaning of Race, pp. 109–14.

33   Pick, Faces of Degeneration, p. 7.

34   Ibid., p. 21.

35   Malik, The Meaning of Race, p. 111.

36   Robert Young, Colonial Desire. Hybridity in Theory, Culture and Race, London, Routledge, 1995.

37   Ibid., p. 19.

38   Ibid., pp. 99–109.

39   See, for example, Homi Bhabha, The Location of Culture, London, Routledge, 1994; Richard Hyam, Empire and Sexuality. The British Experience, Manchester, Manchester University Press, 1991; McClintock, Imperial Leather; Patrick Williams and Laura Chrisman (eds), Colonial Discourse and Postcolonial Theory. A Reader, Brighton, Harvester Press, 1993; Young, Colonial Desire.

40   Joseph Salter, The Asiatics in England. Sketches of Sixteen Years' Work Among Orientals, London, Seeley and Co., 1873, p. 40.

41   Ibid., p. 20.

42   Ibid., p. ii.

43   Ibid., pp. 21–2.

44   Thomas Archer, The Pauper, the Thief and the Convict. Sketches of Some of their Homes, Haunts, and Habits, London, Groombridge and Sons, 1865, p. 133. James Greenwood was also a regular visitor – see his 'An opium smoke in Tiger Bay', in In Strange Company: Being the Experiences of a Roving Correspondent, London, King, 1874, and 'A visit to Tiger Bay', in The Wilds of London, London, Chatto and Windus, 1874.

45   J.C. Parkinson, Places and People, Being Studies from Life, London, Tinsley Bros., 1869, pp. 25–6. This was a collection of articles previously published in Dickens's All the Year Round, Tinsley's Magazine and the Daily News.

46   J. Ewing Ritchie, Days and Nights in London; or, Studies in Black and Grey, London, Tinsley, 1880, pp. 178–9.

47   Anon., Wonderful London. Its Lights and Shadows of Humour and Sadness, London, Tinsley, 1878, p. 337.

48   Ibid., p. 339.

49   Hippolyte Taine, Notes on England, London, Strahan, 1873, pp. 33–4. The observations were originally published in Paris Temps, and almost simultaneously in English translation in the Daily News. Extracts were published widely in the Athenaeum,

Saturday Review, Spectator, Edinburgh Review and *Westminster Review*, and thus provided a source for much middle-class discussion.

50 *Stories and Episodes from Home Mission Work*, London, Society for Promoting the Employment of Additional Curates, 1881, pp. 76, 100. This was a collection of articles previously published in the society's journal *The Home Field*.

51 *Ibid.*, p. 77. The recent work of Antoinette Burton has studied similar responses of a different class of Indian travellers in the late nineteenth-century metropolis. Various educated middle-class Indians migrated to England in order to gain medical or legal qualifications, or simply to explore for themselves British culture. They recorded their observations in letters, travelogues and newpaper articles which reveal how they sought to transform themselves from objects of spectacle to carriers of Western mores, but how 'unmannered and coercive' Western civilization could be. This colonial encounter, Burton concludes, could unsettle power relations of the imperial formation in the metropolis. (Antoinette Burton, 'Making a spectacle of empire: Indian travellers in fin-de-siècle London', *History Workshop Journal*, 42, 1996, pp. 96–117, and *At the Heart of Empire. Indians and the Colonial Encounter in late Victorian Britain*, Berkeley, University of California Press, 1998.)

52 See Judith Walkowitz, *City of Dreadful Delight. Narratives of Sexual Danger in Late-Victorian London*, London, Virago, 1994; and Elizabeth Wilson, *The Sphinx in the City. Urban Life, the Control of Disorder, and Women*, London, Virago, 1991.

53 Anon., *Wonderful London*, p. 215.

54 Stedman Jones, *Outcast London*, especially Chapter 16.

55 Walkowitz, *City of Dreadful Delight*, p. 38.

56 [Andrew Mearns], *The Bitter Cry of Outcast London. An Inquiry into the Condition of the Abject Poor*, London, Clarke and Co., 1883, reprinted with an introduction by A.S. Wohl by Leicester University Press in 1970. Mearns was a member of the London Congregational Union, but was aided by members of the London City Mission and the East London Tabernacle. The introduction provides a measured assessment of the impact of the pamphlet.

57 *Ibid.*, p. 56. This was the only phrase in the pamphlet to be capitalized.

58 *Ibid.*, p. 60. This was a misquote from one of George Sims's articles that appeared earlier in the year in *Pictorial World*.

59 *Ibid.*, p. 61.

60 *Ibid.*, p. 69.

61 George Sims, *How the Poor Live, and Horrible London*, London, Chatto and Windus, 1889. The articles were originally published in *Pictorial World* and the *Daily News*. Sims claimed with some hyperbole that the 'author of *The Bitter Cry of Outcast London* derived the greatest assistance from these while compiling his famous pamphlet' (Preface).

62 *Ibid.*, p. 44.

63 *Ibid.*, p. 54.

64 H.J. Goldsmid, *Dottings of a Dosser, being Revelations of the Inner Life of Low London Lodging Houses*, London, Fisher Unwin, 1886.

65 See Stedman Jones, *Outcast London*, and my 'London over the border: a study of West Ham during rapid growth, 1870–1910', unpublished PhD thesis, University of Cambridge, 1984.

66 Charles Booth, *Life and Labour of the People in London*, 10 vols, London, Macmillan, 1887–1902. For useful critical assessments of Booth see David Englander, 'Comparisons and contrasts: Henry Mayhew and Charles Booth as social investigators', in David Englander and Rosemary O'Day (eds), *Retrieved Riches. Social Investigation in Britain, 1880–1914*, London, Scolar, 1995; Stedman Jones, *Outcast London*; Walkowitz, *City of Dreadful Delight*.

67 Walkowitz, *City of Dreadful Delight*, p. 33.

68 Stedman Jones, *Outcast London*, p. 128.

69 The point is well made by Jose Harris that the widespread currency of the language of degeneracy did not always reflect a commitment to the intellectual framework of social Darwinism. See Jose Harris, 'Between civic virtue and social darwinism: the

concept of the residuum', in Englander and O'Day (eds), *Retrieved Riches*.

70 Booth, *Life and Labour*, Vol. I, p. 64, cited in Walkowitz, *City of Dreadful Delight*, p. 34.

71 Walkowitz, *City of Dreadful Delight*, p. 36. For the description of Jews in Booth, see David Englander, 'Booth's Jews: the presentation of Jews and Judaism in *Life and Labour of the People in London*', *Victorian Studies*, 32, 1989.

72 H. Walker, *East London. Sketches of Christian Work and Workers*, London, Religious Tract Society, 1896, p. 17.

73 *Ibid.*, p. 27.

74 Walter Besant, *East London*, London, Chatto and Windus, 1901, p. 199.

75 F. Hird, *The Cry of the Children. An Exposure of Certain British Industries in which Children are Iniquitously Employed*, London, Bowden, 1898, p. 61.

76 George Haw, *No Room to Live. The Plaint of Overcrowded London*, London, Wells Gardner, 1900, p. 76.

77 Arnold White, *The Problems of a Great City*, London, Remington, 1886. A wide traveller with a deep interest in social problems, White had contested Mile End as a Tory candidate in 1886, and was to contest Tyneside in 1892 and 1895. His racism in publications such as *The Modern Jew*, *English Democracy* and *Efficiency and Empire* became increasingly shrill. He was sent to prison in 1903 for contempt, but liberated by public subscription, and gave evidence to the inquiry which established the 1905 Aliens Act.

78 *Ibid.*, p. 12.

79 *Ibid.*, pp. 14, 48, 227.

80 William Booth, *In Darkest England and the Way Out*, London, Salvation Army, 1890. The book was in part at least ghost-written by W.E. Stead, editor of the *Pall Mall Gazette*, who had five years previously been responsible for one of the most successful endeavours of sensational journalism. His investigation of juvenile prostitution in the 'Maiden tribute of modern Babylon' had an estimated circulation of one and a half million copies. The whole episode is well discussed in Walkowitz, *City of Dreadful Delight*.

81 Booth, *In Darkest England*, p. 9.

82 *Ibid.*, p. 10.

83 *Ibid.*, p. 13.

84 Stedman Jones, *Outcast London*, p. 312.

85 The metaphor of the heart of empire became popular, particularly in titles of books such as Charles F.G. Masterman (ed.), *The Heart of the Empire. Discussions of Problems of Modern City Life in England, with an Essay on Imperialism*, London, Fisher Unwin, 1902; George Haw, *Britain's Homes. A Study of the Empire's Heart-Disease*, London, Clarion Press, 1902; and L. Cope Cornford, *The Canker at the Heart. Being Studies from the Life of the Poor*, London, Grant Richards, 1905.

86 Haw, *Britain's Homes*, p. 53.

87 W. Evans-Gordon, *The Alien Immigrant*, London, Heinemann, 1903, p. 9.

88 Mark Harrison, *Crowds and History. Mass Phenomena in English Towns, 1790–1835*, Cambridge, Cambridge University Press, 1988, pp. 6–8; Malik, *The Meaning of Race*, pp. 104–9. The gendering of the crowd is discussed by McClintock, *Imperial Leather*, p. 119, and Wilson, *The Sphinx in the City*, p. 7, who writes: 'At the heart of the urban labyrinth lurked not the Minotaur, a bull-like male monster, but the female Sphinx, the "strangling one", who was so called because she strangled all those who could not answer her riddle: female sexuality, womanhood out of control, lost nature, loss of identity'.

89 Pick, *Faces of Degeneration*, pp. 4, 223.

90 Young, *Colonial Desire*, p. 19.

91 Masterman (ed.), *The Heart of the Empire*, reprinted Brighton, Harvester Press, 1973.

92 *Ibid.*, p. v.

93 *Ibid.*, p. 7.

94 Charles F.G. Masterman, *From the Abyss; of its Inhabitants by One of Them*, London, Johnson, 1902, p. 4.

95   *Ibid.*, p. 17.
96   See my 'Sensation of the abyss: the urban poor and modernity', in M. Nava and A. O'Shea (eds), *Modern Times. Reflections on a Century of English Modernity*, London, Routledge, 1996.
97   Jack London, *The People of the Abyss*, London, Nelson, 1904.
98   Ford Madox Ford, *The Soul of London. A Survey of a Great City*, London, Alston Rivers, 1905. A new edition with an introduction by A. Hill has recently been published by Everyman in 1995.
99   *Ibid.*, Introduction, pp. xx–xxi.
100   *Ibid.*, pp. 68–9.
101   For a discussion of the premodern character of casual labour throughout the nineteenth century see my 'Sensation of the abyss'.
102   Nicholas Thomas, *Colonialism's Culture. Anthropology, Travel and Government*, London, Polity Press, 1994, p. 49. The few brief references I have made to this important work rather understate the influence it has had on the development of my thought in this chapter.
103   Philip Curtin, *The Image of Africa. British Ideas and Action, 1780–1850*, Madison, University of Wisconsin Press, 1964, p. 364, cited in Young, *Colonial Desire*, p. 122.
104   Cohen, 'The perversions of inheritance', p. 18.

CHAPTER SEVEN

The great museum of races

With the decline of interest in thuggee and dacoity, and in the years preceding 1857, travel and evangelical narratives displayed little of portent or
originality. Most of the organizing tropes – progress, geography, race, gender, religion – had already been established, and accounts were content to
rework familiar imagery in harsher detail. Joseph Peggs, who had served as
a missionary in Orissa, produced a compilation of lengthy extracts from
previous evangelical accounts exposing the horrors of Hinduism in an
effort to promote the 'temporal and spiritual welfare of India'.[1] Howard
Malcolm from Boston, USA, recounted examples of Hindu idolatry, and
complained of the 'cringing servility' and 'indolent habits' of domestic
servants, minutely divided in the tasks they are expected to undertake.[2]
And in the conviction that 'there was no book on India which associated
the progress of missions with the history, the literature, the customs, and
the mythology of its people, and which combined a general view of this
interesting field, with the advancement of the truth', William Campbell
penned his thoughts on the prospects for Christianity.[3] Here his geographical imagination enjoyed free rein in describing the degeneracy of
Indian people:

> [T]he whole race is destitute of that spirit and firmness, and that courageous
> daring which distinguish their European conquerors.... [W]hether it be the
> influence of climate, or the effect of their own depravity, or the fruit of their
> superstition, or the effeminacy which a long career of despotism is sure to
> produce, the present Hindoos are the children of a degenerate age, and the
> veriest dwarfs, when compared with the heroes and the giants of which their
> history can boast, and who seemed to be more in keeping with the grandeur
> and magnificence of their country.[4]

In a similar vein, Thomas Jervis, the ardent evangelical and self-publicist,
recently appointed provisionally to succeed George Everest as the Surveyor-General of India,[5] attempted to justify his proposals for a great

trigonometric survey by drawing links between the progress of science and humanity. The endeavour of missionaries to 'civilize and bring over the helpless besotted heathen', he declared in an address to the Geographical Section of the British Association for the Advancement of Science, had been fatally weakened by ignorance of the 'climate, the people, or countries they go to':

> We hear of famines, of insurrections, of superstitious and barbarous rites: and are surprised that they should find any place under the milder form of the British sway. To obviate, or alleviate, these evils there is one plain course before us, to know more of the country, and of its people; improving that knowledge to their benefit, and to our honour.[6]

In this endeavour science, in particular geography, had a privileged role to play:

> Subserving the important purpose of exploring the darkest recesses of nature, [science] should also light up the darkest retreats of Humanity.... [I]f we really desire success to the one or to the other, to Science or to Missionary enterprise – we must first improve Geography.[7]

This sense of unease about knowledge of India continued also to pervade travel literature. Major Bevan was 'well aware that many valuable works on India have recently appeared', but claimed that in a country so extensive 'much remains to be collected', particularly by someone who has remained there for long periods.[8] Thirty years in India, Bevan suggests, is sufficient to 'get rid of European prejudices, and to lose those feelings of repulsiveness with which even the most judicious will for a time regard manners and customs essentially different from those to which they have been habituated', and he is critical of the contempt shown by young officers for sepoys under their command, but this does not prevent him lapsing into racist imagery:

> Custom, long and deeply-rooted prejudice, and ignorance (connected no doubt, in part, with the physical character of the people, but attributable still more to the nature and effects ... of the religion they profess, or the civil institutions arising from it) have obscured the reasoning powers of the nation, and blunted the measure of ingenuity which they undoubtedly possess, so as to debar them from the attainment of just principles in philosophy, from the discovery of truth in the sciences; and as a consequence ... from a knowledge of the simplest and most effectual processes in the mechanical and other arts.[9]

He adds, with some prescience, that notwithstanding the timidity of Hindu character, 'there are no people whose resentment is more to be dreaded when once they have formed a revolution to obtain revenge'.[10]

James Massie was also sensitive to the inadequate state of knowledge. Despite the multiplication in recent times of travel accounts, he declared, the 'people of England do not know so much of the country, of the people, or the resources of Hindostan, as is desirable for their mutual interest', and he embarked on a narrative that combined personal observation with gleanings from previous accounts.[11] While dismissing various attempts to retrace the progress of human civilization back to its origins, he acknowledged the 'lamentable truth that myriads of the descendants of Adam ... have reached a depth of degeneracy more frightful and fatal than the gloomiest speculations of these authors'.[12] He had in mind savages to be found in New Zealand, the Caribbean and the Southern Pacific, but then detected among the tribes of India the same characteristics of cruelty, sensuality, bigotry, depravity and filth.[13]

Urban mythology

The concern with degeneration and filth signalled in these writings was something of a departure in representations of Indian culture. Earlier manifestations were to be found in accounts of tribals, but striking was the tendency increasingly to locate these pathologies in areas of indigenous settlement at the heart of colonial power. Here the so-called Black Town areas of Calcutta and Madras featured prominently. Descriptions of these areas were part of a nascent urban mythology that requires brief attention. References to Black Town date to the early nineteenth century, and described its isolation from European settlement: an anonymous civilian talked of how 'Black Calcutta (by which I mean that part where the Natives reside) does not at all interfere with the European part, a great comfort, for the Natives are very dirty and their habitations are mere straw huts'.[14] It was in the first topographical surveys, however, that more detailed pictures were to be found. Hamilton's 1820 survey, for example, decribes it:

> The black town extends along the river to the north, and exhibits a remarkable contrast to the part inhabited by Europeans. Persons who have only seen the latter have little conception of the remainder of the city, but those, who have been led there by their public or private avocations, will bear testimony to the wretched condition of at least six in eight parts of this externally magnificent city. The streets here are narrow, dirty, and impaired; the houses to two storeys are of brick with flat terraced roofs; but the great majority are mud cottages, ... the whole within and without swarming with population.[15]

For Mrs Holland, the Black Town area of Calcutta provided a home 'for all the people of the earth' as well as 'every tribe of Hindoostanee origin',[16] while Josiah Conder focused on its plural sensory experience:

[189]

A constant creaking of cart wheels, which are never greased in India, a constant clamour of voices, and an almost constant thumping and jingling of drums, cymbals, &c...; and add to all this, a villainous smell of garlic, rancid coconut oil, and sour butter, and stagnant ditches, and you will understand the sounds, sights, and smells of what is called the 'Black Town' of Calcutta.[17]

In the course of the troubled 1830s, and paralleling the emergence of harsher racial typologies in the metropolis, a distinct sense of urban pathology was constructed around the presence of the poor. Emma Roberts displayed an acute sense of socio-economic differentiation in Calcutta's cosmopolitan population:

> The Black Town ... extends along the river to the north, and a more wretched-looking place can scarcely be imagined: dirty, crowded, ill-built, and abounding with beggars and bad smells. There is, however, a sort of debateable ground between the mud huts, the small dingy brick tenements, and the mean dilapidated bazaars of the middling and lower classes of natives, which is occupied by handsome houses enclosed in court yards, belonging to Armenian merchants, Parsees, and Bengalee gentlemen of wealth and respectability.[18]

For evangelicals like William Campbell, Madras provided Dantean scenes of urban life:

> But to behold the whole city given up to idolatry, what a sight! Every object brings their gross and degrading superstition to your view; the mark of the beast is engraven on their foreheads.... Your heart sickens within you, while you pass through the streets of Black Town, and behold crowds of immortal beings busy upon the trifles of the hour, almost ready to devour one another to obtain the riches and vanities of earth, panting after worldly fame and renown ... but all without God and without hope, famishing for want of the bread that endureth to life everlasting, and perishing in their sins.[19]

It was about this time that Major Ormstowe, a resident of many years, conducted James Massie through its streets. The major had difficulty in making sense of the sights they encountered:

> What do you call this low, crowded, and almost impenetrable mass of ruinous huts and rude sheds ... with so many entirely naked, squalid, and dirty children running and scrambling about, that it is almost impossible to pass without going over them, through the close, dirty, narrow, and uneven streets? The odour is very offensive, and threatens almost to constrain the mere passenger to inhale infection or disease, from the mixture of decaying vegetation with the secretion of animal matter.[20]

The condemnation of particular constituencies – tribals, criminal bands, the urban poor – has to be seen in the context of more general observations on the Indian people as a whole. Zealous evangelical accounts aside, throughout the 1830s and 1840s there was little evidence of a consensus on the state of Indian civilization. Lt. Col. Davidson casti-gated the 'metaphysicians of Europe' as 'prating jackasses' who 'know nothing of the real nature of man as a sentient being'.[21] We are arrogant, he proceeded to argue, in overvaluing the results of civilization. Indians may have been without the benefits of Christianity and education, but they are a 'clever people, and generally behave with as much sincere re-spect to such of us as deserve their good will'.[22] George Johnson, an advo-cate of the Supreme Court at Calcutta, considered that harsh judgements of the 'native character' derived from an exclusive concern with the machinations of the litigious, and the cheating of petty merchants. It was as if Englishmen were to be judged on the examples set by 'the well known men of straw about the London law courts, and the petty chapmen and dealers of its Rag Fair'.[23] Even the Thugs' arch-enemy Sleeman found among the Indian agricultural classes 'some of the best men I have ever known',[24] and cited with approval the sentiments of Thomas Munro that in general the 'Hindoos are not inferior in civilization to the people of Europe'.[25]

If there was a single work of the time that manifested these tensions, it was the Rev. Buyers's *Recollections of Northern India*. Prompted by the desire to familiarize readers with the moral knowledge of Indian heathens, the missionary at Benares identified a now familiar litany of pathologies. Black Town Madras contains a far greater number of 'beggars and diseased persons' than any other city he had seen.[26] Many of these live in a 'very degraded state'. They have an 'unconquerable indolence' which leads them to prefer begging and thieving to honest labour, as a consequence of which it has proved difficult to 'raise them in the scale of society'.[27] They are cruel to animals, displaying no more care than 'Smithfield drovers, or Whitechapel butchers'.[28] Sepoys are made up of 'the very dregs of society', and even the more permanent native inhabitants of military cantonments are 'often of a low and profligate character'.[29] Representations of Hindus, on the other hand, rely heavily on eighteenth-century orientalist perspec-tives. They are 'neither a rude, ignorant people, nor a nation sunk in bar-barism'. From early ages they have possessed a 'knowledge of letters, ... written systems of religion, and of morals, as well as philosophy and civil law'.[30] The common people have a love of poetry, which in its ideas is as beautiful and true to nature as any in Europe.[31]

Nascent ethnology

No doubt as a response to these manifold tensions and uncertainties, Henry Elliot commenced his pioneering work on the ethnology of India. First published in 1844, his *Memoirs of the History, of Folk-lore, and*

Distribution of the Races of the North Western Provinces of India was intended to complement H.H. Wilson's ambitious glossary of Indian terms, the first parts of which had just been received. Elliott claimed modestly to 'put together a few notices respecting the tribes, customs ... not hitherto recorded.... [W]e are still almost as ignorant of the agricultural classes of these Provinces as we were on the first day of our occupation.'[32] Entries were arranged alphabetically, as in a gazetteer, but what might have worked for geographical locations proved confusing when applied to the great variety of terms related to tribes, castes and customs. After his death the entries were re-arranged by John Beames into sections on castes, customs, revenue terms, and rural life, thereby establishing the basis for a nascent ethnology.

With the consolidation of military authority and suppression of collective criminal activity, a new-found confidence emerged in the 1850s. Even uncertainties on the state of colonial knowledge seemed to dissipate. Capt. Hervey writing in 1850 stated that India was a 'common topic in the ranks of respectable society.... [E]verybody is becoming conversant with the affairs of that portion of the world, of the very locality of which he was formerly so ignorant.'[33] In India, the army was firmly in control. Enemies have been defeated, and the native soldiers, with a 'moral courage second to none in the world ... are much attached to their service'.[34] In 1852 J. Gray invited readers to survey India with a 'natural eye ... in these days of sober peace ... when all that is now heard ... is an occasional shot resounding through the Khyber Pass'.[35]

As they took stock of what had been achieved, evangelicals cautiously expressed satisfaction. The Rev. Wylie, a North American missionary, assessed the impact of the British presence in India:

> Civilization, trade, the spread of knowledge, the destruction of their political ascendancy, and special legal privileges, tend inevitably to lower the Brahmans every where; and a certain inevitable curiosity about Christianity, as the religion of the governing classes, prepares the way for a favourable reception of its teachers.[36]

He prayed that the 'whole of India may speedily fall under the benignant rule of Great Britain, and ... enjoy the blessing and equal justice, and the elevating influence of rulers who know and love "The Truth"'.[37] Elsewhere evangelicals made much of detailed information on missionary activity contained in the 40th Report of the Calcutta Auxiliary Bible Society. The past twenty-five years had witnessed extraordinary progress. At a cost of £190,000 there were now operating in India twenty-two missionary societies employing 443 missionaries, 331 native churches, and 1,347 vernacular schools. Twenty-five printing establishments published the Bible in ten languages and a large variety of tracts.[38] True, it was a cause for some concern that the 'native Protestant flock should be so very small',[39] but no one could deny that 'many inhuman rites' had been suppressed, that where 'crime and cruelty reigned before' British power was now ascendant, that civilization had progressed, that 'Brahminical influence' had declined, and that the zeal for pilgrimages had fallen off.[40] The Report's author, Joseph Mullens, also recorded satisfaction that missionary endeavour in the south had assailed the 'bonds of caste, reverence for the sacred books, veneration for a long-established priesthood, and a blind attachment to their idolatories'.[41]

The most comprehensive and measured assessment of the state of British India on the eve of the uprising was *The Administration of the East India Company; a History of Indian Progress*. Written by the Company's historian John Kaye in 1853, it included on the title page a brief extract from Leopold von Ranke's *Civil Wars and Monarchy in France*: 'the highest praise is due to those who, by their victorious arms, have opened up new scenes for the civilisation of mankind, and overcome barbarism in some important portion of the world'.[42] This, together with title itself, set the narrative. Drawing extensively on published accounts and Company records, Kaye sought eagerly to demonstrate the enlightened nature of contemporary colonial rule:

> The servants of the Company have been for nearly two centuries regarding the natives of India only as so many dark-faced and dark-souled Gentiles, whom it was their mission to over-reach in business, and to overcome in war. But out of these hucksters and spoliators had now arisen a race of embryo statesmen with dawning perceptions of the duties and responsibilities of governments and the rightful claims of the people.[43]

Past abuses of power have arisen out of the imperfect state of our knowledge, but now the government is making every effort to perfect its administration; such 'progressive improvement is all that we have a right to expect'.[44] The problems are considerable. India is a country whose area is 'difficult to compute', whose population is 'difficult to number', and whose people 'present as many varieties of character and language as the entire continent of Europe, and the whole of which are utterly dissimilar to our own'.[45] Despite these, the record on amelioration of the condition of the people, rationalization of justice, civilization of savage tribes, suppression of cruel abominations, and 'general diffusion of enlightenment and truth' reflect no little honour on the 'Company and its servants'.[46] Of particular merit was the elimination of the threats from Thug, dacoit and tribal activities. Thugee is now so well understood, Kaye declares, that there is not an 'intelligent reader ... who does not know what a Thug is'. Even the word itself has entered into the English language.[47] Furthermore a few English officers 'have purged India of this great pollution'. As a system thuggee has been completely destroyed. The 'profession is ruined; the Guild is scattered, never again to be associated into a great corporate body'.[48]

Dacoity also was an institution that for a time resisted the imperatives of colonial knowledge. 'Subdued in one form and in one part of the country', Kaye argues, 'it seemed to take a new life and to break out in another place ... beyond the reach of central supervision.' To grasp the nature of dacoity, gangs were compared to the professional mendicants of London. The 'great outcry' against metropolitan beggars, he pointed out, coincided with the panics about robber gangs in India. There were limits, however, to the analysis, for whereas measures against beggars had driven them into the home counties where there was a 'vast increase in rural mendicity', in Bengal 'dakoitee ... began to centralise itself, and Calcutta was surrounded by banditti' made up of 'an indistinct and heterogeneous *posse comitatus*' rather than 'a great homogeneous guild or brother-hood'.[49] Thuggee provided the authorities with a trope with which to think dacoity. The 'great idea of the hereditary robber-tribes' was conceived, and the 1843 Act, which extended the policing of and thinking behind thuggee to 'hereditary robber castes', was implemented, leading eventually to the defeat and dispersal of many gangs.

The threat from tribals had also been eliminated. They had once been 'beyond measure lawless and intractable'.[50] Unsuccessful attempts were made to subdue them by military means, but it was not until the 'work of civilisation' commenced that the culture of violence into which they had been bred and nurtured was displaced by 'habits of peace and industry'.[51] Much of this had been achieved in the past twenty-five years. In 1825, for example, Bheels were at the 'height of lawlessness'. But the 'schoolmaster has taken the young Bheel in hand' and brought him within the 'pale of civilised life' where he is 'contented to abide'.

Simultaneously, Edward Thornton was engaged on a project to revive Hamilton's pioneering work on the gazetteer. His four-volume *Gazetteer of the Territories under the Government of the East India Company* was published in 1854, followed three years later by a single-volume digest. This project was designed as an 'epitome of all that has yet been written and published', and yet was rather more, for Thornton successfully fixed the location of considerable numbers of cities, towns and villages, as well as territorial boundaries.[52]

Amidst this groundswell of optimism, however, other more troubled voices could be heard. An 1853 petition signed by 1,800 inhabitants of Bengal pressed for a Royal Commission into the condition of its people. It noted that the system of land tenures and abuse of power by zemindars and planters had demoralized and pauperized the 'labouring classes'.[53] Relief of this suffering could no longer be delayed, as 'from the information they have acquired, they fear that the discontent of the rural population is daily increasing, and that a bitter feeling of hatred towards their rulers is being engendered in their minds'. Full and detailed information was urgently required on the police system, the 'harassing exactions and oppressions to which the poor are subject', the provision of education, and the best means of 'alleviating the sufferings and elevating the condition of the people'. The petition was denied; whether a commission could have prevented the subsequent rebellion is a matter of idle speculation, but when sepoys mutinied against their British officers in May 1857 they set in train a series of events, the grotesque dramaturgy of which was to transform the political and cultural landscape of India, and to influence profoundly British mythology of the subcontinent.

1857 and its aftermath

It is well beyond my remit to discuss the revolt of 1857.[54] Suffice it to say that its complexities refute generalizations. Seen variously as the first war of independence, a regressive struggle waged by neo-feudal landed magnates, a peasant uprising against oppressive taxation and loss of customary rights over land, and a civil war between collaborators and anti-colonial fighters, it was probably all these, and more.[55] And it cannot be understood as a completely novel and isolated form of struggle. India under colonial rule had witnessed a virtually continuous series of localized revolts or disturbances against the British and their agents. But if the content of 1857 was not unique in Indian history, its scale was; what defined the rebellion was its ability to bring together previously fragmented and uncoordinated struggles, and raise them to new levels of intensity.

The revolt was confined to the northern Gangetic plain and central India. The south, Bengal and the Punjab remained unscathed, although it was the support from the Sikhs, carefully cultivated by the British since the end of the Anglo-Sikh wars, and the disinclination of the Bengali intelligentsia to throw in their lot with what they considered a backward zemindar revolt, that proved decisive in the course of the struggle. The three centres of the revolt reveal something of its lack of cohesion. The sepoy mutiny at Meerut was followed by a march to Delhi where they became a focus for the grievances of landed magnates, artisans and peasants. In Awadh to the east, an autonomous revolt, fuelled by popular resentment against the recent annexation, inflicted a massive defeat on British forces. And in the insecure Maratha districts of Gwalior and Jhansi, rulers and peasants, galvanized by unquenched hostilities, rose up to defeat the British garrison.

We await a detailed study on precisely how mythology of the rebellion was created, but it is clear that the British newspaper and periodical press played a crucial role.[56] By chance, telegraph cables had just been laid. When they worked, information that had previously taken at least thirty days to reach Britain could now be transmitted instantaneously. Reports of the revolt appeared daily in the British press. These were supplemented by articles in reputable periodicals such as *Bentley's Miscellany, Blackwood's, British Quarterly Review, Eclectic Review* and *Fraser's Magazine*.[57] Such reportage, in particular of the atrocities allegedly committed by the mutineers, no doubt boosted sales, but more importantly they shook to the very foundation any confidence in the information order and in the Company's administration of Indian affairs. In this uncertain climate evangelicals went on the assault, resurrecting the most virulent representations of Indian people. Under the rubric 'The heathen, thine inheritance', John Stevenson sermonized on the 'unexpected and tremendous stroke' that has 'paralyzed all England like an electric shock':

> Sons and daughters of England, unoffending missionaries, women and children, have been barbarously tortured and murdered, with a refinement of cruelty that can be paralleled only by the infernal demons. All the tortures we read of in the Romish inquisition and persecutions, or the torments inflicted by American savages upon their captives, had comparatively a touch of mercy.[58]

This relegation of Indians in the chain of being was accompanied by calls for severe retribution to 're-establish that empire of opinion; – that conviction of our supremacy, and of the irresistible superiority of the Anglo-Saxon race, on which the rule of the British in India depended'. Blame for the outrages was placed firmly at the door of the Company. It has pursued 'worldly gain' at the cost of promotion of Christianity. Only the 'simple operation of wise and good government' can regenerate the 'diabolical depravity of the "natural man"' by attracting him to 'our rule'.[59]

Francis Close, Dean of Carlisle, in a retrospective view of the revolt remembered not only the 'horrors ... on every tongue, and successive telegrams [that] made every heart palpitate', but also the indignation aroused against the 'crooked policy of government, and their cowardly abandonment of religious principle'.[60] The same concern was expressed by the Presbyterian missionary James McKee. The reason why India has lagged so far behind the South Sea Islanders in their progress toward civilization is that 'Hindooism is one of the most formidable systems of error ever Satan reared ... the greatest obstacle to progress – the all but insurmountable difficulty against which we have been contending – is, HINDOOISM SUPPORTED BY THE BRITISH GOVERNMENT'.[61] Meanwhile, the Rev. Murray Mitchell, missionary of the Free Church of Scotland at Bombay, noted the lessons that had been learnt. Until recent events, there was a tendency to 'speak in very mitigated condemnation, not to say approbation, of heathen religions'.[62] This 'grievous folly', however, has now ceased, and no one denies that 'the dark places of the earth are full of the habitations of cruelty', and that the heathen are 'without understanding, ... implacable, unmerciful'. The natives of India have a 'character combining many of the attributes of the child with the savage, with a tendency to rush ... from one feeling to the opposite'. Under these circumstances,

> that device of which many of us were so fond, that of *divide et impera* – of playing off the prejudices of one Indian race against another ... has been proved to be utterly fallacious. Moslem and Hindu can unite for a time against the Christian foreigner, although, the moment he is disposed of, they are ready to fly at each other's throats.... Not until India is Christian will her endlessly varied and jarring races coalesce into true union and harmony, [and] either the principles of our rule be understood, or its burden be endured, except with sullen, smouldering discontent and hatred.[63]

Expressing faith in the impulses of modernization, however, Mitchell argues that public improvements are taking place on an unprecedented scale. These will provide propitious conditions, he concludes, for the 'Oriental mind is touched by the spirit of European progress' and Christians will bring Indians willingly to the 'cause of truth'.[64]

Travel narratives of the time display the same intensification of racial attitudes. The rich young sisters Madeline and Rosalind Wallace-Dunlop decided to visit their brother in Meerut, returning to England a month before the mutiny broke out. Their journal was published in 1858.[65] 'One only has to glance at this work', suggests Ketaki Kushari Dyson, 'to understand how inevitable the rebellion of 1857 was',[66] for beneath the light-hearted descriptions of the frivolities of British life in India there is a thinly disguised contempt for Indians, especially rural labourers. Their culture, colour, language, smell and appearance are all described, but in ways that seem to convey a sense of the unreality of an apocalyptic other-worldliness. Porters who carried the sisters' carriage across a river were seen as a 'swarm of yelling, screaming black Coolies'; mid-stream the sisters were 'surrounded by water, and completely at the mercy of a set of demon-like beings'.[67] At a village fête, one of the sisters remarked, 'the hideous music, yelling, and shouting, nasal singing, uncouth gestures, and strange garb of these demoniacal looking natives, strongly reminded me of the pictures of Pandemonium'.[68] At a distance Rajput women appeared 'very becoming', but a 'nearer approach dispels the illusion. Their clothes are filthy dirty, and their hair guiltless of any attempt to smooth or arrange it.'[69] Communication was a problem. Before leaving England the sisters were given a copy of 'Forbes Manual' to study. They found it 'utterly useless' for the phrases were 'far above the comprehension of common servants'. In contrast, 'Hindostanee ... is a frightful language, only sounding pretty from the rosy lips of little English children, a medium that might beautify any jargon'.[70] None of this, however, can be explained as reactions of guileless young travellers. If anything, their brother Robert, Magistrate at Meerut, expressed an even stronger sense of racial and class contempt for Indians. He had the 'most absurd horror of a native's coming near him: he declared he could detect the copperish smell of the colouring matter in their skins the instant they entered the room, and he would much sooner be touched by a toad than by one of their clammy hands'.[71]

Nor were seasoned journalists exempt from the use of such rhetoric. The special correspondent of *The Times*, William Russell, who had been sent in 1858 to cover the suppression of the rebellion, described the approach to Calcutta:

> It was a most wonderful and striking picture – nothing I have ever seen came near to it for variety and effect. The black figures, streaked with white waist-bands and turbans – the contrast between the repose of the groups seated near each fire with the energetic, active, and ceaseless movement of those who were running about – ... those wild weird men dancing like demons. – 'Pooh! what is this dreadful smell – like – like coarse roasting meat?' I glanced at my companion ... and in reply to my look, he said, 'It's one of the BURN-ING GHAUTS! Boatmen! boatmen! pull for your lives!'.... I remember such another horror in an old book of travels – 'cannibals feasting by moonlight.'[72]

The eponymous Cadwalladar Cummerbund called on artistic and literary imaginations to describe the seemingly ineffable bazaars of Calcutta:

> But though insuggestive of the poetical, Calcutta bazaars afford a fine field for the talents of such men as Leech and Dickens; the former might find grotesque subjects for his pencil at every step, and the latter could alone do justice to their ridiculous characteristics. For want of a master mind to evolve it, what a mine of drollery remains yet undeveloped in the antediluvian appearance of the gharries patronized by the poorer classes of babboos.... [T]hese and a hundred other odd sights peculiar to Calcutta, yet await a 'coming man' to place them vividly before the mind's eye.[73]

He also surveyed the 'dusky Venuses' at that privileged site of imperial concern, the Churrock Pooja, and expressed disappointment. Thick lips and bluff noses are not poetical images, he declared. 'What', asks some sceptical young lady, 'were their eyes not black, then?':

> Most assuredly, my dear, but so were their skins.... Your beautiful blue or jet black orbs ... contrast with cheeks blending the lily and the rose, and a swan-like neck of pearly whiteness ... but, black cheeks – black lips – black neck – black hair – black everything! what do they picture but a chimney sweep?[74]

The events of 1857 impacted on British colonial policy. Conventionally thought as constituting a profound rupture, they are better seen as a quickening of measures that had already been set in motion. Following years of growing disaffection with the Company's management of Indian affairs, control was finally wrested by the government, and placed in the hands of a Secretary of State for India. Queen Victoria made conciliatory gestures in her proclamation of 1858. She promised benevolent rule, and an end to the corrupt failure to abide by the terms of treaties entered into with Indian princes. The army switched recruitment to the Punjab and Nepal, plunging the previously favoured areas of Benares and Awadh into economic recession. Simultaneously, the proportion of European troops was doubled. In order to restore finances after the massive debts incurred by 1857, an income tax was levied on urban elites; more fundamentally, the political economy of India was oriented toward the export of agricultural raw materials.

In this period of post-traumatic shock and ensuing stabilization more measured responses to Indian affairs were heard. Kaye, who had written with such calm authority on the good government of the Company, now reflected cautiously on its collapse. His *History of the Indian Mutiny*, commenced in 1864 but published over thirty years later, points to a profound failure of the information order.[75] The empirical knowledge accumulated on India was unable to predict the revolt because it had revealed nothing about Indian customs and beliefs except their outward appearances. The events of the revolt cruelly exposed these weaknesses. Local information networks operated effectively to convey news among the peasantry, but in ways that mystified colonial authorities. The infamous case of chapatis passed from village to village, somehow portentous of a momentous event, created an instant myth emblematic of the unease at the core of colonial knowledge.[76]

Robert Montgomery Martin, who had thirty years previously made available the pioneering survey of Francis Buchanan, also considered the state of India. The 'calamitous tempest' of 1857–58 swept away fictions of the 'Company's dominions', and we have been brought to face the truth that 'England has become identified with Hindostan'.[77] The recent government of India has been found wanting of those necessary virtues of Christian justice, mercy and charity, but there is reason to hope that parliamentary and public opinion are coming to recognize the 'primary duty and even political expediency of *Justice to India*'.[78] Some of the problems that beset the previous administration remain. The 'wild races' such as Mughs and Kookis which live in a savage state east of Bengal continue to plunder villages, forcing inhabitants to desert them. 'Prejudices of caste, of creed and custom' obstruct the creation of national unity among the 'millions of heterogeneous races', and it may be many years before they ultimately yield to the 'humanizing influences of a higher civilization' and so prepare 'all classes for national freedom and self-government'.[79] And yet the new administration is a modernizing one. Past treatment of the people of India as inferior is passing; the new functionaries are from every stratum of British society, and they are brought into contact with 'intelligent and gentlemanly Hindoos'. The spread of education, instruction in medicine, engineering and the 'higher branches of human knowledge', and promotion of 'unfettered enterprise and capital' will 'raise the tone of native society, and enable the upper classes of both races to meet on a more equal footing'.[80]

Sensitive to a more religious modernity, the Rev. John Barton inquired into the impact on the 'Hindu mind' of forty years' contact not only with 'missionary effort, but with the indirectly Christianizing influences of English literature, English political and commercial activity, and, above all, of a government which ... has always been conducted ... with the most scrupulous integrity'.[81] The results, he concluded, were far more momentous than those which the 'railroad progress of scientific discovery has effected within the last century in England'. Few were more involved in this modern civilizing mission than Mary Carpenter.[82] She proudly included a passage written in her notebook by her host, S. Tagore, an Indian Christian:

> What was India a few years ago? ... We see a nation domineered over by caste and idolatry – a nation of which the men are completely enslaved to custom, and the women kept down and tyrannised over by the men ... a nation which has long since ceased to be progressive, and of which inertia and stationariness is the natural condition.... India sank down under the weight of the accumulated corruption of ages; foreign influences were requisite to rouse her.[83]

It could well have been Carpenter's anthem, for as a committed educator and reformer she did much during her time in India to promote the education of the young as a means of overcoming this inertia. In an address on the reformatory school system, Carpenter drew out the lessons from recent intervention of the British. Twenty years ago, she said, a number of benevolent reformers had tried to educate children from the very lowest orders, not to 'raise them out of their proper spheres, but to enable them to work honestly and fitly for their appointed vocations'. The result was a gradual conversion of 'young savages into respectable men and women'.[84] Such reforms could with benefit be introduced in India, although, she added, the lot of a class even lower than these – the roving street Arabs – will continue to exercise the 'best and deepest thinkers, and students of political economy'.[85] So too will the many tribes in the hills who live in a 'completely savage state ... almost entirely unclothed, and looking as if a civilized idea never entered their heads'. For until

> we make every effort ... to educate those who are more within our reach ... and we have taught them a language which will bring them into sympathy,

not only with their rulers, but with the educated portion of their country-men, we shall have little hope of reaching the barbaric life in our midst.[86]

At the heart of Carpenter's concerns, therefore, lay fears about the existing state of knowledge of India. 'The British public', she wrote, 'is ... very little informed of the actual condition and wants of that great country and its inhabitants, beyond what may be gathered from official or from missionary reports.' Any progress was entirely dependent upon a 'more familiar knowledge' between both countries.[87] Doubtless to this end she was instrumental in establishing a Bengal branch of the Social Sciences Association of Great Britain, with areas of interest and inquiry in law, education, health, trade, labour and agriculture.[88]

Despite continued anxieties about the information order, with political stabilization came a renewed sense of optimism about the future of colonial rule. During a sermon delivered at Westminster Abbey at the consecration of George Cotton as Bishop of Calcutta in 1858, the Rev. Vaughan declared that 1857 had given missions a political prominence that they had not received since 1813. Some extreme sentiments were expressed on the danger that they posed to the future of the empire, but calmer and more moderate voices had prevailed. These urged the need for wisdom and a deeper sense of responsibility towards India; calls were renewed for 'labourers in that great field of evangelistic work', a special fund was established, missionary studentships were formed, and a new bishop was 'sent forth to quicken the energies and regulate the labours of missionaries ... [and] to build up again from its ruins a Church distressed and desolate and baptized in blood'.[89] Cotton himself later recorded in his journal that he 'dwelt with mixed feelings of regret and hopefulness on the well-known fact that it was chiefly among the lowest castes ... that Christianity had made ... substantial progress, ... and looked to the introduction and improvement of the ryots, and to the extension of female education throughout India, as the most hopeful agency for promoting the ultimate evangelisation of the country'.[90]

William Butler, entranced as a child by 'amazing descriptions of Oriental magnificence recorded by Sir Thomas Roe' and other tales of the Mughal court, now recognized that the authors had drawn largely 'upon their imagination'.[91] Armed with this, he attacked the enemies of Christian civilization. Brahmans 'hate that republican Christianity which declares that "God hath made of one blood all nations of men"'. There was a time when they could be regarded as the 'learned class of India', but education has moved on, rendering their chronology, geography, astronomy and history 'wild and exaggerated falsehoods'.[92] Above these 'elements of wrath and hatred', however, were the 'criminal classes ... who only needed the sanction of their Brahmins and Fakirs' to rise up in their 'hour of opportunity against the Christian civilization', fought against Christian knowledge for 'possession of the bright land of the Veda, and for the perpetual supremacy over its 200,000,000 men!'[93] In this struggle for supremacy, Butler was able to report, there had been a dramatic increase in missionary activity since 1857.[94]

In no area was this more evident than in women's missions, which expanded rapidly in the decades after 1857. As in the metropolis, women had previously played an auxiliary role in evangelical endeavour. For the most part women were expected to support the activities of male evangelicals, although occasionally, because allowed exclusive access, they had pioneered house-to-house visitations, particularly to the zenanas, the female areas in high-caste households. Amidst fears that the rebellion had taken place because of corrupt ideas taught by heathen mothers, emphasis was now placed on the moral regeneration of indigenous families.[95] Thus in a move mutually reinforcing that in the metropolis, new opportunities were provided for female evangelicals to promote English middle-class domestic ideals through extended house visitations.

Similar, but perhaps more guarded optimism was expressed over ten years later by Herbert Blackett, late of the Cambridge Mission to Delhi. Despite the large and increasing numbers of missions now working in India there remains about one missionary to every 500,000 people. Furthermore, Christianity faces many serious obstacles. Apart from the difficulties of the caste system, the moral and intellectual condition of the people is low. Under these circumstances, the wonder is not that so little but that so much has been achieved. There are signs of transition, for even if the effects of Christianity are not yet palpable, the influence of English government and education is felt everywhere. The 'iron rules of caste' have been mitigated by modernizing impulses of education and the railways, and the 'ancient reverence for Brahmans has suffered much'.[96] James Bradbury, thirty-four years in India as a LMS missionary, looked optimistically to the potential for conversion among aboriginal tribes:

> [N]o institution was ever formed that afforded greater facilities to strengthen the arm of oppression and uphold the reign of terror than caste.... The absence of a corrupt priesthood in most of the tribes will, in the event of missions being established among them, contribute in no ordinary degree to their moral and spiritual improvement. No set of men ever exercised a more powerful and destructive influence over a people and maintained it under a better appearance of outward sanctity, than the brahmans.[97]

The record of missionary activity among tribes previously thought the most potent threat to colonial rule was particularly pleasing:

> The results to evangelize the mountaineers and foresters is of an encouraging nature. The mission among the Coles, who inhabit the hilly country of

Chota Nagpore, is one of the most prosperous in the Bengal presidency. More than 40,000 of the tribe have embraced the Christian faith.[98]

Travel accounts of the time reproduced more strident racial stereotypes, particularly of tribal peoples. In 1871 E.C.P. Hull's new vade-mecum appeared, which attempted to 'fill the void' in ordinary handbooks by describing everyday life in India.[99] In India, it informed the readers, there are 'many different races, bearing little resemblance to each other'. In general the Hindus have 'handsome, well-formed features.... Here is the open forehead, the aquiline nose, the well-cut lip.' Some of the 'hill or jungle tribes', however, possess characteristics 'which one is accustomed to look for only in Africa – frizzled hair, thick lips, and flattened nose.... Others are similar as to nose and lips, but have coarse, dark hair, not unlike the aborigines of Australia.'[100] In rather more interesting ways, Hull outlined the promise of Western modernity in the post-1857 era:

> Then when we get into the railway carriage, and are whirled way at thirty miles an hour, what an incongruity we ourselves become! Sped along by the iron horse, we pass villages of the fashion of 2000 years ago; huts and temples and cultivation, repeated from generation to generation.... [T]he anni-hilation of the rebel armies of 1857, produced a conviction among the people of India of the irresistible sovereignty of Anglo-Saxonism over their country, and with such a conviction immense obstacles to the progress of European civilization must necessarily be removed. There now appears ... the promise of a long period of calm having dawned on the political horizon of India.[101]

The most popular and authoritative handbooks, however, were the series prepared by Capt. Eastwick, and published over 1859–83.[102] The preface to the first edition spoke of 'special want' for a handbook now that England and India have been brought closer by 'almost continuous steam communication, ... the electric telegraph', and by a 'sympathy which even the recent abortive attempt to dissever the two countries ... has tended to evoke'. The vastness and diversity of India, however, and the uncertainty of information we have 'render a Handbook of India a much more arduous undertaking than the Handbook of most other countries'. To address these problems, and provide a work 'as useful as possible to the servants of government, and persons resident in India, as well as the mere traveller', many detailed statistics and much primary information have been provided.[103] Included were figures on population from the Census, although this did not prevent recourse to racialized classifications. In Bengal, for example,

> we have a people physically distinct from any other people in India. Living in a network of rivers and morasses, and nourished on a watery rice diet, the semi-amphibious Bengali in appearance belongs to a weak and puny race....

[T]he Uriyas have developed a peculiar physiognomy and character from their isolated position. They are even more timid than Bengalis. Conservative to a degree, they are wanting in enterprise, evidence a thorough dislike of all modern improvements, and are the most bigoted priest-ridden people in India.... The Hindustanis of Bihar ... are more decidedly Aryan than any of the other races of Bengal, and partly from climate, partly from their more substantial diet, and partly from a larger infusion of Aryan blood, are hardier and more manly than the Bengalis.[104]

This concoction of environmentalism, physiology and genetics is applied to the various peoples encountered to produce a consciously hierarchical taxonomy. The Thakars of the Punjab hills are a 'good looking and well made race', the Paharis of Kashmir a 'strong, hardy race, of a powerful frame, [with] straight foreheads, and noses markedly hooked', the Kolis are 'undoubtedly aborigines, and belong to the dark races', and the Waralis have hair 'black and lank, their bodies were oiled; and altogether they had a very wild appearance'.

The 1857 rebellion had exposed the inadequacies of the information order. Once the shock waves had died down, colonial authorities, evangelicals and reformers, many of whom saw themselves as modernizers, began to address with renewed urgency the attendant demands for relevant and reliable information. They were abetted by a rapid expansion of the communications network, and the establishment of educational institutions, printing presses and libraries by an English-educated elite.[105] With some irony, though, this same expansion in communications promoted the development of indigenous forms of information, and these came to challenge the dominant order, exerting even more pressure to maintain its authority. Information, however, was not the same as knowledge, and so no amount of empirical detail was guaranteed to provide understanding of India's diversity. Prior to 1857 evangelical narratives, travel accounts and surveys attempted to capture this through a totalizing vision based on empirical observation. Now, under pressure to reform, and out of a recognition of epistemological failure, totalization not only intensified but was organized by certain assumptions about the essential features of Indian society. It was at this moment that traditional India was discovered, and caste emerged as the great metanarrative of Indian culture.

Discovery of caste

The notion of caste emerged during the formative stages of the British imagination of India. The first serious attempt to understand Hindu mythology in its own terms, Henry Lord's *Discovery of the Sect of the Banians* (1630), discussed the creation of the caste system, and Ovington's *A Voyage to Surat in the Year 1689* found among the banias twenty-four 'casts, or Sects, who both refrain from an indiscriminate mixture in Marriages, and from eating together in common'.[106] It was not until the end of the eighteenth century, however, that caste was subjected to scholarly analysis. William Robertson's survey of ancient India included a detailed examination of the caste system:

> Such arbitrary arrangements seem ... to be adverse to improvement either in science or in the arts; and by forming around the different orders of men artificial barriers, which it would be impious to pass, tend to circumscribe the operations of the human mind within a narrower sphere than nature has allotted to them.... The regulations of Indian policy, with respect to the different orders of men, must necessarily check genius in its career, and confine to the functions of an inferior cast, talents fitted to shine in an higher sphere.[107]

The objects of civil government, however, are to meet the needs of the many rather than the few. The first Indian legislators, therefore,

> set apart certain races of men for each of the various professions and arts necessary in a well ordered society, and appointed the exercise of them to be transmitted from father to son in succession. This system, although extremely repugnant to the ideas which we ... have formed, will be found ... better adapted to attain the end in view, than a careless observer, at first sight, is apt to imagine.[108]

Concurrently, the French Jesuit missionary Abbe Dubois completed his *Description of the Character, Manners, and Customs of the People of India*, which with the active support of British authorities was published in English in 1816.[109] Dubois confronted criticisms of the caste system as useless, ridiculous and a threat to good order:

> I believe caste division to be in many respects the chef-d'oeuvre, the happiest effort, of Hindu legislation. I am persuaded that it is simply and solely due to the distribution of the people into castes that India did not lapse into a state of barbarism, and that she preserved and perfected the arts and sciences of civilization whilst most other nations of the earth remained in a state of barbarism.[110]

Thus, for Dubois, the caste system kept 'within the bounds of duty' the lower orders of Indian society, who without such moral restraint would have lapsed into a state 'worse than the hordes of cannibals'. It had also preserved Indian laws, religions and customs from foreign invasion. Under these circumstances, Dubois reasoned, Christianity was doomed to fail in India, and colonial authorities should refrain from undue interference in Indian culture.

In the period leading up to the adoption of the pious clause in 1813, these views held sway among Company officials and did much to bolster opposition to evangelical activity. And they survived for some time after. Anglican missionary societies such as the Society for Promoting Christian Knowledge and the Society for Propagating the Gospel – ever suspicious of evangelical zeal – considered caste a religious ordering with which missionaries should not interfere. Heber's sympathy for Indian culture led him to counsel tolerance for practices that were institutional or cultural rather than purely idolatrous.[111] These sentiments could even be found among influential circles as late as 1858, when Bishop Cotton opposed a move to abolish the caste system on the grounds that in the absence of the civilizing influence of Christianity it prevented India from collapse into anarchy.[112] The assault by evangelicals, however, gradually weakened its hold, and over time, particularly when inflected by racial coding, the negative stereotype of a caste-ridden Hinduism intensified.

Caste attracted the hostility of evangelicals because it was seen as a powerful barrier to conversion, enlightenment and progress, and the mainstay of arguments against intervention in Indian customs. And yet caste was understood with neither rigour nor consistency. Dubois's support for caste had coexisted with a revulsion toward Hinduism, as if the former was a civil institution. Others such as William Carey saw the two as mutually supportive and inextricable. Lacking precision, the term caste was used interchangeably with race, sect, tribe and even nation to denote a population seen to possess common traits. Indeed, it was this versatility that promoted the cavalier use of caste to provide pseudo-scientific status to theories on the nature of Indian society. Charles Grant considered caste to be one of the defining features of 'Hindoo character', and as an example described dacoits as 'castes of robbers and thieves'.[113] For others, caste was a means of explaining differentiation. James Forbes subdivided the four varnas into eighty-four castes, attributing differences to geographical factors, and spelled out the implicit racial hierarchization when he noted that 'inferior castes are of a darker complexion than the superior Hindoos'.[114]

We might have expected better of James Mill. His damning indictment of Indian history and culture, published in the same year as the study of Dubois, was written with customary utilitarian rigour. And yet the *History of British India* falters on the matter of caste. Mill's target was Brahmanism, which he considered a despotic system of priestcraft that had for centuries enslaved the Indian people. Ideologically, it was sustained by gross superstition, socially and politically by caste. In caste, he thus proposed, we have the key to understanding India: 'On this division of the people, and the privileges or disadvantages annexed to the several castes, the whole frame of Hindu society so much depends that it is an object of primary importance and merits full elucidation'.[115] This was not a work, however, of sociological sophistication. On Mill's voyage to discover in caste the essence of India he was not equipped with the tools of social analysis, let alone the eyes of a diligent observer; his idea of caste was purely textualist.[116] For despite hostility to the benign views of orientalists on the achievements of Indian civilization, Mill derived his understanding of caste almost exclusively from their work on ancient vedic scripts, in particular Jones's translation of *The Laws of Manu*. The result was a routine account of the varnas, which was then used inconsistently to expose the corrupt, absolute and enervating nature of Brahmanic authority.[117]

During the troubled period of colonial expansion when a certain loss of faith occurred in the promise of missionary endeavour, Brahmanic tyranny more than the caste system *per se* was viewed as the rotten core of Indian society and the barrier to progress. William Ward's influential study *A View of the History, Literature, and Religion of the Hindoos* sought to understand the universal appeal of idolatry and superstition. The many coincidences in mythologies of heathen nations, he surmised, have arisen from the 'common depravity' of men who reject Christianity. The manifest effect of idolatry 'is an immersion into grossest moral darkness'; 'no where have these features presented a more disgusting and horrible appearance than among the Hindoos',[118] for the Hindu system is 'wholly the work of brahmuns' who have 'placed themselves above kings in honour, and laid the whole nation at their feet'.[119]

Here was a theme that, drawing upon Protestant myths of an idolatrous, priest-ridden papacy,[120] or the anti-clericalism of the Enlightenment, could unite the followers of both Dubois and Mill. In contrast, the idea of caste was more contentious and seemingly less amenable to empirical observation, as a result of which it continued to be used loosely as a descriptive term. Walter Hamilton's pioneering survey of 1820, for example, noted that 'were it not for the uncharitable operation of caste, [the Bengalese] would be a friendly and inoffensive race. They have a thorough contempt for all other nations and castes ... whom they consider impure and degraded.'[121] Lt. Col. Fitzclarence, scourge of the Pindaris, saw Christian converts as 'the vilest wretches of the lowest class, or of no caste', who choose to call themselves of 'master's caste'.[122] And Francis Buchanan blamed the 'doctrine of caste' for the large presence of the necessitous poor.[123]

Until 1857 the notion of caste was little developed beyond its use to understand criminal and tribal activity.[124] Despite the continued lack of precision, a certain consensus was established in Protestant circles on its inherent malignancy. Wilson, Bishop of Calcutta, summed up the prevailing mood:

> The distinction of castes ... must be abandoned, decidedly, immediately, finally.... The Gospel recognizes no distinctions such as those of castes, imposed by a heathen usage, bearing in some respects a supposed religious

obligation, condemning those in the lower ranks to perpetual abasement, placing an immovable barrier against all general advance and improvement in society.[125]

After reverberations from the revolt had died down, colonial authorities, now under the direct control of the British state, turned to the serious and urgent task of providing more systematic, comprehensive and classified knowledge of Indian people. This was not a radical shift in strategy. As we have seen, from the time of Buchanan's surveys early in the century, various attempts had been made to survey aspects of Indian culture and polity. They tended to have a regional basis, or were focused on particular types of information such as settlement or land revenue records. But it was these surveys – partial, diverse and incommensurable – that set the stage for the massive ethnological project of the post-1857 period.

Certain clearly defined objectives had to be met. To prevent mutinous impulses in the army, 'brahmanized' Indians needed to be replaced by recruits from manly, 'casteless' (and hence safer) areas such as the Punjab and Nepal. And in order to reduce pressure on peasant populations that had joined the revolt, the first moves were made to extend representative power to small groups on provincial legislative councils.[126] Overall, however, the sense of urgency sprang from the recognition of inadequacies in the knowledge order due not only to the paucity of reliable comparative data, but also to the epistemologies that had so inconsistently and unsuccessfully framed previous knowledge production. Solutions were sought in the discipline of ethnology, the emergence of which in this period was prompted by a desire to confer scientific status on the human sciences through quantitative work on people in the 'laboratory of mankind'.[127] But if the perspective was provided by ethnology, the focal point was caste, thought no longer in doctrinal or academic terms, but as a matter of colonial policy.

The literature created by this project is so vast it demands separate study.[128] All I can do here is attempt to bring out some of the more significant features. Two projects dominated knowledge production in India during the second half of the nineteenth century. The Census was introduced in the 1850s, and initially was organized on a provincial basis.[129] Thus the North-Western Provinces were surveyed in 1853, and the Punjab in 1855. Plans for the introduction in 1861 of an all-India decennial Census along the lines of that of Britain were thwarted by the rebellion. The first was therefore undertaken in 1871. Over time it grew into the most extensive enumeration of a population ever taken; the 1961 Census, completed nearly twenty years after its inception, appeared in over 1,600 volumes.

In the shadow of the Census, and dependent upon it for much of the statistical data, was *The Imperial Gazetteer*. Although a series of studies was inaugurated with the ill-fated Buchanan surveys, and followed by Hamilton and Thornton, serious work began in 1869 when William Hunter was directed by the government to undertake a statistical survey of India. Unhappy with the meagre and 'heterogeneous incompleteness' of previous local surveys, most of which had involved extravagant outlays, the Governor-General required Hamilton to visit the various provincial governments with a view to 'submit a comprehensive scheme for utilizing the information already collected; for prescribing the principles' to be adopted; and 'for the consolidation into one work of the whole of the materials that may be available'.[130] The models he chose were *Aini-i-Akbari* of 1580 and Napoleon's *Description de L'Egypt* of 1821: 'It was my hope', he declared, 'to make a memorial of England's work in India, more lasting, because truer and more complete, than these monuments of Mughal Empire and of French ambition':

> Nothing is more costly than ignorance. I believe that, in spite of its many defects, this work will prove a memorable episode in the long battle against ignorance; a breakwater against the tide of prejudice and false opinions flowing down upon us from the past, and the foundation for a truer and wider knowledge of India in time to come. Its aim has been, not literary graces, nor scientific discovery, nor antiquarian research; but an earnest endeavour to render India better governed, because better understood.[131]

With an army of co-workers he compiled information on each of the 240 districts, publishing the findings in over a hundred volumes. These were later condensed into the nine volumes of *The Imperial Gazetteer*.[132] Other series followed; together they were a unique achievement.

In both projects caste was used as a fundamental category of classification. From the outset the Census had a strong interest in ethnology as a means of organizing a massive amount of seemingly disparate data. Thus in addition to age, marital status and sex, the 1871 Census included details of caste and religion in spite of the very real uncertainties that existed. W.R. Cornish, who supervised the Census for Madras, suggested that caste was a 'subject upon which no two divisions or sub-divisions of the people themselves are agreed and upon which European authorities who have paid any attention to it differ hopelessly'.[133] Later, the supervisor of the 1901 Bombay Census, R.E. Enthoven, argued that the concept of caste used in the Census is 'so hopelessly vague that our figures are useless', and urged it be abandoned. In the event, the recording of caste took on a life of its own. Early in the twentieth century separate 'Castes and Tribes' volumes appeared; Indians consulted them to assess the condition and progress of castes with which they increasingly identified.

Race and progress

Hunter organized the *Gazetteer* as a narrative of progress, but faced the same problems in organizing data as did superintendents of the Census. Like them he had recourse to caste since, as he stated, 'The Census proves that this classification remains the fundamental one to the present day'.[134] He traced the 'ethnical basis of caste' to the fourfold division of the Vedas. The practical application of this conception of caste, however, proved impossible, for Hunter was astute enough to recognize that this classification had only limited value in understanding the complexities of social and religious divisions in Indian society. In a way redolent of Mill, and even Marx, he attempted to overcome this problem by proposing that the division into varnas is modified by other factors:

> But while caste has thus its foundations deep in the distinctions of race, its superstructure is regulated by another system of division, based on the occupations of the people. The early classification of the people may be expressed either ethnically as 'twice-born' Aryans, and 'once-born' non-Aryans; or socially, as priests, warriors, husbandmen, and serfs. On these two principles of classification, according to race and to employment, still further modified by geographical position, has been built up the ethnical and social organization of Indian caste. From the resulting cross-division arises an excessive complexity which renders any brief exposition of caste superficial.[135]

This elaboration also proved unworkable. Not only did it render any uniform plan impossible, but the sheer diversity of India's regions and peoples resisted statistical appropriation. Overall the project produced 'unhappy results' for the investigators; the 'distinctive features of caste, creed, language and the different levels of existence obtaining, tended to undermine the energy and interest of the work'.[136]

Hunter's thinking on caste was influenced by the Rev. Sherring, who simultaneously was working on his major study *Hindu Tribes and Castes*.[137] 'It appears strange', Sherring declared at the outset, 'that hitherto no one has attempted to give in English a consecutive and detailed account of the castes of India', and he proceeds to make the observation to his 'numerous native friends' that his study has not been undertaken out of 'admiration or respect for ... the peculiar institution of caste'. To the contrary, caste is a 'monstrous engine of pride, dissension, and shame, which could only have been invented by an utterly diseased condition of human society'.[138] Sherring confronts some of the terminological confusion surrounding caste evident in previous writing:

> It is common to speak of the castes of India in their relation to the Hindu religion; and in that light they may be very properly regarded. Yet they sustain another highly important relation. Ethnologically they are so many tribes

and clans, with separate histories and customs. The members of a caste are, doubtless, united together by peculiar sacred and social ties. In addition, they bear a tribal relation to one another of great significance. Each caste … is in fact a tribe governed by laws of the most impervious character.[139]

There is a certain logic to these arguments, but it is a flimsy one. The distinction between religiously based and sanctioned castes and ethnologically based tribes lacked rigour, and therefore could not be applied with any degree of consistency. Sherring confusingly organized the first volume around studies of 'Brahmanical tribes' such as the 'Kshatriya or Rajputs', the 'mixed castes and tribes' of the 'Vaisyas and Sudras', and 'aboriginal tribes and lower castes'. This conspicuous lack of success in elaborating the complexities of the caste system did not compromise in any way Sherring's narrative of racial progress. European education, he claimed, was undermining the divine authority of the Brahman, and forcing him to give way to the Kayasth (writer caste) and Vaisya (trading caste) who are 'seizing the golden opportunities that education, civilization, and a thousand favourable circumstances' offer.[140] Caste relationships have been transformed. Middle and lower castes, which because of their 'presumed impurity of blood, and inherent inferiority, owing … to the operation of divine laws' had been prevented from escaping from 'prejudice and tyranny', now enjoyed under the influence of British rule the fundamental rights to social and political equality. Even the 'most untamed and vagabond' tribes have been reformed by the 'steady and onward progress of civilization' in India.[141]

This picture of social mobility, however, stands in sharp contrast to the racial hierarchy outlined in Sherring's account of the 'natural history' of Hindu caste. There is in India, he stated, 'an infinite variety of physiognomy, colour, and physique', and he proceeded to provide a taxonomy:

> The fair-faced, keen-eyed, aquiline-nosed, and intellectual Brahmin, the stalwart and commanding Rajpoot, the supple Banniah, the conceited yet able Kayasth, or writer, the clever barhai, or carpenter, the heavy-browed lohar, or blacksmith, the wiry and laborious Kumbhi, or agriculturalist, the short and handsome chamar, the dark Pasi, the darker Dom, the wild and semi-barbarous aborigines, and hundreds of other tribes and castes, are in reality so many distinct types of the human family.[142]

Sherring acknowledged the necessary albeit limited nature of such a roughly drawn hierarchy. In reality, he argued, 'the boundary lines dividing the vast Hindu race into multitudinous clans' are 'beyond computation'.[143] Nowhere, however, does he inquire into how this racial hierarchy is affected by the social transformations brought about by British rule. In important respects Sherring was emblematic of changes that were taking place in the production of knowledge. First, there is in his work a move –

faltering and inconsistent though it might have been – from textual-based theories of caste to ones incorporating observable socio-cultural factors. Secondly, we can also detect a shift that in the long term eclipsed evangelical perspectives. It was significant that Sherring was an Anglican who clearly subscribed to older concerns about Brahmanical tyranny. But his condemnations of the caste system were based less on biblical exegesis than on secular, empirical arguments. Thirdly, he consolidated and systematized racial theories of the caste system. In all these, foundations were being laid for the massive intervention of colonial anthropology made by the Census and imperial gazetteers.[144]

Race and progress provided the articulating principles. Neither was required,[145] but they had by this time proved their value and versatility in helping to make sense of the complexities of Indian history and society. The idea of progress had since the eighteenth century framed British perspectives on the backwardness of Indian society, and been used to justify colonial expansion. Race, in part the progeny of progress, developed later, and had in embryonic form informed discussions on those features of Indian society that were seen as barriers to the march of civilization. Used in combination toward the end of the nineteenth century, they were to act as a powerful motif. Consider, for example, Hunter's account of the origins of Indian society:

> Our earliest glimpses of India disclose two races struggling for the soil. The one was a fair-skinned people, which had lately entered by the north-western passes; a people of ARYAN, literally 'noble' lineage, speaking a stately language, worshipping friendly and powerful gods. The other was a race of a lower type, who had long dwelt in the land, and whom the lordly new-comers drove back before them into the mountains, or reduced to servitude on the plains. The comparatively pure descendants of these two races were in 1872 nearly equal in numbers ... the intermediate castes, sprung chiefly from the ruder stock, make up the mass of the Indian population.[146]

This Aryan theory of race in its most modern manifestation went to the heart of the matter. The history of India was the history of a grim struggle between noble Aryans of Indo-European origin and debased aboriginal races. In this war against savagery the 'conquering stock' of Aryans had triumphed. Where racial mixing occurred, however, degeneration had followed since the purity of Aryan sentiment had become contaminated with base superstition. Founded on readings of Vedic scriptures, endowed with status by Jones's discovery of the commonality of Indo-Aryan languages, this theory was now embraced by ethnologists. In doing so, writers such as Hunter temporalized notions of the caste system, for whereas orientalists had thought of it primarily in terms of cultural difference, ethnologists increasingly located it hierarchically within evolutionary schema. This is nicely illustrated by Hunter. In attempting to demonstrate the lineages of cultural prejudice in early racial struggles he looked to the ancient texts, and found there 'scornful epithets for the primitive tribes'. The Aryan, with 'his finely-formed features, loathed the squat Mongolian faces of the Aborigines'. Vedic songs abound with references to tribal people as 'noseless', 'disturbers of sacrifices', 'gross feeders on flesh', 'lawless', 'without gods' and 'without rites'. These peoples were from the plains, where

> they have lain hidden away in the recesses of the mountains, like the remains of extinct animals which palaeontologists find in hill caves. India thus forms a great museum of races, in which we can study man from his lowest to his highest stages of culture. The specimens are not fossils or dry bones, but living communities, to whose widely-diverse conditions we have to adapt our administration and our laws.[147]

Hunter proceeds to catalogue and classify the specimens on display using the full repertoire – and terminological confusion – of nineteenth-century racial imagery. The Brahmans, for example, are

> the result of nearly 3000 years of hereditary education and self-restraint; and they have evolved a type of mankind quite distinct from the surrounding population. Even the passing traveller in India marks them out, alike from the bronze-cheeked, large-limbed, leisure-loving Rajput or warrior caste of Aryan descent; and from the dark-skinned, flat-nosed, thick-lipped low-castes of non-Aryan origin, with their short bodies and bullet heads. The Brahman stands apart from both; tall and slim, with finely modelled lips and nose, fair complexion, high forehead, and somewhat cocoa-nut shaped skull.... He is an example of a class becoming the ruling power in a country, not by force of arms, but by the vigour of hereditary culture and temperance.[148]

Caste thus conceived was not merely an invention of European writers, nor a direct appropriation of ancient Indian thought and practice, but rather the outcome of an ongoing dialogue between the two. This may help to explain the continued imprecision; it certainly accounts for the contrasts in the approaches of Hunter and other prominent ethnologists such as William Crooke, Herbert Risley and Denzil Ibbetson.[149]

From these debates emerged a renewed concern with the degeneration of Indian society. Articulated to notions of caste and race, effeminacy came to be singled out as a crucial symptom of inevitable decline.[150] As we have seen, many of the early travel accounts commented on the passive and effeminate nature of Bengalis, and the trope continued to feature in contemporary comment, most notably in the writings of Macaulay. After the troubles of 1857 – from which Bengal had remained remote – ethnology provided the means of putting the whole matter on a scientific basis. Hunter and his contemporaries displayed a clear sense of racial vigour, but it was with the extensive studies of Risley that effeminacy became a key signifier of degeneration. He concluded that the people of Bengal were of the Mongolo-Dravidian racial stock. They were slightly built and of low stature, an effeminacy he attributed to an enervating climate and diet, and the early maternity of Bengali women.[151] These ideas were used to great effect to deal with the challenge posed by the Indian middle class to rights and privileges seen to be the preserve of the British. Faced with mounting pressure for reform, British commentators directed attention to the effeminacy of this Western-educated elite. So what had previously been a category applied fairly loosely to the population of Bengal as a whole, was now directed specifically to its bhadralok elite, and the 'Bengali babu' emerged as a figure of ridicule quite unfit for the manly demands of imperial administration.

With the publication of the 1891 Census for Bengal, revised and expanded into the 1908 *Tribes and Castes of Bengal*, Risley established himself as the leading figure in colonial ethnology. Using the full range of techniques, including anthropometry, and abandoning occupational categories of classification in favour of Brahmanic sociology, Risley sought to prove the primordial role of caste in Indian society. The key to understanding its historic role was race:

> race sentiment, … far from being a figment of the intolerant pride of the Brahman, rests upon a foundation of fact which scientific methods confirm, that it has shaped the intricate groupings of the caste system, and has preserved the Aryan type in comparative purity throughout Northern India.[152]

Risley considered India an ideal laboratory of racial science. Ultimately, his experimental work expressed, and to an extent ameliorated, the ritual anxieties of the Brahman elite, and the racial anxieties of the empire at a time of rapid change.[153] His findings provided succour to higher castes fearing loss of authority, simultaneously laying the foundation for the rise of communalism. And in pointing to caste as both the bastion against anarchy and the single greatest obstacle to change, he warned Indian and European modernizers of the potentially catastrophic nature of change promoted by idealism. The racial inferiority of Indians justified, even demanded, their continued dominance by Britain. It was, concludes Dirks, a 'bloody legacy that continues to exact a mounting toll'.[154] With perhaps less momentous consequences, ethnology impacted also on the information order. The long shadow cast by the Census and *Imperial Gazetteer* eclipsed all other forms of knowledge production. In the last thirty years of the nineteenth century few evangelical or travel accounts of note appeared; those that did tended to reproduce familiar imagery which contributed little to the state of knowledge on Indian society.

Notes

1 Joseph Peggs, *Ghaut Murders in India. An Appeal to British Humanity and Justice Respecting the Practice of Exposing the Sick on the Banks of the Ganges*, London, Seeley, 1830.
2 Howard Malcolm, *Travels in South East Asia, embracing Hindustan, Malaya, Siam and China; with Notices of Numerous Missionary Stations*, London, Charles Tilt, 1839, p. 8.
3 William Campbell, *British India in its Relation to the Decline of Hindooism, and the Progress of Christianity ...*, London, Snow, 1839, p. iii.
4 *Ibid.*, pp. 9–10.
5 For details of Jervis's manoeuvres see Matthew Edney, *Mapping and Empire. The Geographical Construction of British India, 1765–1843*, Chicago, University of Chicago Press, 1997.
6 Major Thomas Jervis, *Address ... Descriptive of the State, Progress, and Prospects of the Various Surveys, and other Scientific Enquiries, instituted by the Hon. East India Company throughout Asia*, Torquay, Private Circulation, 1838, p. 44. As part of his campaign to have his provisional appointment as Surveyor-General confirmed, Jervis arranged to have the address printed privately. It was then distributed with covering hand-written notes to influential contacts, all to no avail.
7 *Ibid.*, p. 10.
8 Major H. Bevan, *Thirty Years in India: or, A Soldier's Reminiscences of Nature and European Life in the Presidencies, from 1808 to 1838*, London, Pelham Richardson, 1839, p. vi.
9 *Ibid.*, p. 321.
10 *Ibid.*, p. 146.
11 James Massie, *Continental India*, London, Ward, 1840, pp. xiii–xiv.
12 *Ibid.*, p. 82.
13 *Ibid.*, p. 254.
14 Anon., 'A young civilian in Bengal in 1805', *Bengal Past and Present*, 29, 1805, p. 125.
15 Walter Hamilton, *A Geographical, Statistical and Historical Description of Hindostan, and the Adjacent Countries*, London, Murray, 1820, pp. 51–2.
16 Mrs B.H. Holland, *The Young Cadet; or Henry Delamere's Voyage to India*, London, John Harris, 1827, p. 81.
17 Josiah Conder, *The Modern Traveller. A Description, Geographical, Historical and Topographical of the Various Countries of the Globe*, 30 vols, London, Duncan, 1830, Vol. III, pp. 49–50.
18 Emma Roberts, *Scenes and Characteristics of Hindostan with Sketches of Anglo-Indian Society*, London, Allen, 1835, pp. 13–14.
19 Campbell, *British India in its Relation to the Decline of Hindooism*, p. 5.
20 Massie, *Continental India*, pp. 99–100.
21 C.J.C. Davidson, *Diary of Travels and Adventures in Upper India*, London, Henry Colburn, 1843, p. 338.
22 *Ibid.*, p. 6.
23 George Johnson, *The Stranger in India; or, Three Years in Calcutta*, London, Colburn, 1843, p. 188.
24 William Sleeman, *Rambles and Recollections of an Indian Official*, London, Hatchard, 1844, p. 76.
25 *Ibid.*, p. 4.
26 Rev. W. Buyers, *Recollections of Northern India; with Observations on the Origin, Customs, and Moral Sentiments of the Hindoos, and Remarks on the Country, and Principal Places on the Ganges, &c.*, London, Snow, 1848, p. 23.
27 *Ibid.*, p. 25.
28 *Ibid.*, p. 184.
29 *Ibid.*, p. 209.
30 *Ibid.*, p. 408.
31 *Ibid.*, p. 198.

32 Henry Elliot, *Memoirs of the History, of Folk-lore, and Distribution of Races of the North Western Provinces of India*, edited, revised and rearranged by John Beames, London, Trubner, 1869, pp. xv–xvi.

33 A. Hervey, *Ten Years in India; or, The Life of a Young Officer*, London, Schoberl, 1850, pp. iv–v.

34 *Ibid.*, p. 88. A note of caution is struck, however, on the treatment meted out by young officers. They talk of *'those horrible black nigger sepoys* [and] look down on them as brute beasts' (p. 88), and as long as this continues, Hervey concludes, 'the poor soldier will be maltreated until his meek and humble spirit becomes roused, his pride hurt, and the consequences are attended with fearful results' (p. 90).

35 J. Gray, *Life in Bombay, and the Neighbouring Out-Stations*, London, Bentley, 1852, p. viii.

36 M. Wylie, *Bengal as a Field of Missions*, London, Dalton, 1854, p. 209.

37 *Ibid.*, pp. 35–6.

38 Joseph Mullens, *Revised Statistics of Missions in India and Ceylon, compiled at the Request of the Calcutta Missionary Conference, by Rev. Joseph Mullens*, Calcutta, Baptist Mission Press, 1852.

39 [Anon.], *A Voice from Bombay in Western India – in Behalf of the Spiritual Wants of a Population of 550,000 Souls in Heathen Darkness*, London, Seeleys, 1852, p. 11.

40 [M. Wylie], *The Bible in India*, London, Dalton, 1853, p. 14.

41 Joseph Mullens, *Missions in South India*, London, Dalton, 1854, p. 3.

42 John Kaye, *The Administration of the East India Company; a History of Indian Progress*, London, Bentley, 1853.

43 *Ibid.*, p. 3.

44 *Ibid.*, p. 9.

45 *Ibid.*, pp. 13–14.

46 *Ibid.*, pp. 14–16.

47 *Ibid.*, pp. 356–7.

48 *Ibid.*, p. 376.

49 *Ibid.*, p. 407.

50 *Ibid.*, p. 471.

51 *Ibid.*, p. 488.

52 Edward Thornton, *A Gazetteer of the Territories under the Government of the East India Company, and of the Native States on the Continent of India*, London, Allen, 1857.

53 *Petition of the Calcutta Missionaries, for a Royal Commission to Enquire into the Condition of the People of Bengal*, London, Sanders, Cones and Co., 1856, p. 16.

54 For an extensive and useful annotated bibliography, see P.J.O. Taylor (ed.), *A Companion to the 'Indian Mutiny' of 1857*, Delhi, Oxford University Press, 1996.

55 I have relied here on the scholarly syntheses provided in C.A. Bayly, *Indian Society and the Making of the British Empire. The New Cambridge History of India* Vol. II.1, Cambridge, Cambridge University Press, 1988, and Sugata Bose and Ayesha Jalal, *Modern South Asia. History, Culture, Political Economy*, Delhi, Oxford University Press, 1999.

56 For a more general survey of the role of the press in reporting India, see David Finkelstein and Douglas Peers (eds), *Negotiating India in the Nineteenth-Century Media*, Basingstoke, Macmillan, 2000.

57 Eugenie Palmegiano, *The British Empire in the Victorian Press, 1832–1867. A Bibliography*, New York, Garland, 1987.

58 Rev. John Stevenson, *A Sermon, for the Benefit of the Sufferers in India, on the Goodness and Severity of God. Preached at Tinwell, Rutland, 20 September 1857*, Stamford, Langley, 1857, p. 6.

59 *Ibid.*, p. 11.

60 Francis Close, *An Indian Retrospect, or, What has Christian England done for Heathen India?*, London, Hatchard, 1858, p. 3.

61 James McKee, *Obstacles to the Progress of Christianity in India*, Belfast, Belfast News-Letter, 1858, pp. 4–5.

62 Rev. J. Murray Mitchell, *Indian Missions; Viewed in Connexion with the Mutiny and other Recent Events*, London, Nisbet, 1859, p. 6.
63 *Ibid.*, p. 16.
64 *Ibid.*, p. 24.
65 Madeline and Rosalind Wallace-Dunlop, *A Timely Retreat; or, A Year in Bengal before the Mutinies. By Two Sisters*, 2 vols, London, Bentley, 1858.
66 Kataki Kushari Dyson, *A Various Universe. A Study of the Journals of British Men and Women in the Indian Subcontinent, 1765–1856*, Delhi, Oxford University Press, 1978, p. 320.
67 Wallace-Dunlop, *A Timely Retreat*, Vol. I, p. 98.
68 *Ibid.*, p. 112.
69 *Ibid.*, Vol. II, pp. 8–9.
70 *Ibid.*, pp. 89–90.
71 *Ibid.*, p. 90.
72 William H. Russell, *My Diary in India in the Year 1858–59*, London, 1860, pp. 125–6.
73 Cadwalladar Cummerbund, *From Southampton to Calcutta*, London, Saunders, Otley and Co., 1860, p. 228.
74 *Ibid.*, pp. 171–2.
75 John Kaye, *Kaye's and Malleson's History of the Indian Mutiny of 1857–8*, 4 vols, London, 1897–98. The first three volumes were written by Kaye; a fourth was intended but Kaye died before it could be completed. It was finished by G.B. Malleson. Based on extensive research of contemporary evidence, it remains the most authoritative account of the nineteenth century.
76 For the best analyses of Kaye's chapatis and the role of rumour see Ranajit Guha, *Elementary Aspects of Peasant Insurgency in Colonial India*, Delhi, Oxford University Press, 1983, and Homi Bhabha, 'By bread alone: signs of violence in the mid-nineteenth century', in *The Location of Culture*, London, Routledge, 1994.
77 R. Montgomery Martin, *The Progress and Present State of British India*, London, Sampson Low, 1862, pp. vi–vii.
78 *Ibid.*, p. x.
79 *Ibid.*, p. 293.
80 *Ibid.*, pp. 294–5.
81 Rev. John Barton, *The Educated Classes of Calcutta, viewed in regard to their Accessibility to Missionary Effort*, London, Church Missionary House, 1864, p. 5.
82 For the background to the increased involvement of women like Mary Carpenter in missionary work after 1857 see Steven Maugham, 'Civic culture, women's foreign missions, and the British imperial imagination, 1860–1914', in Frank Trentmann (ed.), *Paradoxes of Civil Society. New Perspectives on Modern German and British History*, New York, Berghahn, 2000.
83 Mary Carpenter, *Six Months in India*, 2 vols, London, Longmans, Green and Co., 1868, Vol. II, pp. 80–1.
84 Mary Carpenter, *Addresses to the Hindoos, delivered in India*, London, Longmans, Green and Co., 1867, p. 5.
85 *Ibid.*, p. 6.
86 Carpenter, *Six Months in India*, Vol. II, p. 108.
87 *Ibid.*, p. 55. See also Antoinette Burton's study of this text, 'Fearful bodies into disciplined subjects: pleasure, romance and the family drama of colonial reform in Mary Carpenter's *Six Months in India*', *Signs*, 20:3, Spring 1995, pp. 545–74.
88 Carpenter, *Addresses to the Hindoos*, p. 8.
89 *Memoir of George E.L. Cotton, Bishop of Calcutta, and Metropolitan. With Selections from his Journals and Correspondence. Edited by Mrs. Cotton*, London, Longmans, Green and Co., 1871, pp. 80–1.
90 *Ibid.*, p. 331.
91 William Butler, *The Land of the Veda, being Personal Reminiscences of India; its People, Castes, Thugs, and Fakirs ...*, New York, Phillips and Hunt, 1871, p. 11.
92 *Ibid.*, p. 40.
93 *Ibid.*, p. 402.

94 See the tables reproduced on pp. 529–31.
95 Maughan, 'Civic culture, women's foreign missions, and the British imperial imagination'.
96 Herbert Blackett, *Two Years in an Indian Mission*, London, SPCK, 1884, pp. 9–10, 12, 15.
97 James Bradbury, *India, its Condition, Religion and Missions*, London, Snow, 1884, p. 8.
98 *Ibid.*, p. 24.
99 E.C.P. Hull, *The European in India; or, Anglo-Indian's Vade Mecum*, London, King, 1871, p. viii.
100 *Ibid.*, p. 39.
101 *Ibid.*, pp. 43, 45.
102 [Edward Eastwick], *Handbook of the Madras Presidency*, London, Murray, 1879; *Handbook of the Bombay Presidency*, London, Murray, 1881; *Handbook of the Bengal Presidency*, London, Murray, 1882; *Handbook of the Panjab, Rajputana, Kashmir and Upper Sindh*, London, Murray, 1883. These were condensed into a single volume in 1892, which was revised seven times in the ensuing decade.
103 Cited in *Handbook of the Madras Presidency*, pp. xi–xii.
104 *Handbook of the Bengal Presidency*, pp. 34–5.
105 C.A. Bayly, *Empire and Information. Intelligence Gathering and Social Communication in India, 1780–1870*, Cambridge, Cambridge University Press, 1996, p. 338.
106 Cited in Susan Bayly, *Caste, Society and Politics in India from the Eighteenth Century to the Modern Age. The New Cambridge History of Modern India* Vol. IV.3, Cambridge, Cambridge University Press, 1999, p. 106.
107 William Robertson, *An Historical Disquisition concerning the Knowledge which the Ancients had of India*, London, Cadell and Davies, 1817 [1791], p. 200.
108 *Ibid.*, p. 201.
109 Abbe J.A. Dubois, *Description of the Character, Manners, and Customs of the People of India, and of Their Institutions, Religious and Civil*, translated and edited by Henry Beauchamp as *Hindu Manners, Customs and Ceremonies*, Oxford, Clarendon Press, 1906. The origins and publication of the manuscript are well described by Nicholas Dirks, *Castes of Mind. Colonialism and the Making of Modern India*, Princeton, Princeton University Press, 2001.
110 Cited in Dirks, *Castes of Mind*, p. 24.
111 Duncan Forester, *Caste and Christianity. Attitudes and Policies on Caste of Anglo-Saxon Protestant Missions in India*, London, Curzon Press, 1980, p. 35.
112 G.A. Oddie, *Social Protest in India. British Protestant Missionaries and Social Reforms, 1850–1900*, Delhi, Manoher, 1979, p. 56.
113 Charles Grant, *Observations on the State of Society among the Asiatic Subjects of Great Britain, particularly with reference to Morals; and on the Means of Improving it. – Written chiefly in the Year 1792*, Parliamentary Papers, 1813, p. 28.
114 James Forbes, *Oriental Memoirs*, 4 vols, London, White, Cochrane and Co., 1813, Vol. I, p. 73.
115 Cited in Ronald Inden, *Imagining India*, Bloomington, Indiana University Press, 2000 [1990], p. 57.
116 Dirks, *Castes of Mind*, p. 34.
117 In fairness, Mill was later to develop his ideas in the 1824 supplement of the *Encyclopaedia Britannica*. He located caste within the broad history of the division of labour, and the transition from a pastoral to an agricultural mode of production. Contradictions between the economic and religious exigencies, however, remained unresolved. See Louis Dumont, *Homo Hierachicus. The Caste System and its Implications*, Chicago, University of Chicago Press, 1980 [1966], p. 24.
118 William Ward, *A View of the History, Literature, and Religion of the Hindoos*, 4 vols, London, British Missionary Society, 1817–20, Vol. III, p. xxviii.
119 *Ibid.*, p. 69.
120 Bayly, *Caste, Society and Politics in India*, p. 110.
121 Walter Hamilton, *A Geographical, Statistical and Historical Description of Hindostan*,

and the Adjacent Countries, London, Murray, 1820, p. 102.
122 Lt. Col. Fitzclarence, Journal of a Route across India, through Egypt to England in the latter end of the Year 1817, and the beginning of 1818, London, Murray, 1819, p. 105.
123 R. Montgomery Martin, The History, Antiquities, Topography, and Statistics of Eastern India, 3 vols, London, Allen, 1838, Vol. I, p. 126.
124 This tends to be suggested not only by the lack of reference in travel and evangelical accounts, but also by silences on this period in all of the recent studies. Dumont, Dirks, Inden and Bayly have little to say, choosing instead to jump from Mill to 1857, even to Risley at the end of the century. The intellectual history of Western conceptions of caste awaits its scholar.
125 Cited in Forrester, Caste and Christianity, p. 38.
126 Bayly, Caste, Society and Politics in India, p. 122.
127 Christopher Pinney, 'Colonial anthropology in the "laboratory of mankind"', in C.A. Bayly (ed.), The Raj. India and the British 1600–1946, London, National Portrait Gallery Publications, 1990, pp. 252–63.
128 For an early but worthy foray into it, see S.B. Chaudhuri, History of the Gazetteers of India, Delhi, Ministry of Education, 1964.
129 Kenneth Jones, 'Religious identity and the Indian Census', in N. Gerald Barrier (ed.), The Census in British India. New Perspectives, Delhi, Manohar, 1981. For a useful bibliography on the Census, see Richard Martin, 'Bibliographic notes on the Indian Census', in the same collection.
130 William Hunter, The Imperial Gazetteer of India, London, Trubner, 1881, p. ix.
131 Ibid., p. xxx.
132 By far the most accessible and popular form of the Gazetteer, however, was the updated single-volume digest Hunter compiled in 1886 (William Hunter, The Indian Empire. Its People, History and Products, London, Trubner, 1886).
133 Cited in Frank Conlon. 'The Census of India as a source for the historical study of religion and caste', in Barrier (ed.), The Census in British India, p. 108.
134 Hunter, The Indian Empire, p. 192.
135 Ibid., p. 192.
136 Chaudhuri, History of the Gazetteers of India, p. 16.
137 Rev. M.A. Sherring, Hindu Tribes and Castes, 3 vols, London, Trubner, 1872–81. Vol. I dealing with Brahmanical, Kshatriya or Rajpoot tribes, mixed castes and tribes of Vaisyas and Sudras, and Aboriginal tribes and inferior castes around Benares appeared in 1872, Vol. II covering the north-west frontier and central provinces appeared in 1879, and Vol. III covering Rajputna and Madras appeared in 1881, after Sherring's death. Also important at the time were the writings of George Campbell: for example, 'On the races of India as traced in existing tribes and castes', Quarterly Ethnological Journal, 1:2, 1876.
138 Sherring, Hindu Tribes and Castes, Vol. I, p. iv.
139 Ibid., p. xxiii.
140 Ibid., pp. 4–5.
141 Ibid., p. 387.
142 Ibid., Vol. III, p. 218.
143 Ibid., p. 219.
144 The broad contours of this intervention have recently been traced by Bayly, Caste, Society and Politics in India, and Dirks, Castes of Mind.
145 In what remains one of the most perceptive discussions of how racial categories were applied in India, Peter Robb has argued that late nineteenth-century perceptions of Indian society 'did not require the term "race", but that was the word around which they were to gather' (Peter Robb, 'South Asia and the concept of race', in Robb (ed.), The Concept of Race in South Asia, Delhi, Oxford University Press, 1997). The same obtains for 'progress'.
146 Hunter, The Indian Empire, p. 52.
147 Ibid., p. 54.
148 Ibid., p. 96.
149 William Crooke, The Native Races of the British Empire: Natives of Northern India,

London, 1907; Herbert Risley, *The People of India*, London, 1908; Denzil Ibbetson, *Panjab Castes*, Delhi, Low Price Publications, 1993, first published as part of the 1881 Census of the Panjab. Crooke and Ibbetson, while sharing with Hunter founding concepts on civilization and Aryan stock, dismissed the excesses of racial theory (Susan Bayly, 'Caste and "race" in colonial ethnography', in Robb (ed.), *The Concept of Race in South Asia*, p. 205). Both emphasized the role of occupation. 'The whole basis of diversity of caste', wrote Ibbetson, 'is diversity of occupation' (Ibbetson, *Panjab Castes*, p. 3).

150 Mrinalini Sinha, *Colonial Masculinity. The 'Manly Englishman' and the 'Effeminate Bengali' in the Late Nineteenth Century*, Manchester, Manchester University Press, 1995.

151 *Ibid.*, p. 20.

152 Cited in Dirks, *Castes of Mind*, p. 213.

153 *Ibid.*, p. 225.

154 *Ibid.*, p. 227.

Conclusion

I embarked on this study in the belief rather than the conviction that the nineteenth-century metropolitan poor should be seen as an object of imperial, not merely domestic concern. Well known from writings on the poor were the frequent references to non-European peoples and places. Henry Mayhew found 'wandering tribes', George Sims 'savage tribes of outcast Blackamoors', and William Booth 'pygmies' on the streets of London; J.C. Parkinson discovered the orient in Bluegate Fields, and Charles Masterman likened the abyss of the East End to a tropical forest. On reflection, I found this evidence unconvincing. Such metaphors could have been little more than reflections of contemporary linguistic practices; they did not in themselves prove the existence of imperial discourses.

More compelling were the explicit references in evangelical writings to the situation in India. Frederick Meyrick looked to the 1857 revolt and found there a portent for a pauper population living beyond the 'wholesome restraint' of Christianity. And Joseph Mullens compared the heathenism of London to that of Calcutta, concluding that both constituencies faced eternal damnation. Here, to my mind, were discourses that drew upon imperial concerns to construct narratives of progress. This seemed a more productive way of proceeding, and so I studied evangelical and travel writings on the metropolitan poor and India in order to understand better the ways in which they were structured by, and the mechanisms they displayed to express fears about, the progress of imperial modernity.

Although I anticipated certain homologies between constructions of the metropolitan poor and colonial subjects, there were few direct cross-references. Travel and evangelical narratives on London infrequently acknowledged the existence of writings on India; conversely, apart from passing mention of the need of a Dickens to describe Indian life, travellers in India did not seem drawn to the style or vocabulary of urban explorers such as Mayhew or Greenwood. What became apparent was that these homologies operated at a deeper structural level, and it was to parallels in narrative form, chronology and rhetoric that I should look for evidence of their existence.

Bernard Cohn's suggestion of the creation of a unitary field between Britain and India in the late eighteenth century seemed to provide a good working model of how such homologies may have arisen. Prior to this period links between the literary appropriation of the metropolis and India were tenuous. Despite the crucial role of travel narratives in promoting nascent Enlightenment thought and the attraction of the East for eighteenth-century writers, the metropolitan literary imagination remained insular to the point of deprecating travel, particularly in pursuit of imperial ambition. With the ascent of British power in India and the attendant demand for information, argues Cohn, metropolis and colony were brought onto a common terrain, the boundaries of which were defined by the production of knowledge, namely, the project to gather, order and classify useful information on topography, history, population, trade and culture, and make it available in various forms. The field was cultivated by an empiricist methodology and epistemology; more importantly, I felt, it had an articulating principle of progress. The idea of progress – thought exclusively in terms of Western civilization – took hold at precisely that moment when the unitary field was created, and came to be of critical importance in structuring narratives of metropolis and colony, particularly by identifying antithetical forces seen to threaten the future of the imperial nation.

Much of this study, therefore, has focused on the faltering attempts by various agencies to know and hence control perceived threats to British commercial, political and cultural authority in London and India during the long nineteenth century, and make known their deliberations to a general readership. Travel accounts and evangelical writings exerted the formative influence on perceptions of London and India. Government and East India Company reports and detailed statistical surveys were not read widely; rather it was the likes of Colquhoun, Egan, Mayhew, Mearns and Booth who revealed London, and Grant, Ward, Forbes, Heber, Montgomery Martin and Kaye who revealed India to the British public.

The transformation of London in the late eighteenth century engendered literary forms and modes of inquiry that strove to see, define and understand its poor. The intervention of Colquhoun was instrumental in discovering the residuum, but his intervention was part of a wider concern to make sense of social relationships that could no longer be captured by descriptive and anecdotal taxonomies of diverse paupers preying upon an unwary bourgeoisie moving about the streets of the metropolis. For now recognition was forced that poverty was the inevitable concomitant of prosperity, the pathological consequences of which had to be controlled, initially by revealing 'suppressed connections' of the social order in its totality. Thus the historical insight to be gained from knowledge of the immense and plural unity of the metropolis was part of the same project to confront the forces of disorder that threatened the commercial progress of the nation.

Semi-factual accounts are more difficult to place. They shared a totalizing vision, but in stumbling pursuit drew freely upon diverse genres and inhabited awkwardly contradictory epistemologies. Egan's *Life in London* was an early and enormously popular account of the high and low in metropolitan life, but in many respects a transitional work. Its depiction of the grotesque and exotic among underworld characters encountered on the tour may have drawn upon Elizabethan popular literature and its eighteenth-century successors, and yet its narrative devices and concerns anticipated much of the work of urban travellers and novelists.

Responding to failures of the previous century to represent the diversity of metropolitan life, Colquhoun and Egan in their different ways opened up radically new projects of knowledge production. Colquhoun brought the systematic use of statistical materials to reveal the extent of criminal activity. This delinquency, he anticipated, placed before his readers in such a detailed and prominent manner, must excite astonishment. Egan, on the other hand, represented the new ambulatory observer attempting to capture the dislocating experiences of the metropolis by first-hand observation. Theoretical knowledge – that derived from the closet – was incapable of ascertaining real life; the object of his heroes was to see its quotidian plurality through direct experience of London's streets and diverse haunts.

Although India was distant, it was arguably no less known to the bourgeois reader than East London, and presented the same problems for those wishing to address the prevailing state of ignorance. Robertson and Mill pursued theoretical inquiry without ever visiting India. For Mill this was a point of principle; a man could, he argued in stark contrast to his contemporary Egan, gain more knowledge of India in 'his closet in England than he could during the course of longest life, by the use of eyes and ears in India'. Travel writers, on the other hand, celebrated the virtues of first-hand observation. Predating by some years the genre of urban travel, Forster, Kindersley, Nugent, Forbes and Graham struggled to grasp and represent the mysterious complexities of Indian life. Sensitive to the fanciful nature of previous accounts, they strove for veracity based on personal experience. Forster, in a move anticipating many nineteenth-century urban travellers, relied on disguise and knowledge of indigenous languages to gain access to Indian culture.

If anything united the imagery in these early accounts it was plurality and contradiction. Following a century in which knowledge of India and metropolitan low life advanced little, travellers to India reproduced variously tropes of depraved and barbarous customs described in previous accounts, stereotypical characterizations based on environmentalism, and more sympathetic orientalist perspectives. In a metropolitan context, tricks-of-the-town narratives traceable to the writings of Elizabethan pamphleteers had in the course of the eighteenth century degenerated into stale formulae, then to be displaced by the intervention of Colquhoun. In contrast to the finely resolved taxonomies of exotic criminal activity, Colquhoun created an endemic, predatory and organized underclass located in the riverside areas of East London. This shift was profoundly to influence the criminalization of collective activity in the nineteenth century.

Less riven by internal contradiction was the intervention of evangelicals. Informed by coherent and powerful narratives on the revelation of divine grace, evangelicalism brought together groups of people from various social backgrounds committed to missionary work wherever the need was recognized. The Clapham Sect, for example, united the efforts of influential persons including Wilberforce, Bernard, Grant and Colquhoun to fight on the fronts of abolition, poverty and conversion of the heathen. Their members were largely responsible for the pioneering work of the Society for Bettering the Condition of the Poor (SBCP), various schemes to relieve distress in the metropolis, and the campaign to eradicate restrictions on missionary activity in India culminating in the introduction of the pious clause in the Company's charter of 1813.

It was the Baptists, however, who spearheaded missionary work in India, to be followed by the LMS and the CMS. Such work was commenced some forty years before serious evangelical activity in the metropolis. The result was that significant strands of evangelical thought were developed in India and then applied to the metropolitan poor. While the SBCP was encouraging the moral regeneration of the poor through frugality, self-help, industry and purity, Grant wrote in the immediate aftermath of the French Revolution of the necessity of reconciling the depraved and corrupt natives in India to British rule. He conceded that Indians had never existed in a savage state but proposed that any attempt to convert them to light, knowledge and hence improvement would be mitigated by the debilitating influence of climate, despotic government, caste and Hindu mythology. Carey at the Serampur Mission inhabited a more inclusive vision of humanity, and yet could justify foreign work on the grounds that barbarous, poor and naked heathens in India were denied the truth through lack of Bibles and Protestant ministers. Over time evangelical attitudes hardened. Thus in the writings of Claudius Buchanan and Ward we see an embryonic racial separateness and virulent demonization of the rites and superstitions of a heathen and degraded population lost in a state of darkness, ideas that were to influence evangelical sentiment in both metropolis and India throughout the nineteenth century.

With the emergence around 1813 of a certain consensus on the nature of imperial rule, projects were initiated to create a totalizing vision of India. The Company commissioned Francis Buchanan to undertake a survey of its territories. A product of the Scottish Enlightenment, Buchanan brought to the work a scientific and empiricist methodology. Little was of necessity excluded from his inquiry, and he recorded with unprecedented accuracy details of topography, trade, agriculture, population and flora. In contrast, the information used in Hamilton's *East India Gazetteer* (1815) was not gathered from empirical inquiry, and the publication was not initiated by the Company, but it was part of the same desire to think India in a more rational, ordered and coherent fashion. Finally, Forbes's *Oriental Memoirs* (1813) marked a defining moment in the travel literature of India. The product of an obsessive and protracted interest, it strove diligently to record a more complete picture of India's natural and human landscape.

These three projects in their different ways were the product of a new empiricist mode of observation that attempted a total vision of India, but simultaneously recognized the vision's inherent instability. Despite the vaulting ambition that drove the work, at its core remained a sense of epistemological insecurity. Buchanan, overwhelmed by the task, was forced to rely on sources over which he had no control and in which he had little confidence. The material he accumulated was never published. This has conventionally been blamed on the worsening relationship between Buchanan and the Company, but more likely it signalled a failure to comprehend and organize the massive body of inchoate material. Hamilton faced similar problems. Soon after the publication of his *Gazetteer* he embarked on a project to reduce the geography of India to a more systematic form, but was forced to recognize the impossibility of providing reliable information on so vast a country. And Forbes's *Memoirs* was ultimately not only an awkward mix of materials gathered from incommensurable modes of inquiry, but also a project framed by a profound shift in consciousness from an orientalist sympathy with Indian culture, to a hard-line evangelical condemnation of it.

Modes of inquiry in a metropolitan context displayed the same modernizing impulses. In the work of Egan and his contemporaries we can detect for the first time an attempt to grasp London's diversity combined with recognition of its futility. Although Egan, Smeeton, Badcock and James Grant drew upon a distinct urban mentality, they were conscious of the limited potential of eighteenth-century literary appropriations to comprehend London's immense, labyrinthine totality. They therefore developed novel ways of representing the metropolis based on their status as observing subjects. Its totality, however, lay beyond the reach of their awkward compilation of fiction, first-hand observation and extracts from previously published materials. Likewise, Mayhew's project to capture London's street life, in part by allowing the poor to speak, was brought to the point of collapse by the sheer mass of material seemingly beyond classification. Ultimately, London – like India – remained ineffable.

This epistemological insecurity combined with a mounting sense of political crisis fostered the racialization of imperial and metropolitan subjects. The form, chronology and rhetoric of these racializations are similar enough to suggest they were part of the same process. In both contexts the 1830s and 1840s were critical to order and progress. Domestically, the 1832 Reform Act, the 1834 Poor Law Amendment Act and the 1835 Municipal Corporations Act had transformed class relationships and installed a harsher disciplinary regime confident enough to confront chartist agitation. However, the 1842 Chadwick Report on the sanitary condition of the labouring population, journalistic and evangelical accounts of metropolitan life, and the popularity of urban novels, most notably those of Dickens, rediscovered the poor and reminded a middle-class public that the relative tranquillity of the period in the immediate aftermath of social and political turmoil could be shattered. Colonial rule was also transformed during this period. Enlightenment universalism had failed to challenge the British sense of innate superiority over Asians and Africans. Even British orientalists, while celebrating the richness and longevity of Indian culture, and the common heritage of Indo-European languages, derided contemporary Indian society and remained aloof from its people. But such attitudes were not rigid and impacted little on the hierarchies of colonial administration; only under the new imperial ethos of the early nineteenth century were indigenous rulers excluded from positions of colonial authority, the British elite removed from the influence of indigenous culture, and marginal groups subjected to investigation and control.

Many social and political factors accelerated the tendency around 1840 to construct class and imperial relationships in terms of race. The abolition of slavery, expansion of imperial rule, and rediscovery of the metropolitan poor threw into stark relief a range of concerns, resolution of which was thought possible only through measures predicated on the racialization of subject peoples. If the Anglo-Saxon race was to progress, in other words, critical problems such as wage labour, citizenship, rationality, hybridity, sexuality, civilization, order, hierarchy had to be addressed, and all of these had an urgency in both imperial and metropolitan contexts.

Travel and evangelical writings in India had from the end of the eighteenth century displayed various forms of embryonic racist sentiment. Environmentalism and zealous religious orthodoxy created regional stereotypes. Bengalis, for example, were represented as an effeminate, enervated, idolatrous and uncivilized people, seen occasionally as a race apart. Over time, and used in combination with class-based and gender-based discourses, these sentiments became harsher and more elaborate, and were generalized to encompass the whole of India. The existence of threatening forces of disorder beyond the knowledge of British authority provided the initial impulse. Thus dacoits, Thugs and tribals were singled out as objects of particular concern, and attracted the most vicious forms of racial coding. They were represented in ways redolent of the criminalization of the metropolitan residuum by Colquhoun and Mayhew. Here too were nomadic, predatory, organized, secretive and hereditary gangs acting outside the law to plunder innocent victims. Their sheer unknowability prompted detailed investigations centred on the re-construction of criminal biographies and the decipherment of cant. Many were used as specimens to test – and bolster – nascent theories on racial physiognomy. And to counter their activities wholesale changes were introduced in surveillance, policing and the operation of law.

With the suppression of dacoity and thuggee, the steady growth in missionary work and improvements in the information order, a certain optimism prevailed in the late 1840s and early 1850s. The 1857 revolt shattered this complacency, and confirmed the worst fears of the British about the latent threat from a population living in a darkness and degradation. Some of these fears reverberated in the metropolis as evangelicals like Meyrick pointed to the disastrous consequences of allowing a sub-merged population to continue to live beyond the influence of (Christian) civilization. The aftermath of 1857 coincided with a sense of crisis in the metropolis as fears of social disorder and imperial decline mounted. In this climate racial theory intensified and took a sinister and menacing turn. Race was increasingly articulated with the tropes of degeneration, dirt and blackness; together they were used to explain the social pathology of the residuum and the savagery of imperial subjects, both of which constituted potent threats to the future of the Anglo-Saxon race.

This agenda attracted the attention of the Victorian intelligentsia. Scientists, anthropologists, linguists, philosophers, cultural theorists, political scientists, theologians, historians and writers employed their talents to reveal the dimensions of race, as a result of which racial attitudes were articulated much more pervasively than heretofore, and their own disciplines were energized and empowered. Race became an intellectual and political testing ground for many of the fledgling sciences; the metropolis and India provided the laboratories. It was in this period that London was transformed from Egan's cyclopaedia to Sims's dangerous labyrinth of darkness and contamination, Mullens compared the heathenism of London to that of Calcutta, and the Anglo-Saxon subject was valorized in defence against threats from degeneration and hybridity.

This agenda, however, prompted different responses to anxieties about the future of the imperial formation. In India, racial fears were augmented by renewed uncertainties over the state of colonial knowledge. To address these, authorities instigated totalizing projects best represented by the Census and the *Imperial Gazetteer*. These massive endeavours were framed loosely by ethnological categories, by far the most important of which was caste, which was erected as the metanarrative of Indian history and culture. It explained contemporary society as the outcome of the primeval struggle between light-skinned Aryans of Indo-European stock and dark-skinned, indigenous and debased races. Extant hierarchical ordering was therefore described in evolutionary terms, and complex racial taxonomies emerged based on notions of racial purity. In the metropolis, travel writing identified the degenerative tendencies of racial mixing, and threats posed by internal orients. Intimations of class rather than caste informed these perspectives, but during the political crises of the late 1880s the crowd, transgressing the spatial confines of East London, entered into the symbolic sites of bourgeois fears.

Integral also was Charles Booth's project systematically to map London in its totality. Comparable in scale and ambition with Hunter's *Imperial Gazetteer*, Booth's volumes comprised the most comprehensive and detailed attempt to record the spatial, material, occupational and, to a lesser extent, cultural aspects of metropolitan life. His social categories were based loosely on class rather than caste but there was the same recognition of degenerative strains in the imperial formation. To say that in Booth the residuum equates with Hunter's aborigines greatly oversimplifies the complexities of ways in which both constituencies were constructed, and yet in terms of narratives of racial conflict between a bourgeois/Aryan elite and a low other the parallels are striking. With the emergence of such massive projects of knowledge production in the latter stages of the nineteenth century, the influence of travel and evangelical writing receded. In the metropolis a modernist sensibility in the writings of Masterman, Madox Ford and London called upon a repertoire of degeneration and racial decline to articulate fears of crowds from the abyss. In India, there was, well, Kipling. Fascinating though it may be to explore connections within this body of work – the use of jungle as metaphor in Masterman and Kipling is one that immediately springs to mind – there is neither space nor time here.

So, to conclude, does the production of knowledge in travel and evangelical writings of the nineteenth century reveal the establishment and retention of a unitary field between metropolis and India? The internal coherence and integrity of evangelical narratives and the common objective of mission work to provide spiritual salvation to heathen populations created strong homologies. Evangelical perspectives on the nature of these populations and the work to be undertaken with them originated, it has to be recalled, in the colonial 'periphery' and were then applied to the metropolis some years later. The emphasis on spiritual rather than political or material salvation, particularly when confronted by constituencies that seemed impervious to their influence, did not override social or cultural differences, but did engender a degree of stability and continuity at times of profound political change. Travel writings were less coherent. They drew contradictorily and differentially upon longer traditions to produce epistemologically insecure visions of both metropolis and colony. Overarching both genres – and arguably the field of knowledge production as a whole – were narratives of progress. It was these that at times of political unease and perceived crisis in the information order engendered racialized and totalizing visions, which eventually rendered obsolete the projects of travellers and evangelicals to create a knowledge of India.

INDEX

Printed in the United Kingdom by
Lightning Source UK Ltd., Milton Keynes
137948UK00001B/14/P